# GOOD FOUNDATIONS
*Author: Paul Glinkowski · Photographer: Phil Sayer*

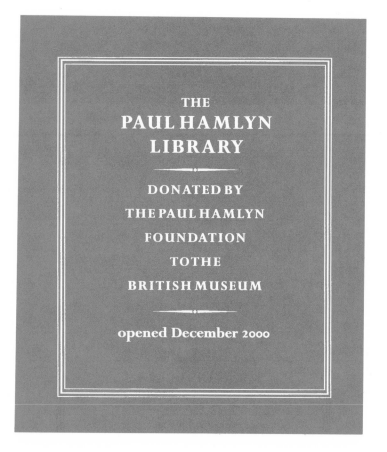

THE
**PAUL HAMLYN
LIBRARY**

DONATED BY
THE PAUL HAMLYN
FOUNDATION
TO THE
BRITISH MUSEUM

opened December 2000

# GOOD FOUNDATIONS

Trusts & Foundations and the Arts in the United Kingdom

Author: Paul Glinkowski · Photographer: Phil Sayer

VOLUME I

The Rootstein Hopkins Foundation: *A Case Study*

ATTRIBUTIONS

Paul Glinkowski, Rootstein Hopkins Research Fellow, has been the main researcher on this book as well as the principal author. I am grateful to Michael Southgate, Chairman of the Rootstein Hopkins Foundation, for the Foreword he has written on behalf of the Foundation's trustees, and I am indebted to Professor Mel Gooding for his role as Associate Editor in addition to the insights provided by his own text. Phil Sayer's photographic essay supplies a vivid visual parallel to the writing, and his perceptions have been an important catalyst throughout the project. Angus Hyland and Zara Moore of Pentagram have been generous in their detailed focus on the book's design as it has developed.

*Professor Rod Bugg, Project Director*

PROJECT STEERING AND EDITORIAL GROUP

Chair: Professor Rod Bugg (Wimbledon College of Art)
Paul Glinkowski (Wimbledon College of Art)
Professor Eileen Hogan (trustee: the Rootstein Hopkins Foundation)
Deirdre Hopkins (trustee: the Rootstein Hopkins Foundation)
Angus Hyland (Pentagram)
Dr Malcolm Quinn (Wimbledon College of Art)
Phil Sayer
Professor Anita Taylor (Wimbledon College of Art)

DESIGN

Pentagram (Angus Hyland and Zara Moore)

ACKNOWLEDGEMENTS

This book commemorates a decade-long conversation between the trustees of the Rootstein Hopkins Foundation and a wide range of people whose lives are rooted in the visual arts in Britain. The trustees would like to thank the many voices and energies which have helped to make this publication possible, in particular all the contributors to the book and Wimbledon College of Art.

In addition to the many individuals who generously gave up their valuable time to be interviewed for this research project, Paul Glinkowski would like to thank Professor Anne Bamford, Dr Eleonora Belfiore and Rose Challies for their input into the design of the impact study, and Jane Bailey, Claire Foss, Charlotte Kelley and Dr Susie Morrow for their unfailing good humour and support.

# CONTENTS

# FOREWORD

*by Michael Southgate, Chair of the Trustees, the Rootstein Hopkins Foundation*

It is a wonder to me, as indeed it was to Adel and Rick Hopkins, the founders and benefactors of the Rootstein Hopkins Foundation, that there should have been a Foundation at all; that through the success of the Rootstein business enough money was accumulated to make it possible. As with all self-made businesses, timing was everything. In the early 1960s change was in the air, hair got longer, skirts unthinkably shorter, and Time magazine declared that London was 'swinging'. Department stores needed a new image to go with this exciting era. The young fashion designers complained to Adel that their clothes looked quite wrong in the store windows of Regent Street and Knightsbridge. The problem was the mannequins; the tall, elongated, tortured attitudes of 1950s couture no longer suited the new vibrant look of the Carnaby Street 'dolly bird'.

The outcome was that Adel Rootstein became a self-taught mannequin designer. Her husband Rick later joined the company as Managing Director and Rootsteins went on to design and manufacture the most famous fashion mannequins in the world. They made props for department store displays and for the theatre, beautiful, fanciful creations that always had charm, and yet also had glamour, a look that became very 'Rootstein'.

In the course of their working day, both Adel and Rick interacted with artists of many kinds: sculptors, portrait painters, wigmakers, hairdressers, and of course fashion designers. All were highly skilled in their fields, and all were necessary for the design, manufacture and marketing of the finished product. Adel and Rick were, in their way, artists themselves and it seems rather unfair that, because they were both so competent at managing a business, their considerable creative abilities have tended to be overlooked.

Throughout the years of building an internationally successful business, Adel had harboured a deep-felt desire to go to art school, which she was fortunate to be able to do in the final few years of her life. Her experiences at the Slade School of Fine Art, where she gained a degree, gave Adel an insight into how difficult it can be for aspiring artists to finance themselves. This awareness set the path for the direction that the Rootstein Hopkins Foundation has subsequently taken. Our overall aim has been to help artists to further their education and to develop and share with the public their creative talents. Drawing and painting were preoccupations for both Rick and Adel and this is reflected in the support offered by the Foundation to practitioners working in the broader context of the visual arts.

The trustees of the Rootstein Hopkins Foundation are delighted to have commissioned this publication, which we hope will provide thought-provoking and timely insights into the work of the independent trusts and foundations that support the arts in the United Kingdom today. Trusts and foundations often prefer to conduct their business in a discreet and understated manner, and for this reason their contribution to the arts is perhaps yet to be fully appreciated and acknowledged. The publication in 2006 of *Experience and Experiment*, which commemorates the fiftieth anniversary of the Calouste Gulbenkian Foundation, did much to address this deficit. The aim of this volume, which represents the fruits of a two-year research project at Wimbledon College of Art, is to raise still further an awareness of the state of this important sector and to provoke debate about its future. It is the hope of the Rootstein Hopkins Foundation trustees, both past and present, that this book will assist other foundations to learn from our experiences and to find new and exciting ways to support 'the artist'.

# INTRODUCTION

*by Professor Rod Bugg, Director of the Rootstein Hopkins Research Project
at Wimbledon College of Art, University of the Arts London*

Early in 2004 the trustees of the Rootstein Hopkins Foundation made the decision that, as one of their final acts, a record should be created of what the Foundation had set out to do and what it had achieved since its establishment in 1990. They wished to reflect upon and evaluate the impact that a small grant-giving charity such as theirs could have within a relatively short life span and to make that reflection available for the benefit of the wider community of art professionals, academics and others working in the field of the visual arts.

The charitable foundation had been set up through profits earned in a highly creative business, which had produced a range of display mannequins for the fashion industry that were quite different in character from any seen before. It seems fitting, given such groundbreaking origins, that the trustees should seek to leave an imaginative and innovative legacy of value to future artists, scholars and funders of the arts in the form of this book.

As guardians of the funds, the trustees will have disbursed around £8,000,000 over the fourteen-year period from 1995, when the first grant was given, until 2008, the agreed date for winding down the Foundation. They felt their story might influence others to realise how a relatively modest sum of money, in trust terms, can make a positive and significant intervention in the lives and ambitions of cash-strapped artists and art students, the careers of art teachers, the practices and capabilities of arts venues and museums, and in colleges of art and design.

The founders of the Rootstein Hopkins Foundation had a long-term interest in and concern for art education. In his essay A History and Analysis of a Grant-Giving Trust, Paul Glinkowski provides a detailed insight into the evolution of the Foundation. He details how, within its original charitable intentions, there was an aim to establish a new art school, and how after careful scrutiny this initiative was found to be flawed. The trustees then turned their thoughts to alternative ways in which to assist effectively, or to otherwise act as catalysts, within the existing art school landscape. In the years that followed they worked with a number of colleges and universities to build good relationships, through their support for staff sabbaticals and through major projects with institutions throughout the country.

Faced with the challenge of how to mark the wind down of the charity, it was no surprise that they should turn to the colleges in thinking through how to record their grant-giving activities and the impact of their work. They decided to invite a number of colleges to come forward with ideas as to how this might be achieved. This book, *Good Foundations*, is the outcome of that process. It is the product of a proposal from Wimbledon School of Art (now a College of the University of the Arts London) to set up a research project to evaluate the work of the Foundation through text and images, presented in parallel as photographic and written essays. Glinkowski, the appointed Rootstein Hopkins Research Fellow at Wimbledon and the principal author of this book, has worked with a team, made up of representatives from the Rootstein Hopkins trustees, academics, the photographer Phil Sayer and Angus Hyland from the design consultancy Pentagram, to achieve this and to present the work of the Foundation alongside a major analytical study of the role of trust funding in supporting the arts.

The location of the Rootstein Hopkins project at Wimbledon was significant in setting the work in the context of key research initiatives in art and theatre practice and impact assessment at the College. Wimbledon's history of commitment to drawing – evidenced through the Centre for Drawing, the Wimbledon Figurative Drawing Fellowships (these grew out of the earlier Linbury Fellowships) and the Jerwood Drawing Prize, hosted at the College – mirrored the Foundation's abiding interest in this area, which is reflected in much of its grant-giving. Similarly, the College's work in costume and theatre relates closely to the earlier activities of the Rootstein Hopkins Group Ltd. The project was developed alongside the Engine Room at Wimbledon, the College's focus for knowledge transfer and community engagement, which has undertaken a range of projects involving impact assessment related to the arts.

The two-volume integrated design of this book reflects the duality of emphasis that emerged as the research programme unfolded. Volume I, which includes Sayer's photographic essay, is focused firmly on the Rootstein Hopkins Foundation: its history and an analysis of the outcomes of its funding. Volume II widens the horizons of enquiry, presenting analyses and discussion of the bigger picture of support for the arts in this country, philanthropic and otherwise, at the beginning of the twenty-first century.

In Volume I, the documentation and evaluation of the Foundation's activities is developed by Glinkowski through the examination, in an original and searching way, of the various questions arising from the issues confronted by the Foundation and by similar grant-giving bodies. This draws on extensive case studies of the grant recipients, the goal being to provide a unique scholarly insight to the holistic range of benefits and effects that can follow on from an act of funding.

Sayer's images were commissioned to provide a visual essay telling its own complementary story and furnishing further insights into the people, places and activities central to the Rootstein Hopkins narrative. As well as portraying the trustees at work, the photographs document a range of the recipients and projects featured in the text as case studies, alongside some of the 'spend out' projects that were funded subsequent to the period covered by the impact study.

The impact study was of necessity retrospective. In the period since the study was initiated, the Foundation has made a series of major awards to a wide range of organisations. These are outlined in my own essay, *Spend Out or Legacy?*, which reflects the Foundation's priorities once the decision was taken to disburse its remaining resources. As I will demonstrate, the same priorities that underpinned the Foundation's earlier funding programmes were sustained during the 'spend out', with concentration remaining on the artist and centred around the themes of artists, studios, galleries, archives, art colleges and education.

Volume II, edited and prefaced by Professor Mel Gooding, begins with Glinkowski's detailed exploration of the recent history and present funding position of the arts in the United Kingdom. Glinkowski highlights the current policy context within which debates about arts funding and the philanthropic role are being aired. He concludes by considering the common practices and approaches of a number of trusts and foundations in the independent funding sector.

Two essays by leading experts in the fields of arts development and arts funding – Marjorie Allthorpe-Guyton, Director of Visual Arts at Arts Council England until 2006, and Timothy Llewellyn, Director of the Henry Moore Foundation until May 2007 – follow, and together help further to position the work of the trusts and foundations sector in terms of a national map. These essays, which provide different views and approaches gained through many years' experience of working at the coalface of private and public sector arts funding, extend and develop the questions raised by Glinkowski.

In my role as Director of the Rootstein Hopkins Research Project at Wimbledon I have chaired the editorial group. The trustees' hunch was right; the story that has emerged from the research has proved to be well worth telling. The intimate scale of the Foundation, the incremental and slowly evolving changes within its membership, and the unconditional nature of so much of its grant-giving have all contributed to its unique character, a flavour of which is, fittingly, preserved within the pages of this book.

# THE ROOTSTEIN HOPKINS FOUNDATION: A HISTORY AND ANALYSIS OF A GRANT-GIVING TRUST

*by Paul Glinkowski*

Origins and founders: a fortune made in fashion

The Rootstein Hopkins Foundation was established on 25 October 1990 by the husband-and-wife partnership of Richard [Rick] and Adel Hopkins [née Rootstein], who were at that time the principal directors and shareholders of a private limited company, the Rootstein Hopkins Group Ltd. The idea to create a charitable foundation had first been proposed in correspondence with lawyers in 1984, in the context of planning for the sale of the Rootstein business, which the Hopkinses had developed into a global market leader in the design and manufacture of display mannequins for the fashion industry.

As is often the case with philanthropic enterprises, in the early planning phase of the Foundation public spiritedness was combined with pragmatism. The vehicle of the charitable trust or foundation was suggested by the couple's legal and financial advisors as a mechanism to mitigate the Capital Transfer Tax liability when the business came to be sold; the maximum amount of profit from the business could thereby be safeguarded for charitable purposes. At this time, the mid-1980s, the object that the Rootstein Hopkins Foundation would serve had not been decided. The couple were, however, life-long devotees of the arts, particularly the visual arts, and Adel was already developing an ambition to become a painter in her retirement.

Rick and Adel Hopkins possessed many of the characteristics often found in philanthropists: they were self-made business people, who had built up a highly profitable company on the basis of hard work, enterprise and creativity; they were both immigrants to the United Kingdom – Rick from Canada, Adel from South Africa – who wanted to give something back to the country that had given them a home and had provided the context for their success; they were a childless couple, used to living comfortably within their means, who decided, in later life, that they could use some of their surplus wealth to support areas of public good which, over the years, had given them considerable pleasure and stimulation.

Michael Southgate, a long-time friend and the Creative Director of the company, who has chaired the trustees of the Rootstein Hopkins Foundation since July 2000, remembers their situation well: 'Their personal needs were modest,' he says, 'in forty years their lifestyle hardly changed. Despite their success, Adel had just a small car and Rick continued to use public transport. The business was their life. When it became clear that the company would have to be sold, the plan was devised to create a charity.'

Rick and Adel had both chosen to settle in London when they came to the United Kingdom at the start of the 1950s. By the time they first met – when they were both in their early twenties – they had already begun to carve out individual careers in the display industry. The personal devotion and creative symbiosis that was to define their relationship for the next forty years is evident in an interview Adel gave to the *Sunday Express* in 1980, in which she recalls her earliest memories of Rick: 'I worked for Aquascutum, where I met the man who was going to become my husband – Rick Hopkins,' she says. 'The minute I saw him I thought the world had fallen on my head. When I met him, I suddenly began to love and understand things about figures and fashion and combining three dimensional things with visual images.'

Adel managed to translate the combination of visual awareness and fashion sense that Rick had helped to instil in her into the product that was to make both their fortunes: the Adel Rootstein display mannequin. When Adel Rootstein Ltd was founded, in 1959, the mannequin was ripe for reinvention. With the arrival of the Swinging Sixties, the mannequins used in the department stores seemed out of touch with the clothes being made by a new young generation of fashion designers. Adel saw that the mannequin needed to move with the rapidly changing times. Shop windows were suddenly becoming street theatre; they were more creative, a way of telling stories.

Adel's innovation was to design mannequins in the image of the fashion models and celebrities of the day. Michael Southgate recalls the breakthrough moment: 'Adel said, "If we're Swinging London, we should be doing mannequins of people that are making London swing." And that's the idea that formed the company. The timing was perfect. Adel had this incredible insight into what was hot, what was next, who was interesting. An aquiline nose, or an unusual bone structure, was far more appealing to her than conventional beauty.' A typical example was Rootstein's first big success – Twiggy. 'She had a physique like a boy and this clown-like make up,' recalls Southgate. 'Adel said, "We should do that girl." By the time we got her mannequin on the market (it takes about six months), Twiggy was already well known in London. In fact, she was a sensation. Nobody knew the name Adel Rootstein, but we became "the company that did Twiggy". From then on, Adel just had a fantastic record of always picking what was the next wave, the next kind of person.'

The new, individualised mannequin was a great success on both sides of the Atlantic and by the end of the 1960s Adel Rootstein Ltd was on its way to becoming a global brand. By the time Rick retired from the business, in 1996, Rootstein's place in the annals of late twentieth-century fashion was secure. In February of that year, in an article in the *Independent*, Lesley Gillilan paid tribute to its achievements: 'Adel Rootstein's factory is supernaturally successful,' she wrote. 'In the fashion industry it is universally revered; no other producer of mannequins approaches it for prestige.'

## A commitment to art

By the late 1980s, Adel had already decided to retire from Rootstein's. Adel and Rick were making plans to sell the company and to set up a charitable foundation; at the same time, Adel's creative energies became firmly focused on the visual arts. Not having attained the qualifications usually required to embark on a fine art degree course, she had negotiated an arrangement with the Slade School of Fine Art by which she paid a fee to attend the school on an informal basis. When Bernard Cohen was appointed as the new Slade Professor and head of school in the summer of 1988, he decided that this arrangement would have to change. Cohen, who was to become one of the original trustees of the Rootstein Hopkins Foundation, recalls vividly his first encounter with Adel – who was busy working in one of the studios at the Slade – on the eve of the new academic year in September 1988. 'She greeted me,' says Cohen, 'with the words, "Ah, you're my new little professor. Now are you going to be a good professor?" And I said, "Yes, I'm going to try to be a good professor, but the first thing I have to do is to broach this thing with you." And I was looking and looking at the work. I had no idea who she was at that time. The name Rootstein didn't mean anything at all to me. And I explained to her that I thought her work was very impressive. I saw that she was surrounded by a lot of extremely good paintings; more than a year's worth of degree-level painting. And so I said to Adel, "Why don't you take a degree?" She said, "Well what do I have to do?" And I said, "All you have to do is turn up on Monday morning of the first day of term with a portfolio." And she said. "And I'd be in?" And I said, "Yes, you'd be in, if you agree to follow the course for four years." It wasn't that I was squeezing someone in through a back door without having the justification to do it. No, I thought that she was an exceptional talent.'

The next four years, which Adel spent as a dedicated student at the Slade, were to influence profoundly the direction that the Rootstein Hopkins Foundation – which was still little more than the germ of an idea in 1988 – was to take. It was at the Slade that Adel began to develop both her commitment to art and her instinct for philanthropy.

'Adel was a woman in her late fifties, but she set the pace for everyone,' says Cohen. This was true on the theoretical side as well as on the creative. 'One day,' Cohen recalls, 'she said to me, "I don't know anything about colour and no one here seems to be lecturing about colour." And I said: "Well, colour is a very difficult thing, unless you get the right person to do it." And I said, "My funding is at zero at the moment, there's no way that I can provide someone." And she said, "Well, I'll provide. Who would you get?" And I said, "The best man I can think of is Martin Kemp." And she said, "Well, here you are," and she wrote me out a cheque to cover the cost of Martin's fees.

'Everything Adel did was on behalf of the school. If she saw that something was inadequate for the students she would provide it, in the gentlest way. If she saw a student was struggling because clearly they couldn't afford decent brushes, the next thing was that they would find a pile of brushes in front of them. She had become a mixture of mother, aunt and benefactor, but in the gentlest possible way. Never, ever would she say, "I think you should do this, I think you should do that." It would always be, "Is the school a bit short of this? Or, a bit short of that?" Always extremely respectful.'

Sadly, Adel Hopkins was unable fully to realise the potential that she had begun to show at the Slade, or the dream she had forged there of becoming a serious painter in later life. Adel was diagnosed with terminal cancer in the early summer of 1992, just as she was completing her studies, and she died in September that year, a few weeks after learning that she had gained her degree.

## Shawfield House: the demise of an art school vision

The Rootstein Hopkins Foundation was set up in October 1990, just as Adel was beginning her third year at the Slade. Adel had retired from Adel Rootstein Ltd, Rick remained as the Managing Director, and negotiations were underway to sell the company. The couple had two key concerns in arranging for the disposal of their business: that the future of its employees – who they regarded almost as surrogate family members – should be safeguarded; and that the showroom and head office, Shawfield House, a characterful Georgian building occupying a prime site just off the Kings Road in Chelsea, should be taken out of the business and gifted to the Rootstein Hopkins Foundation. Shawfield House was, in fact, to be both the Foundation's principal asset and source of income and the focus for its initial objective: 'to establish a school of fine art'.

The art school vision was very much that of Adel who, it seems, wanted to build an academy of like-minded artists around her once she had graduated from the Slade. Although it was never explicitly stated in the records of the Foundation, Adel, who was strongly committed to the figurative tradition of painting, may have had in mind as a model the short-lived but influential private art school that was set up at 316 Euston Road, London, in February 1938, by William Coldstream (who was later to precede Bernard Cohen as Slade Professor), Victor Pasmore and Claude Rogers. As a deliberate reaction to avant-gardism, the Euston Road School advocated the painting of traditional subjects in a realist manner. The school attracted high profile associates, such as Augustus John, Vanessa Bell, Duncan Grant and Paul Nash, and by September 1939, when it closed, at the outbreak of the Second World War, it had rapidly attained a high reputation.

Shawfield House was 'settled' on the Rootstein Hopkins Foundation in January 1992, when negotiations with the new Japanese owners of the Rootstein business, the Yoshichu Mannequin Company, were concluded. Adel included in the settlement a personal donation to the Foundation of £80,000, to secure for herself a studio for life within Shawfield House. Sadly, for Adel 'for life' was to mean only a few short months; she died on 20 September that same year.

Almost immediately then, with the death of Adel, the objective of creating an art school lost its original impetus. Even at that early point, there were some doubts amongst the remaining trustees – Rick Hopkins, Michael Southgate, Professor Bernard Cohen and Graham Feldman (a long time friend and business advisor to Rick and Adel) – concerning the practical viability of the proposal. Notwithstanding these doubts, the trustees were, initially, determined to try to remain faithful to Adel's vision for the Foundation and on 20 April 1993, in their first annual meeting following her death, they agreed unanimously 'to occupy and develop Shawfield House as studios and a gallery'. This was to happen in 2002, the point at which the building (which had been leased back to the new owners of the Rootstein company for ten years when the business was sold) would become physically available. The trustees anticipated that the income generated in the intervening period – an annual rent from Shawfield House of £116,000, plus the capital realised on investments – would be 'sufficient to allow building work and to provide a fund for part of the bursaries and expenses'. Artists would be given a rent-free studio for six to twelve months and a small allowance for materials, and they would have a gallery at their disposal on the premises. There would be a concentration on figurative art, 'with special emphasis on the live model'.

The focus on Shawfield House as a site for some form of art school or artists' studios only began to fall away when Rick Hopkins, who had agreed to stay on at Adel Rootstein Ltd as Managing Director for five years after the sale of the company, retired from business at the end of 1996. He was then free to give the Foundation his undivided attention and formally took over as Chair of the charity at a meeting of the trustees on 23 January 1997. A feasibility study commissioned by Rick towards the end of 1997, which was carried out by independent consultant Robert Halsall, confirmed that the proposition to set up a school of art at Shawfield House was unrealistic. 'In considering the market needs, practical and financial implications of founding a new School of Fine Art,' Halsall advised, 'I believe it will be impossible to gain public funds to deliver a Higher Education programme and the charity would have to charge students full fees in the region of £7,000 per annum, thus excluding all but wealthy overseas students.' Halsall concluded that the Foundation was better placed to make a greater contribution to what had until that point been regarded as its secondary objective: 'promoting the study and research of fine arts' through the giving of grants to artists and to arts organisations.

In the light of Robert Halsall's feasibility report, the Rootstein Hopkins Foundation prepared a request to the Charity Commission to amend its trust deed and, on 16 December 1998, the original commitment 'to establish a school of art' was finally removed. From now on, the focus of the Foundation would be solely on grant-giving, to support 'research and practice of art in all its branches, but in particular painting, drawing, sculpture, photography, fine and applied art'.

## The beginnings of grant-giving: learning the ropes

The Rootstein Hopkins Foundation had, in fact, been making exploratory forays into grant-making since 1995. Anxious, after five years of relative dormancy, to be seen to be fulfilling its charitable objects – and concerned that the Charity Commission might take a dim view of the fact that it was accumulating expendable capital year on year (from the rental on Shawfield House) without any signs of charitable expenditure or activity – it had devised a number of awards which it felt would reflect the character and interests of the Foundation and which would meet needs that were not at that time fully being addressed by other funders.

The challenge for the Foundation was, how should it approach the business of grant-giving? The four surviving founding members had been joined in January 1993 by Jacqueline (Jackie) Morreau, a painter whom Adel had befriended and greatly admired. Professor Cohen was responsible for administering a programme of travel awards for recent graduates, the Boise scholarships, through a committee that operated from the Slade School of Fine Art. It seemed sensible to the Rootstein Hopkins Foundation trustees, then, that in the first instance they should form an association with the Slade.

Although it was instructive for the Rootstein Hopkins trustees, the relationship with the Boise committee was not ideal. There was a concern that the committee was too large and unwieldy, and the Rootstein Hopkins Foundation representatives on the panel did not necessarily agree with the selections made. There was an uncomfortable sense that the Foundation was not fully responsible for the destiny of its own grants.

The Foundation's relationship with the Boise committee lasted from 1995 until 1998, during which time it awarded one travel grant per year to a recently graduated young artist. The Foundation had also began to offer a number of other awards – an artists' support award, a sabbatical award, a mature student award, and an award to enable international student exchanges – which were granted and administered directly by the Rootstein Hopkins Foundation trustees. Right from the start, its grant-giving had two clear areas of focus: supporting fine art education, and helping emerging artists to realise their potential.

The process by which new categories of grants were identified was a responsive one. Jackie Morreau had become aware, through working alongside other artists in collective studios in London, that a small amount of financial support given at a pivotal moment could be of enormous help in enabling promising, but not yet fully successful, artists to take forward their careers; and so the artists' support grant (later known as the project grant) was developed. In 1995, Helen Slater, a woman in her early forties who had gained a place on an MA degree course at the Slade, wrote to Rick Hopkins to highlight how difficult it was for the over-35s to secure public funding to cover fees; an annual grant to assist a mature student was the result. The fact that Adel had, just a few years earlier, gained so much from the experience of being a mature student at the Slade and had observed the financial difficulties faced by the less well-off students there, was undoubtedly a factor in the trustees' decision to commit to this particular category of award.

Thus began a gradual evolution of areas, categories and conditions of grant-giving, which would continue for the next decade. This incremental process – based on refinement by trial and error – reflects the informal, and in some ways unashamedly old-fashioned, culture of the Foundation; a culture based more upon personal networks and an instinct to do good, than upon a rigorously evidence-based or policy-driven, strategic plan. Looking back, Jane Hartwell, who served as a Rootstein Hopkins Foundation trustee from 1997 to 2003, regards this culture in positive terms. 'It will be a loss to the art world when they eventually wind up,' she says. 'None of the people involved came from a fundraising background and it was done from a warm spirit of wanting to help people. It was a philanthropic gesture to the art world, which probably helped a lot of people who wouldn't otherwise have got support. They are quite old fashioned in a good way; you wouldn't want to run every institution like that, but it is good that they are there as well.'

## Awards by nomination, or by open application? A funder's dilemma

The Rootstein Hopkins Foundation is unusual amongst independent trusts in that, from its earliest days of grant-giving, it has chosen to give awards to individual artists as well as to institutions that support artists, such as art colleges. For reasons of accountability (being able to track and to monitor how an award is spent) most grant-givers prefer only to fund formally constituted organisations; many, indeed, will only fund registered charities. The Rootstein Hopkins Foundation's willingness to offer direct support to the individual artist stems partly from the self-reliant attitude of its founders, particularly Adel. As the Foundation's current Chair, Michael Southgate, puts it: 'We want to try to help people who wouldn't necessarily get help through the normal system; it's a philosophy that reflects Adel's independent thinking.'

Some of the Foundation's earliest awards, the travel awards given in conjunction with the Boise committee, were in fact given to young artists who might be said to be more in tune with 'the normal system'. The recipient of the first such award in 1995, Ishbel Myerscough, for example, went on to win the BP National Portrait Award in that same year and has subsequently enjoyed a sustained and successful career. The candidates for these early Rootstein Hopkins travel awards were nominated by a small group of art world professionals – curators, dealers and art school tutors – who were chosen as nominators because they were well placed to spot emerging talent. This process created an instant shortlist and helped to ensure a high calibre of applicant.

When the Foundation decided to act independently of the Boise committee and to set up its own awards, it had to confront one of the key questions perennially faced by grant-makers: how could it reach and attract the right kind and quality of applicant? The original plan was to seek the co-operation of art schools by inviting them to nominate candidates for the awards. As Maureen Fawsitt, the Secretary of the Rootstein Hopkins Foundation from 1997 until 2005, recalls: 'We contacted lots of colleges all over the country, but we got very little response. They were all so busy. We realised that it wasn't going to work that way and that we would have to throw it open to general application.' Trustee Graham Feldman remembers being surprised by the lack of interest and co-operation from the colleges. 'When we originally approached them, they wouldn't even put up a notice saying that the grants were available,' he recalls. 'The feeling was that they weren't really interested. Our problem from the very beginning was how to get the information out to the people who might want to receive the grant.'

The solution eventually decided upon – one which the Foundation has followed annually since 1997 – was to promote the awards to artists nationally through an advertisement in *a-n Magazine* (formerly known as *Artists' Newsletter*). This approach had quite a dramatic impact, as Maureen Fawsitt recalls: 'To begin with we were inundated. We got a huge amount of applications and a lot of them were not really very good. We realised at that point that we would have to make some conditions. It was decided after about the first or second year that applicants had to have a minimum of a BA degree. Everything evolved over time.'

As well as putting a new strain on the administrative capacities of the Foundation, the open application approach helped to hasten the departure of one of its founder trustees. Professor Cohen, who had expressed his concerns about the high level of bureaucracy that the new process would involve, resigned from the Foundation in February 1998, following the first round of grant-giving by open application.

The open application approach, which the Foundation has applied to all its awards for individual artists, has proved to be a mixed blessing. On the one hand, it has ensured that the Foundation attracts applications from the kind of artists that Adel might have wished to encourage: those who have not yet found their place in the system. On the other hand, it places a significant annual burden on the trustees' voluntary time and the Foundation's limited administrative resources. It also produces a ratio of unsuccessful to successful applications of around 30 to 1, which is extremely high in comparison to other grant-making trusts. 'Sometimes people do complain about the quality of the work,' says trustee Jackie Morreau, 'but we've always found enough worthwhile artists to fund.'

The Rootstein Hopkins Foundation's commitment to support the individual artist proved to be a compelling incentive when it sought to recruit new trustees. Jane Hartwell, for example, was well aware, from her role as Exhibitions Organiser at the Morley Gallery, London, of the difficulties that artists face in raising funding. 'There are so few organisations that actually focus on the artist,' she says, 'for small projects as well as big ones. I know how difficult it is for people just to get the money to transport works for an exhibition, or to print invitations to the private view. There aren't many other places you can go to for that amount of money, which will help to get a project off the ground. If you go to the Arts Council, there's so much competition. You have to fill in complicated application forms and fit in with their priorities. The Rootstein Hopkins Foundation seemed an easier route, with a wide range of grants, so I was very keen to be part of that organisation.'

It is a point of view shared by a current trustee, Ian Cole, who joined the Foundation shortly after Jane Hartwell departed in 2003. 'I know from my own experience of working with artists,' says Cole, 'that it can be sometimes very, very difficult for them to find even small amounts of money to finance things that they consider to be of pivotal importance. And if you can give somebody a few thousand pounds, if that's what it takes, to enable them to realise an ambition that's well set out and proposed, and which might, on some level, actually make a difference, then it seems a worthwhile thing to do.'

## Awards to institutions: From minor to major

Although nearly two-thirds of the awards given in the Rootstein Hopkins Foundation's first ten years of grant-making went directly to artists (fifty-one out of the seventy-eight awards made between 1995 and 2004 went to individual artists), as the decade progressed, there developed an increasing emphasis on grants to institutions. Whereas the grants given to individuals were always for small or modest amounts – from around £1,500 to cover student course fees, to £12,000 to enable an art college lecturer to take a six-month sabbatical – an increase in the expendable capital that the Foundation had at its disposal, coupled with an awareness of the needs faced by certain major organisations, encouraged the trustees to consider sizeable donations to institutions. This culminated, in 2001, in two awards of £500,000 each: one to the British Museum and the other to London College of Fashion.

The earliest institutional grant was, in fact, awarded as early as 1995, shortly after the first award to an individual artist was decided through the Boise committee. Eight thousand pounds was given to the London College of Printing and Distributive

Trades to enable two of its students to exchange for a term with two students from the Fashion Institute of Design and Merchandising, Los Angeles. Occasional awards to benefit students preparing for a career in the fashion industry, the industry upon which the wealth of the Rootstein Hopkins Foundation was based, have remained an ongoing feature of the Foundation's grant-giving, as indeed has the commitment to support international student exchange.

A shift in emphasis from the individual to the institution – a shift that is reflected in the amounts and proportion of money given, rather than in the numbers of grants awarded – came about as a consequence of the amendment to the Foundation's trust deed in December 1998. Once it had been confirmed that the Rootstein Hopkins Foundation no longer sought to establish a school of fine art, the trustees immediately decided that the substantial reserves that had been accumulating to the Foundation to meet that objective should begin to be distributed in the form of grants.

In 1999 a capital grant was added to the Foundation's list of annual awards. Principally targeted at art colleges, though opened up on occasion to other kinds of visual arts organisation, the capital grant is designed to meet the need either for new equipment or for small-scale building-related projects. As Deirdre Hopkins – the widow of Rick Hopkins, who became a trustee of the Foundation following her husband's death in June 2000 – explains, the philosophy behind the capital grant is utilitarian: 'It is to benefit the greatest number of students and staff for the longest possible time. For the last five or six years we've been providing computer suites. This reflects what the colleges tell us are the present priority needs within art and design education.'

Deirdre Hopkins, who taught for a number of years at the colleges now known as London College of Fashion and London College of Communications, is one of several current trustees to have direct experience of the art school system. This in-house expertise has made it easier for the Foundation to target the capital award, which it does by selective invitation to apply rather than by an open call for proposals. By comparison with the nationally advertised awards to individual artists, the process for identifying projects and areas of need operates relatively informally, but it is nevertheless an informed one. 'The capital grant is not advertised,' says Deirdre Hopkins. 'Individual trustees encourage colleges to apply. As a trustee, I visit art schools all the time. Talking to the staff reveals potential projects and future plans. Often, out of these discussions, you can identify areas where money would actually make quite a lot of difference and an idea for a capital grant will emerge.'

By 2000, the amount of surplus capital available to the Foundation for distribution to meet its charitable mission had reached over £1,000,000. The trustees decided in December of that year that 'it would now be prudent to make substantial one-time distributions from these past reserves'. In the following spring, two major awards were confirmed. £500,000 was given as an endowment to the British Museum to create a permanent fund for the ongoing purchase of works for the Museum's Prints and Drawings Collection, principally by living artists resident in the United Kingdom. Again, the idea for this award had its origins in the personal experience and insight of one of the trustees, Jackie Morreau, who was profoundly aware of the value to contemporary artists – in terms of professional status, public recognition and self esteem – of having their work represented in an important national collection. 'That has always seemed to me one of the goals of most artists,' says Morreau. 'Frances Carey, who was then the curator of the Prints and Drawings Collection at the British Museum, was always quite prepared to look at anybody's work. I thought that was very democratic of her. She bought some of my work for the Collection in 1991 and then again in 1995. I was so thrilled when they first bought some. I thought, "this is what artists want; they want their work to be in a permanent collection where other people can go and look at it if they want to." So I proposed that the Foundation should give the British Museum an award.'

The second major award went to London College of Fashion: £500,000 to create the Rootstein Hopkins Space, a new multi-purpose facility which would be available for use for fashion shows, exhibitions, conferences and seminars, by each of the colleges which together make up the University of the Arts London (which was known at the time of the award, in 2001, as the London Institute) . This award enabled the Foundation to meet multiple aims. It satisfied its utilitarian aspiration to offer long-term benefit to a large academic community, which was focused on the visual and creative arts. At the same time, it was a major investment to support the future of fashion, the creative milieu in which the Foundation had its origins. The award to London College of Fashion was an example of the right project finding the right funder at the right time. The trustees had wanted to put something back into the industry that had provided the Foundation with its fortune and it seemed appropriate that London College of Fashion, which is the only higher education institution in the United Kingdom dedicated to this discipline, should be the beneficiary.

## A passion for drawing

Under the terms of its trust deed, the Rootstein Hopkins Foundation has a commitment to support 'art in all its branches, but in particular painting, drawing, sculpture, photography, fine and applied art'. Of these disciplines, drawing has emerged clearly as the most significant beneficiary of the Foundation's support. The reasons for this are twofold. The first is the passion, derived from personal practice and experience, which Rick and Adel Hopkins both felt for art that was rooted in drawing. The second is the perception held by the trustees that in the mid-1990s, relative to the other disciplines that together constitute the contemporary visual arts, the practice of drawing was in particular need of encouragement.

Prior to 1976, when he became a full-time director of Adel Rootstein Ltd, Rick Hopkins had run a successful design company. Deirdre Hopkins recalls that, for Rick, drawing was central to the process of learning how to refine and articulate his ideas. 'He was passionate about the fact that drawing was a rite of passage for an artist,' she says; 'it was how they moved into their work. Rick was a designer and he used drawing like that: as a development tool. It was a passion that he shared with Adel. When, following Rick's death, I had to sort out all of Adel's work and send it over to her family, I discovered books and books full of drawings.'

Rick and Adel were concerned that, with contemporary art becoming an increasingly plural field, the position of drawing was under threat. Deirdre Hopkins recalls her husband's conviction that something needed to be done to reverse what he regarded as the decline of the discipline. 'Rick was upset by what had happened to drawing with the onset of modernism and abstract painting,' she says. 'He was concerned that the practice of going "straight to canvas", made fashionable by such high profile painters as Jackson Pollock, had given a green light to young artists to dismiss the importance of drawing. He felt there was a danger that we might lose the skill completely.'

In 1995, the year in which the trustees began to define their grant-giving priorities, it seemed to them that drawing was in danger of losing its status as an indispensable discipline within the visual arts. Moreover, its position was at risk of being further undermined by developments within fine art higher education. Art students were gaining access to an increasing range of media and technologies (in particular, digital technologies); with the advent of modular courses, less emphasis was being placed on the painstaking acquisition of traditional skills and techniques.

It is understandable, then, given both the enthusiasms of its founders and the historical moment at which it emerged, that the Rootstein Hopkins Foundation should have evolved into a consistent and proactive champion of drawing. Support for drawing is reflected right across the range of its awards: the major endowment made in 2001 to the Prints and Drawings Collection at the British Museum will ensure that graphic work by living artists will continue in perpetuity to have a place in the holdings of one of this country's most important cultural institutions; capital funding awarded in 2004 has enabled Wimbledon College of Art to create The Observatory, a space designed to facilitate observation-based work in drawing and lens-based media; funding awarded to the Royal College of Art over an extended period, from 1997 to 2004, has given support to doctoral students whose work is focused on the discipline of drawing; over a five-year period, from 2001 to 2005, the Rootstein Hopkins Foundation sponsored two student prizes to be awarded each year as part of the prestigious Jerwood Prize for Drawing; and numerous awards have been made to support and encourage individual artists whose practice is, in some way, rooted in drawing.

In addition to the substantial investment they made possible through the Rootstein Hopkins Foundation, Rick and Adel each made generous personal donations to help sustain and promote the discipline of drawing within higher education. When Adel died in 1992, in order to encourage the practice of drawing from the figure, she left a substantial legacy to the Slade School of Fine Art so that students there could have access to life models. Under the terms of Rick's will, which were enacted following his death in June 2000, a large sum of money was set aside to found the first perma-nent Chair of Drawing to be based at a British university. The Chair was settled on the University of the Arts London, and, in 2004, Stephen Farthing was appointed as the inaugural Rootstein Hopkins Professor of Drawing.

From the figurative to the experimental: a revival in drawing leads to a shifting sense of practice

Jane Hartwell recalls that the initial thrust of the Foundation's support for drawing was firmly towards conventional forms of practice. 'Particularly when Rick was alive,' she says, 'there was very much a focus on the more traditional: for example, the figu-rative. I felt that we could have been a bit more adventurous in some ways. But Rick was Chair and had a lot of influence over what we did. In some ways, we weren't looking at the cutting edge of art. But, I think that the trustees were happy about that because it was felt that the cutting edge was getting quite a lot of exposure anyway.' Supporting what appear to be unpopular causes – causes that the more mainstream public or commercial sector agencies seem unwilling to invest in – is often held to be an important function of independent grant-giving trusts and foundations. And in the mid-1990s, from an arts funding point of view, figurative drawing had become an unpopular cause.

In the period from 1995 to 2007, however, during which the Rootstein Hopkins Foundation has engaged in grant-giving, drawing seems to have gained a new impetus. The new professorship at the University of the Arts London, and another at the University of the West of England, where Deanna Petherbridge was appointed the first Arnolfini Professor of Drawing in 2002, have helped to reaffirm the academic status of the discipline; high profile annual events, such as The Big Draw and the Jerwood Prize for Drawing, have brought it back into the public eye; figure-based drawing is recognised as an important component in the work of some of the best known of the so-called Young British Artists, such as Tracy Emin and the Chapman brothers. There has been talk in the art world of a 'drawing revival'. It could be claimed, with some justification, that over the last decade drawing has managed to reassert its position as a vigorous and vibrant discipline within the varied portfolio of techniques and approaches that constitute the contemporary visual arts.

Responding, perhaps, to this resurgence of confidence in drawing, the Rootstein Hopkins Foundation appears over time to have embraced a bolder definition of what might constitute contemporary drawing practice. A clear shift in emphasis is recognised by the original trustees. Michael Southgate, for example, observes that: 'The priorities have changed tremendously over the years. Adel was really only interested in promoting figurative drawing. She felt that true figurative drawing was getting pushed out of the curriculum in all of the colleges. It didn't seem to be fashionable. And that was what interested her.' The Foundation's willingness, at times, to embrace more experimental drawing practices might also be related to the changing composition and the growing expertise of its trustees. Ian Cole, who joined the trustees in 2003, is keen that the Foundation should keep itself open to an expanded sense of what drawing might be. 'I regard drawing as quite a broad church,' he says. 'It can apply to a whole range of things which, on the face of it, are probably quite a long way from picking up a piece of charcoal and making a mark.'

An experimental approach to drawing is particularly evident in the work of some of the individual artists that the Foundation has sponsored in recent years. A good example is the work of Yuen-Yi Lo, who received an award in 2002 to enable her to travel to the Jiangyong region of the Hunan Province in China. Yuen-Yi's purpose was to research Nushu, a secret script and dialect developed by the women of that region, who had historically been denied access to education and thus were marginalised from the official language of their male-dominated community. The data collected on the field trip to China provided essential raw material for the PhD that Yuen-Yi Lo completed at Wimbledon College of Art between 2001 and 2005. Although Yuen-Yi describes her practice as based in the discipline of drawing, the art work that has resulted from this project was presented for her doctoral examination as a mixed-media installation, incorporating graphic work, printed textiles, burnt wood and an audio track based on field recordings of women chanting in the Nushu dialect. 'Nushu is a means for women to produce autobiography,' says Yuen-Yi. 'My practice of drawing – or my creative practice – is written in this women's autobiography. It is an intervention into the writing of man.'

## The governance of the Rootstein Hopkins Foundation: a gradual evolution

As is often the case in small private charities, the turnover of Rootstein Hopkins Foundation trustees has been limited, and carefully managed. Over time, the effect has been to turn the Foundation from an organisation governed by a 'family and friends' culture into one in which professional art world expertise has gained the ascendancy. In its eighteen-year history, from 1990 to 2007, the Foundation has had a total of just ten trustees. Of the five original trustees, the two founder members, Adel and Rick Hopkins, died in 1992 and 2000 respectively. Michael Southgate and Graham Feldman – both friends and business associates of Adel and Rick – have served the full eighteen years. The fifth inaugural trustee, Professor Cohen, resigned in 1998. The painter Jackie Morreau, who joined the Foundation in 1993, several months after the death of Adel, remains a trustee. Jane Hartwell, the Exhibitions Organiser at the Morley Gallery, served for seven years, from 1997 to 2003. Deirdre Hopkins joined the trustees in 2000, shortly after the death of her husband, Rick. Ian Cole and Professor Eileen Hogan are the most recent appointees, taking up their posts in 2003.

Over the course of eighteen years, the balance within the trustees has shifted significantly. In the beginning, with the exception of Professor Cohen, the Foundation was governed by experienced and successful business people who, although they might have considered themselves to be creative individuals in their own right, had a strong but essentially non-professional interest in the visual arts. In identifying who the founder trustees should be, ties of friendship appear to have taken priority. It was not until December 1998, when the trust deed was amended, primarily to remove the original object of creating a school of fine art, that 'the future minimum require-ments' for the governance of the trust were formally considered and defined. From that date on, the trust deed has stated that: 'The Trustees will comprise a majority of artists or art-related professionals, a successful Director or former Director of a commercial enterprise and an Accountant.' The introduction of this new governance clause into the deed, which tips the balance in favour of artistic expertise, reflected the key role that artists and art professionals – Jackie Morreau, Jane Hartwell and Professor Cohen – had played in the development of the trust: from its initial concept, focused on the art school vision, to a grant-giving body responsible for disbursing tens of thousands of pounds each year to artists and to arts organisations.

The aim is to achieve a blend of artistic vision tempered by fiscal prudence, and so a guarantee of business experience has been written into the long-term formula for the governance of the Foundation. In the minutes of a trustees' meeting in April 1998, Rick Hopkins is recorded as having said that the balance of the trustees should be 'loaded in favour of artists and/or gallery owners, but there must be some who can protect the finances'. Graham Feldman, who has played the accountant's role for the Foundation throughout its history, maintains a clear sense of the pragmatic nature of his contribution. 'I'm the philistine amongst the artists,' he says, modestly. 'I deal with the lawyers and do the returns for the Charity Commission and make sure that we act in accordance with the law. The others are more interested in the art side. I'm just facilitating them to do what they should be doing. My role is much more about telling them what they are allowed to do, rather than telling them what to do.'

The three trustees who have been appointed since the founding deed was amended in December 1998 all have considerable experience of the visual arts, particularly in relation to education. Professor Eileen Hogan who joined the trustees in 2003, at the same time as Ian Cole, is a well regarded painter who has also enjoyed a distinguished career in higher education. Ian Cole was a former Head of Education and Public Programmes at the Museum of Modern Art Oxford (now known as Modern Art Oxford). Along with her experience of teaching at various colleges of what is now the University of the Arts London, Deirdre Hopkins – like Adel before her – brings to the Foundation a personal understanding of what it is to be a mature student of the visual arts. She studied for a BA degree in the History of Art, Design and Architecture at Kingston University in the late 1990s.

The blend of business background and artistic experience, long-term service and 'new blood', loyalty to the enthusiasms of the founders and a more dispassionate, expert point of view, makes for a rich and distinctive culture of governance within the trust. 'It's an enjoyably eccentric group of people,' says Professor Hogan. 'That is one of the interesting things about it. I think it was very courageous more recently to bring in people who didn't know Rick and Adel, who have professional but different expertise. Everybody has their own strengths and brings an idiosyncratic ingredient to the group and generally it works very well. It evolved because of Adel, and it was very much based on her and Rick's interests. If you set up a trust that's run by friends and relatives there is a great deal of emotion involved, but that also means that there is tremendous commitment and an independence of approach.'

Jackie Morreau acknowledges that working within such a highly-charged culture can sometimes be a strain. 'It takes a lot of psychic energy,' she says. 'I think we have a kind of divide between those people who knew Adel, and feel that it's important to follow what she wanted, and those who didn't know her.' Four of the six current trustees retain powerful memories of Rick and Adel. Deirdre Hopkins recognises that this can, at times, be problematic. 'There is this enormous emotional undertow to the whole thing,' she says, 'which makes for a very strong culture. But I think we all try very hard to do what Rick and Adel wanted. And I don't think that we do too bad a job.'

Taking the initiative: A learning curve

In addition to providing the expertise necessary for making sound judgements in relation to grant-making, the arts professionals amongst the trustees have on occasion encouraged the Rootstein Hopkins Foundation to be more proactive in the delivery of its charitable objects. There are two moments in its history when the Foundation has adopted what might be described as an engaged, or hands-on, rather than a reactive, approach to achieving its mission: in 2002 it staged *Chosen*, an exhibition of work by some of the artists who had been the recipients of its awards; and in 2004 it entered into discussions with a number of art colleges to develop a pathfinding research project. This research project would identify the outcomes of the Foundation's investment in the visual arts and, at the same time, would begin to map and to analyse the work of other grant-giving trusts that currently support the arts in the United Kingdom. It is this latter project, realised through a fellowship based at Wimbledon College of Art, which has resulted in this publication.

*Chosen* took place following a long period of gestation. Jane Hartwell first proposed the idea of an exhibition of past grant winners in November 1998. The trustees agreed that such an exhibition could help to raise the profile of the Rootstein Hopkins Foundation and, as a result, a higher quality of applicant might be attracted to apply. The 'exhibition of past winners' was discussed at a succession of trustees meetings and it was eventually decided that it should be held in 2002, to take advantage of the publicity generated by the two major awards made in 2001, to the British Museum and to London College of Fashion. The trustees anticipated that *Chosen* would be the first of an annual series of exhibitions, 'which will show off the best of what the Rootstein Hopkins Foundation does'.

The exhibition was developed and managed by an independent curator, Suimee Keelan. The choice of artists was determined by a selection committee made up of Keelan and two of the trustees, Jane Hartwell and Jackie Morreau. Eight artists – Virginia Bodman, Andrew Ekins, Brian Grassom, Susan Miller, Duncan Newton, Jayne Parker, Srinivas Surti and Frances Turner – were selected to exhibit their work in the recently opened Rootstein Hopkins Space at London College of Fashion, from 11 July to 7 August 2002. A series of talks by participating artists and a one-day seminar entitled *Patronage in the 21st Century* provided an educational strand to the event. The exhibitors represented a wide range of visual arts practice. As Chris Horrocks wrote in his essay for the catalogue that accompanied *Chosen*: 'While their different methods, materials and references converge at some levels, their varied approaches suggest that pluralism in painting, sculpture and installation is the order of the day.'

The artists who featured in the show were on the whole positive about the experience. Looking back on it from the perspective of 2005, Virginia Bodman commented: 'I was fortunate to get selected for the *Chosen* exhibition. It was good to meet the trustees again. The Rootstein Hopkins Space wasn't ideal – it had a red carpet – but it worked fine for my work.' The inter-generational nature of the show meant that younger artists could learn from working alongside their more experienced peers. For Srinivas Surti, who was preparing during the summer of 2002 for his MA degree show at Central Saint Martins College of Art and Design, taking part in *Chosen* was particularly instructive. 'I learned a lot from exhibiting with Jayne Parker,' he said. 'She really stood her ground as to how her work was to be shown, which taught me how to operate in that sort of exhibition context. It made me realise that it is really important as an artist to be assertive about how your work should be seen.'

The Rootstein Hopkins Foundation trustees were keen to regard *Chosen* as a learning experience. The time and location of the exhibition were both felt to have been somewhat problematic. Holding the event during the summer vacation inevitably meant that fewer students and staff from the London Institute could attend. With hindsight, Jane Hartwell felt that the venue was not ideal. 'The Rootstein Hopkins Space isn't known as a dedicated gallery,' she said, 'and the end of July is a difficult time of year. So, as an exercise to celebrate what we'd done and to raise our profile, I don't know how successful it was.' There were, however, definite plusses to the event. 'It was fantastic for the trustees to see the work of some of the people we'd supported,' said Hartwell, 'and, I would imagine, for those people to exhibit.' The mixed success of *Chosen*, combined with a re-evaluation of spending priorities, led the trustees to abandon plans to repeat the exhibition annually.

## Looking back and taking stock

An important, unforeseen outcome of staging the exhibition was that the Rootstein Hopkins Foundation became more reflective about its activities, and more eager to learn about what its investment had achieved. The process of identifying artists to include in the exhibition revealed that the Foundation's light-touch philosophy, which might be described as grant-giving without strings, had had its limitations. This philosophy, and what it leads to in practice, is summed up by Deirdre Hopkins. 'We get letters from a lot of awardees saying, "Thank you very much, this is what I did", she says. 'But that is not a formal requirement. The award is an absolute gift. Having made the decision, that's it: do with it what you will. I think that is the way it should be.'

By comparison with the burdensome reporting that is increasingly required by other funders, the Rootstein Hopkins Foundation's lack of emphasis on formal accountability was seen as a blessing by many of its awardees. Monica Petzal, the Director of the Foundation for Women's Art (formerly the Museum of Women's Art), which received an award in 1996 to support *From the Interior*, a touring exhibition of work by English and Chinese women artists, takes this view. 'These sorts of awards are critical,' she says, 'particularly because they come with so few strings attached. Applying to public agencies like Arts Council England requires a spectacular amount of work. A light-touch application by letter, directly to the funder, is a gift from the gods. There is great value to philanthropy that is easily and trustworthily given. We still do find the odd person who will say, "We think you're a good thing, have a thousand pounds", but funding has been turned into such an industry. There is very little room left for the personal quirkiness that you get with people who have the money and are able just to do what they want with it.'

For the Foundation, though, the absence of feedback from award winners meant that, where individual artists were concerned, contact was invariably lost; many of them had moved on and, when *Chosen* came to be researched, were hard to trace. There was little visual or written evidence in the Foundation's archive of what had been achieved. 'It was through that exhibition,' says Jane Hartwell, 'that the process of monitoring and recording started. It became apparent that we had to do it.'

The urge to take stock of what had been achieved in a more formal and considered way gained impetus when Professor Hogan joined the trustees. 'My influence has been more external to the actual grant programme,' says Professor Hogan. 'It is more to do with setting up a legacy for the Rootstein Hopkins Foundation. I was very keen on the idea of trying to commission a new piece of research to be that legacy, as well as trying to record what has been done.'

Professor Hogan was aware that, as a consequence of the Labour government's requirement that more rigorous evidence should be produced to justify and account for government expenditure across the public sector, a new emphasis was being placed on measuring the value gained from investment in the arts. Major public sector funders, such as Arts Council England and the Arts and Humanities Research Council, had begun to commission research into 'impact assessment' in order to facilitate the development of the more robust evidence-base that was now felt to be required to legitimise subsidies to the cultural sector.

Encouraged by Professor Hogan, the trustees saw that their desire to investigate the outcomes of the Rootstein Hopkins Foundation's investment in the visual arts could be shaped into a research project that would have a wider public benefit. Appropriately framed, such a project could contribute to current discussions about how to measure impact in the arts. It could also create an opportunity to begin to map and to analyse more broadly the role played by independent trusts and foundations in supporting the contemporary arts in the United Kingdom. Following talks with a number of art colleges, the trustees decided, in 2004, to locate the Rootstein Hopkins Research Fellowship at Wimbledon College of Art.

## Winding up and spending out: leaving a legacy

The process of taking stock, which began with *Chosen* in 2002 and has continued through the work of the Research Fellowship, is a natural consequence of the Rootstein Hopkins Foundation's decision to wind up its affairs in 2008. Most independent trusts are established in the expectation that they will continue in perpetuity. This would probably have been the case with the Rootstein Hopkins Foundation too, had its original plan to establish a school of fine art come to fruition. However, with the early death of Adel and the gradual demise of the art school vision, the Foundation approached the new millennium with a revised charitable mission and with an ageing cohort of trustees. The time had come to think about how, or indeed whether, the Foundation should carry on into the twenty-first century.

'Before Rick died,' says Michael Southgate, 'it became clear that we wouldn't be able to keep the trusteeship going in the same way.' With uncanny prescience, in November 1999, at the final trustees' meeting before his death in June 2000, Rick Hopkins declared that, rather than pass it on to a new generation of trustees, he wished to make plans for the Foundation to be wound up. The reasons he gave were twofold: he was worried that future generations of trustees might not properly understand or implement the intentions of the founders; and he was concerned that, as the culture of the Foundation changed, the burden of the administrative costs might become too great.

Rick had discussed the issue with his wife, Deirdre. 'The concern he expressed to me,' she recalls, 'was that he didn't want the Foundation to carry on with a new generation of trustees who had no understanding of the history or the thrust of the Foundation, of what he and Adel had been trying to do. He was afraid it would just become another large sum of money, given away in a way that they wouldn't have approved of.' Graham Feldman has a similar recollection. 'The worry was that the whole thing would go off at a different tangent and it would not do what was originally intended,' says Feldman. 'We run quite a tight ship in terms of administration costs, and we didn't want to get into a situation where we would be paying more on administration and management than we were giving out in grants.'

When the trustees met in July 2000, barely a month after Rick's death, they agreed to honour his wish that the trust should be dissolved. The rate of grant-giving would be accelerated so that the Foundation's accumulated reserves would, over several years, be dissipated. Then, as it approached January 2006, the date at which the lease on the building would expire, Shawfield House would be sold and the Foundation would 'spend out' the proceeds as soon as was practicably possible. Donees would be sought 'who comply with the Foundation's deed and grant strategy'. And so a target wind-up date of 2008 was set.

This plan has subsequently been followed. The only significant departure from the trustees' expectations was a welcome one. When Shawfield House was put on the market, its value was estimated to be somewhere in the region of £ 2,000,000; when the building was eventually sold in June 2005, following a competitive bidding process, the actual price realised was in excess of £6,000,000. 'We lost the rental on the building,' says Deirdre Hopkins, 'but we gained £6.2 million instead to distribute. This is an exciting prospect for all of the trustees. The final few years are going to be very, very interesting.'

Setting the deadline for the cessation of its activities well in advance, has allowed the Foundation plenty of time to plan for its departure. 'The idea,' says Professor Hogan, 'is to distribute the money to charities that will carry on the work of the trust and are in sympathy with its philosophy.' The 'spending out' phase, as it is known in trusts and foundations sector, will involve the trustees in some challenging decision-making. Will the Foundation continue its support for individual artists, or will the emphasis be towards grants for organisations? Will prestigious, well-known institutions, such as national museums, be prioritised, or is there a case for encouraging artist-led activity? Should the aim be to leave a legacy for the long term, or is there an argument for investing in more immediate, short-term needs? The solution, which Professor Rod Bugg begins to map and to analyse in his essay, will no doubt be a combination of all of these things.

'I know that when we start distributing larger funds, it will probably be to institutions rather than individuals,' says Jackie Morreau. 'I think it would be nice if there could continue to be a fund for individuals, but it's a lot of work; unless, when we stop, we leave a pot of money for somebody else to take charge of. I think that is what will have to happen if we want to keep that branch of it open.'

'Michael Southgate would like a legacy that would be there in perpetuity; something that would go on forever,' says Graham Feldman. 'I think the rest of the trustees would be happy if the name stayed around for another twenty or thirty years. It will certainly stay around at the British Museum; the Rootstein Hopkins Foundation endowment fund will continue there, but that's sort of hidden.' There, but sort of hidden: a fitting description, perhaps, of the understated but valuable contribution that the Rootstein Hopkins Foundation, alongside many other independent trusts and foundations, has made to the arts in the United Kingdom.

# THE IMPACT OF ROOTSTEIN HOPKINS FOUNDATION FUNDING

*by Paul Glinkowski*

## Introduction

A core component of the Rootstein Hopkins Research Fellowship at Wimbledon College of Art was a study to examine the impact of Rootstein Hopkins Foundation (RHF) funding. The purpose of this study, which was based on a series of face-to-face interviews, was to record and to analyse the qualitative experiences and the quantitative outputs described by the individuals and institutions that received awards from the Foundation during the ten-year period from 1995 to 2004. Where possible, the interviewees' testimonies were supported by relevant documentary data (such as artists' CVs, exhibition catalogues or visual documentation of art works and events). The result is a unique piece of research, which provides an insight into the wide range of impacts or effects that have followed on from and, to a greater or lesser extent, appear related to the funding given by an independent grant-making foundation in support of the visual arts in the United Kingdom. The definition of visual arts used for this study embraces fashion, graphic design and digital media practices, as well as more traditional fine art disciplines such as drawing, painting and sculpture. The study aspires to contribute to academic understanding of the relatively new but rapidly expanding field of impact assessment in the context of the arts.

Most of the literature concerning impact studies in the arts agrees that the definition and measurement of the impact, or impacts, resulting from arts activity is highly problematic. In particular, problems arise when trying to demonstrate or attribute a cause and effect relationship between a particular action or event and a given outcome. A perennial difficulty with impact studies is the temptation to over-interpret the connection between, to take the present example, RHF funding and the subsequent successes (or failures) of an individual artist, arts organisation, or project. Because of the often unprovable relationship between cause and effect, it could be argued that it might be better to talk of perceived outcomes or probable effects rather than hard and fast impacts *per se*.

An additional caveat in discussing the impact of RHF funding is that the degree to which this source of funding was crucial to enabling a particular activity to take place varied from project to project. Thirty-six per cent of the participants in the study felt that their activity would probably have gone ahead in some form even without RHF funding, although the majority of those who thought that it would go ahead indicated that having the RHF funding had made a qualitative difference to what it was possible for them to achieve.

Recognising, rather than attempting to resolve or overcome, these limitations, this study adopts an inclusive definition and interpretation of the term 'impact', where an impact is an effect or consequence that is perceived to be related to the project or activity funded by the RHF.

The study focused on Rootstein Hopkins Foundation award winners from 1995 to 2004, the Foundation's first decade of grant-giving. All the award winners who could be traced were invited to take part. It was important to achieve an inclusive rather than a representative sample because part of the *raison d'être* for the study was to provide the RHF with a detailed overview of what had been achieved with its funding. Out of a possible survey sample of 69, a total of 60 grant recipients (41 individuals and 19 institutions) agreed to participate. The sample equates to 87 per cent of the total number of awards given during the survey period (60 out of 69), and represents 97 per cent of the total value of awards given (£1,569,692 out of £1,602,338).

Data was gathered through a series of face-to-face interviews, based upon a questionnaire that was designed to be consistent and appropriate for recipients of both individual and institutional awards. The 60 interviews took place during a four-month period between 3 October 2005 and 1 February 2006. There were two instances in which there was a departure from the standard scenario of a face-to-face interview with either the recipient of an individual award, or with the nominated representative of an institutional award winner. Linda Short (*travel* 2000) had relocated to Australia and agreed to conduct the interview via e-mail. Frances Turner (*travel* 1998) sadly died in July 2003. Frances' partner, Peter Gandy, agreed to provide a proxy interview, from which it was possible to gain a useful third-party account of what had resulted from this award.

## Awards by Category
### Different categories, different awards, different outcomes

An analysis of the material collated from interviews with the recipients of the different types of award that have been offered by the RHF showed that each type of award was associated with different kinds of outcome. The categories of award are: *capital projects; sabbaticals; student fees; students' international exchange; student prizes; collections; projects and exhibitions; and travel*. What follows is a summary of the principal findings for each of the eight categories. The first five of these represent different forms of support for the visual arts within the context of higher education. Four of the categories of award – *sabbaticals, student fees, projects and exhibitions and travel* – were particularly (but not exclusively) targeted at individual artists, whereas *capital projects, students' international exchange, student prizes and collections* were always supported via grants to institutions.

Each category of award is introduced with a brief description of the activities funded, followed by a summary of the impacts that were found to be associated with that type of award. The discussion of each category (with the exception of *student prizes*, where only one recurrent award was made) is augmented by a series of case studies which follow this impact analysis, in which the award recipients' own words are interwoven with an interpretative commentary to highlight the outcomes that resulted from their particular project.

*Support for the visual arts in higher education*

Of the 69 awards made by the RHF in the ten years between 1995 and 2004, 39 (57 per cent) in some way supported the visual arts within the British higher education sector. The £942,078 awarded to these projects represents 59 per cent of the total value of the funding given by the Foundation during this period.

Fifteen awards, worth a total £808,383, were made to higher education institutions. These awards were given either to support the delivery of capital projects, or to enable the recipient institutions to assist specific students by providing international student exchange opportunities, student bursaries, or student prizes.

A further 24 awards, totalling £133,695, were made to individuals who applied to the Foundation in their capacity either as art college lecturers seeking sabbaticals, or as students who needed assistance with their higher education course fees.

*Capital projects*

The majority of the funding targeted by the RHF at the higher education sector was to support the development or enhancement of capital facilities, either within specialist art colleges, or within art faculties in universities. Six capital awards were made, totalling £644,000.

A capital grant, up to a value of £30,000, was first instituted by the Foundation in 1999 and was awarded thereafter on (more or less) an annual basis. An additional award of £500,000 made in 2001 to London College of Fashion, which was described in the Foundation's records as a 'special' award, is classified for the purposes of this study as a capital award, as its purpose was to create a new multi-purpose facility within the college.

All six capital projects had been completed and were considered by the interviewees to be highly successful. Although some of the projects had suffered delays or exceeded initial budget estimates, none of the interviewees reported significant negative outcomes. All six projects were said to have created a base of provision which had subsequently been built upon. All were said to have enhanced the learning experience for students, brought a variety of benefits and opportunities for staff, and created new possibilities for interfacing with external partners and audiences. Five of the six projects reported that RHF funding had helped to lever additional funding, either to support and sustain the initial capital project, or for other purposes.

Three of the six capital awards had led to the creation or enhancement of facilities dedicated to the creative use of digital technologies. Each of these awards had significant outcomes in common, which can be summarised as follows:

- The RHF funding provided a catalyst for rapid growth and investment in new areas of technology-based creative practice.
- The resources created are attractive both to existing and to would-be students and are perceived to give the respective institutions a competitive advantage in the higher education market place.

*LONDON COLLEGE OF PRINTING AND
DISTRIBUTIVE TRADES, SCHOOL OF RETAIL STUDIES
1995 – £8.121
For two students from LCPDT to exchange with two students from the Fashion Institute of Design and Merchandising, Los Angeles, USA.

LONDON COLLEGE OF FASHION,
UNIVERSITY OF THE ARTS LONDON
1997-1999 – £24,000
For two students per year (for three years) from London College of Fashion to exchange with two students from the Fashion Institute of Technology, New York, USA.

NEWCASTLE UNIVERSITY
1997 – £8,000
For two students from Newcastle University to exchange with two students from the Cleveland Institute of Art, Ohio, USA.

GLASGOW SCHOOL OF ART
1998 – £5,000
For six Master of Fine Art (MFA) students from Glasgow School of Art to exchange with students from six different overseas art colleges.

GLASGOW SCHOOL OF ART
1998 – £3,000
For 23 students and staff from the MFA course at Glasgow School of Art to travel to Germany for a week at the invitation of the DAAD programme.

KINGSTON UNIVERSITY
2001-2003 – £30,000
For two students per year (for three years) from Kingston University to exchange with two students from Hong Ik University, Seoul, South Korea.

MANCHESTER METROPOLITAN UNIVERSITY+
2004 – £10,000
For two students from Manchester Metropolitan University to exchange with two students from Hong Kong Polytechnic University, Hong Kong.

* Indicates an award recipient that did not participate in the survey.
+ This award was subsequently repeated for the years 2005 and 2006, which fall outside of the scope of the impact study.

- The quality and ambition of students' creative work was perceived to have improved because of the availability of the new technology.
- The skills gained by students using the facilities had improved their employment prospects; employers, therefore, also benefited from the existence of such facilities.
- Staff as well as students had gained the opportunity for skills enhancement.
- Having such facilities had made technology-based collaborations with external partners more possible.

For Gray's School of Art in Aberdeen, being able to maintain a competitive edge and profile was a particularly important outcome. 'Having state of the art digital resources has given us important credibility relative to other art schools in Scotland and the wider UK,' said its Head of School. 'We are on the edge of the UK and most of the opportunities in fine art are in centres like London and Glasgow. We are always looking at how we can punch above our weight, and this kind of additional funding enables us to do that.'

*Students' international exchange*

An award was initiated in 1995 to enable an art college in the United Kingdom to give a limited number of its students (usually two) the chance to exchange, generally for a period of between two and three months, with students from art colleges overseas. Eight such awards, totalling £88,121, were made during the period to 2004. Sometimes the exchange awards were given on a one-off basis; sometimes funding was awarded over a three-year period to allow the exchanges to be repeated to benefit students from different year groups. In most cases, RHF funding subsidised the visit to the United Kingdom of international students as well as the costs associated with sending the British-based students overseas.

The key benefits described by institutions which had been supported to provide opportunities for international exchange were: gaining access to new perspectives; and networking, on an individual and at an institutional level.

Leo Duff, Director of the Drawing as Process MA programme at Kingston University, believed that the opportunity to spend time in a Korean university had had a powerful creative influence on students from Kingston. 'The whole point of an exchange is for a new cultural experience in art and design to take place and for that to feed new ideas and insights into practice,' she said. 'We have achieved that. All the students who made the exchange – certainly those from here – felt 100 per cent that the experience completely changed the way they saw things; they had their eyes opened to new ways of thinking and working. For each of these postgraduate students, without exception, it has profoundly influenced the direction of their work.'

Sam Ainsley, Head of the MFA programme at Glasgow School of Art, felt that international awareness and networking was becoming increasingly important for artists. 'The current art world is very international and it is important for emerging artists to gain an early sense of how they might operate internationally,' she said. 'All of the people on the exchange that year [1998] made contacts that are ongoing. Some have already resulted in international exhibiting opportunities; others may

List of awards made between 1995 and 2004 to support students' fees (n.b. where an institution has changed its name since the time of the award, the current name is given)

HELEN SLATER
1995 – £2,430
Fees for the first year of an MFA in Printmaking at the Slade School of Fine Art, London.

*SHANTI THOMAS
1997 – £2,500
Fees for an MA in European Fine Art at Winchester School of Art (for a course based in Barcelona).

*JANE HARRIS
1998 – £2,500
Towards the fees for a PhD in Digital Textiles at the Royal College of Art, London.

*LYNNE ROBERTSON
1999 – £1,025
Towards the fees for a BA at Bradford College.

BRIAN GRASSOM
2000 – £2,500
Fees for an MFA at Gray's School of Art, Robert Gordon University, Aberdeen.

SRINIVAS SURTI
2001 – £1,550
Fees for a two-year part-time MFA at Central Saint Martins College of Art and Design, London.

JULIA POLONSKI
2001 – £2,950
Fees for a two-year part-time MFA in Drawing at Wimbledon College of Art. London.

STINA HARRIS
2002 – £2,150
Fees and materials support for an MA in Printmaking at Bradford College.

KAREN COLLEY
2002 – £2,950
Fees for a two-year part-time MFA in Drawing at Wimbledon College of Art, London.

JUNE TRAFFORD
2002 – £2,200
Fees to allow the conversion from a HND course to a BA in Drawing for Fine Art Practice at Swindon College.

EMMA CHURCHILL
2003 – £2,500
Towards the fees for an MA in Contemporary Visual Arts at University College Falmouth.

*EMMA STIBBON
2003 – £1,000
Towards the fees for an MFA at the University of the West of England.

*   Indicates an award recipient who did not participate in the survey

do so in the future.'

For Ainsley, another important dimension of student exchanges was the opportunity to network at an institutional level. 'Each international exchange cements Glasgow School of Art's relationship with the institution we exchange with. We do our best to "keep it live"' she said. 'We now have a drawing research project between Glasgow, Sydney and Beijing, which came about from discussions initiated through the international student exchange programme. It is a valuable catalyst for further links, projects and initiatives.'

Two institutions reported that the international exchange project supported by the RHF had been influential to their institution in demonstrating the importance of such exchanges. The result has been that greater emphasis has subsequently been given to them. In two other cases, however, it had not been possible to sustain the international exchange opportunity once the RHF funding had ended.

Student fees

The RHF made 15 awards between 1995 and 2004 to assist with the fees (and occasionally a proportion of the materials or maintenance costs) of students studying, usually for higher degrees, at British art colleges. Fourteen of these awards, totalling £31,695, were made directly to individual students. One award, worth £71,262 over an eight-year period, was given to an institution, the Royal College of Art, to enable it to assist students who were studying there for a PhD degree.

Eleven of the 14 awards made directly to students were to support Masters-level study, one was to support study at PhD level, and two helped with the fees of undergraduate students. Awards to assist individuals with their course fees ranged from £1,000 to £2,950, making this the lowest category of RHF award by value. In general, the awards were targeted at mature students; most of the recipients were in their thirties or forties.

Eight of the nine individual-award recipients interviewed had successfully completed their studies. One had chosen to intermit (to defer completion) for family reasons. All nine recipients were continuing to pursue their art practice. Four of the seven students who were supported through an institutional award to the Royal College of Art to undertake doctoral research had, at the time of the survey, gained their PhD degrees.

The positive outcomes that were most prevalent in this category of award were: a strong sense of creative and professional advancement; a powerful sense of esteem or endorsement associated with gaining an award; new bodies of art work, which had generally been exhibited in public and had often helped to gain additional opportunities for the artists.

Karen Colley spoke of a clear sense of progress, which she associated with the pursuit of her MA. 'It was as if someone had turned a light on,' she said. 'I developed a lot in terms of my art practice and also in my understanding of the academic side. I now feel more confident about my work. I felt like an amateur before because I was largely self-taught. I now feel equipped to operate as a professional artist.'

Srinivas Surti, who at the time of the interview was both a practising artist and a tutor at an art college, felt that his MA at Central Saint Martins College of Art and

List of awards made between 1995 and 2004 to support students' fees continued

*JANINE BARRACLOUGH
2003 – £2,000
Towards the fees for an MA in Fashion at Central Saint Martins College of Art and Design, London.

PAULA GARCIA STONE
2004 – £2,940
Towards the fees for a part-time MA in Creative Technology at the University of Salford.

ROYAL COLLEGE OF ART, LONDON
1997- 2004 – £71.262
To support, over an eight-year period, the fees and maintenance costs of PhD students with a subject focus on drawing.

* Indicates an award recipient who did not participate in the survey

List of student prize awards made between 1995 and 2004

CHELTENHAM AND GLOUCESTER COLLEGE OF HIGHER EDUCATION, UNIVERSITY OF GLOUCESTERSHIRE
2001 – £5,000
For two student prizes of £500 each to be awarded for a five-year period: 2001 to 2005.

Design had led on directly to new creative and professional opportunities. 'I left Saint Martins with new skills, confidence and qualifications for teaching and with a body of work that helped me to get exhibitions and residency opportunities,' he said. 'I became far more articulate and confident because of Saint Martins. I'd developed the ability and the language to communicate about both my own work and other peoples', which is an essential part of the job. It was massively important in terms of my own education as an artist, and now I am able to pass on the lessons learned to a new generation of students.'

Paula Garcia Stone typified the positive sense of endorsement shared by the majority of the student artists who had received an award from the RHF. 'The main benefit,' she said, 'is the sense of achievement at being given such an award. It is not all about money. I feel honoured to have had the grant. It demonstrates external endorsement for the direction my art is taking. That perhaps is as important as being awarded the money.'

The main problems encountered by artists who had received support with their fees related either to the pressures associated with academic study, or to economic difficulties following art college. However, a relative lack of income is widely accepted as part of the habitus of an early-stage professional artist and it was as likely to be viewed with optimism as with dismay. One artist, for example, observed: 'When I applied for the Rootstein Hopkins award I was on benefits; today I am self-employed as an artist. My income is now from my practice, and having an income allows me to continue to practise. I'm not necessarily better off, but I've been able to invest what I've earned on materials and resources, such as a computer, and I feel better placed to function professionally as an artist.'

*Student prizes*

An exceptional award of £5,000 was made in 2001 to Cheltenham and Gloucester College of Higher Education to enable student prizes to be given as part of a national open-submission competition focused on the discipline of drawing. The competition is currently known as the Jerwood Drawing Prize. In 2003 the administration of the prize (and the RHF funding contribution) transferred from Cheltenham and Gloucester College to Wimbledon College of Art.

The principal impact of offering two student prizes as a component of a major open-submission drawing competition was the encouragement that this gave to student artists to pit their talents against those of their more experienced professional peers. Professor Anita Taylor, who initiated the prize at Cheltenham and Gloucester College and who continues to oversee its administration at Wimbledon College of Art, observed that over the five years in which the RHF had funded the student prizes there had been a discernible increase in both the quantity and quality of student applications. The improvement in quality was reflected in the numbers of students who were being selected for the Jerwood Drawing Prize exhibition, which offers a public showcase for some of the best works submitted to the competition. In 2005 students represented around 25 per cent of the chosen exhibitors. Student artists had also succeeded in winning the non-student prizes. Five Jerwood Drawing Prizes are awarded each year (including the two earmarked specifically for students); in 2005, no fewer

than four went to student artists. The 2001 student prize winner, Lisa Cathro, had her winning drawing, *Construction of Time*, bought by the Prints and Drawings Collection at the British Museum.

'The Jerwood Drawing Prize has become an important stepping-stone for young and emerging artists,' said Taylor. 'The student prizes offer an important incentive for younger artists to participate in a high profile national award alongside major recognised artists. A lot of galleries pick up on artists from the show, including young graduates.'

## Sabbaticals

The RHF made ten sabbatical awards, worth a total of £102,000, during the period from 1995 to 2004. The sabbaticals were given to enable lecturers at British art colleges to spend time away from their professional commitments in order to focus on their art practice for a period of either three or six months; sometimes to work towards a specific outcome (usually an exhibition), sometimes just to develop their studio practice. The recipients had all been teaching for a number of years at the time of their awards. Most had a significant track record of exhibiting and could be described as mid-career artists. Depending on the length of their absence from work, recipients received either £6,000 or £12,000, to compensate for loss of earnings. The most prevalent positive outcomes associated with sabbatical awards were:

- The opportunity for re-evaluation and renewal, both creatively and professionally.
- A powerful sense of freedom from professional constraints and obligations.
- A body of new work, which the artist generally considered to be of some significance within their total oeuvre and which usually became the focus of a solo exhibition.
- Benefits of esteem, which might be of value to the college where the artist worked as well as to the artist.
- Benefits to others, including art colleges, art students, exhibition venues and public audiences.
- The opportunity for international research and/or exhibitions.

Several artists were prompted by their sabbaticals to reassess and renegotiate their commitments to teaching. Chris Jones, for example, said: 'It made me take stock of my situation and re-evaluate the balance between earning a living as a teacher and making art. Now, I teach three days in the University and the rest of the week is either research time or studio time, which psychologically is a big shift.'

Jones was also able to use the time away from teaching to reappraise his all-round creative and professional practice. 'It allows time to think,' said Jones. 'Not just about a particular painting, but about your whole approach to your practice. That can involve a whole host of things, from how to raise your profile, to having new conversations with people about your work and about art in general. All the stuff that goes on around the edge of making work can be followed through more fully. The real value is that it gives you a chance to integrate things within your practice and gives you space to develop. That can be very liberating.'

A sense of liberation was shared by Jayne Parker. 'I earn my living mainly through teaching,' she said, 'and having time away was liberating. I'd been teaching since I left college and this was the first time I had had a chance to stop. Just having the time to think about my own work, rather than other peoples' work, was important; being able to concentrate my energy on my own creative interests – having thinking space. I really valued the time that it gave me.'

For Pam Skelton, the sabbatical allowed her more time to work on a project that was already in progress and that she regards as seminal within her overall creative career: a video installation, *Liquidators*, which has been exhibited in London, Northern Ireland, Finland and Croatia. 'It [the award] coincided with a period of development that was already happening,' recalled Skelton, 'but having those two terms off provided a lot more free time to develop the work. It wasn't just down to the sabbatical, but it enabled me to give time and thought to what I did.'

Virginia Bodman valued the sense of professional recognition and affirmation that came with the sabbatical award. 'The award is a mark of esteem, both personally and externally,' she said. 'It represents validation, and if you live in a place where debate with other artists is limited, it is all the more important to have these external marks of esteem. I felt empowered by that.'

Bodman observed also that the sabbatical had enabled her to forge a qualitatively different type of relationship with her students; a relationship based on their awareness of her as a practising artist, rather than as a teacher. 'I took some of them to my studio to see the work in progress,' she recalled. 'As teaching now seems to me to be focused on "tell" rather than "show", or "do", showing somebody what you mean can sometimes be much more effective. Many students tell me that they appreciate what they describe as the privilege of seeing the work in progress. A lot of the students came to the [subsequent] exhibition at Hexham and this promoted a stimulating dialogue between teacher and student.'

For Paul Butler the award had numerous benefits: 'The salient fact of the sabbatical was that I went over to the States for a month. I visited an old friend, the artist Mary Kelly, at UCLA [University of California, Los Angeles] and then went up to northern California. I took a large number of photographs and did a lot of drawing and it was an enormously successful and stimulating trip. I also went over to New York and made contacts there. It had a lot of very valuable spin-offs. Without question, a sabbatical feeds hugely into your teaching.'

Although the outcomes described by sabbatical award winners were overwhelmingly positive, a negative outcome peculiar to this category of award winner was that 50 per cent of the artists had experienced some sort of difficulty in returning to work. Three artists had found it hard to adjust to academic employment again after a temporary interlude of working as a full-time artist. Duncan Newton said of his return to academic duties: 'Rather than noticing the positive benefits to teaching, more pronounced to me was the difficulty of continuing the same artistic practice having got back into the institution. It was very difficult to acclimatise again to an interrupted mode of practice. That meditative looking that enables you to decide what to do is much more circumscribed when you are teaching. As a consequence, my work shifted to a much smaller scale.'

Two other artists referred to the fact that part-time tutors who pursued sabbatical opportunities could find themselves in a vulnerable situation with regard to their employment. Richard Talbot observed: 'As a part-time teacher, you're always taking a risk if you take a break. The college I was at was not subject to the RAE [Research Assessment Exercise] review, so what I did with my time out was, in some ways, neither here nor there to them.' Both of the artists who raised this issue had subsequently given up part-time teaching posts that they had occupied at the time of the sabbatical, but felt that they were better off for having done so.

### Collections

During the period from 1995 to 2004 the RHF gave £518,000 (32 per cent of the total value of the awards made) to two important national collections which, in quite different ways, support, promote and conserve the contemporary visual arts in the United Kingdom.

In 2000 the Foundation granted the British Museum a one-off award of £500,000 to create a capital endowment which it can draw on, in perpetuity, to purchase works on paper by contemporary artists to add to its Prints and Drawings Collection.

Two awards were made during the period covered by the study (an initial £8,000 in 2001, followed by a further £10,000 in 2004) to support new recordings for the *Artists' Lives* oral history project, which is part of the National Life Stories collection at the British Library. Two subsequent awards were made to *Artists' Lives* in 2005: £26,930 to enable the purchase of digital recording equipment, and a major endowment of £400,000 to ensure that a minimum of four new artists' recordings per year can be made for the foreseeable future.

Where collections are concerned, the purpose of which is to acquire and conserve works, or, in the case of *Artists' Lives* testimonies, for the benefit of future as well as current generations, it is perhaps more appropriate to take a longer-term view of impact than was possible in this study. In the words of Antony Griffiths, Keeper of the Department of Prints and Drawings at the British Museum: 'The benefits rack up over the centuries.' Nevertheless, significant short-term impacts were described, which are highlighted in the case studies that follow.

### Projects and exhibitions

During the period from 1995 to 2004, the RHF made awards totalling £51,760 to 12 individual artists to assist them to make and/or present work. These projects were usually intended to culminate in exhibitions or other forms of presentation of new work in public spaces. The earliest awards of this nature are described in the Foundation's records as 'artists' support' grants. This category of award evolved in 2000 into 'artists' projects' and thereafter was renamed simply 'projects'. The amounts of project funding awarded by the Foundation to individual artists ranged from £2,000 to £6,000.

Two institutions were also awarded a total of £19,500 during the period covered by the study to assist with costs related to exhibitions. The Museum of Women's Art received £7,500 towards an international touring exhibition, *From the Interior*. The

Morley Gallery received £12,000 to help with the costs of two publications produced in association with *Father*, a solo exhibition of the work of Maggi Hambling.

The RHF's project and exhibition awards led to many quantifiable outputs, which are summarised later. Each award had in some way supported the production and/or presentation of a new body of work, usually both. In several instances, work produced with RHF project funding had received exposure in exhibitions additional to those envisaged at the time of the application, or else had been on display for longer than was originally planned. There were two instances, however, in which work intended for exhibition had yet to find an audience. In addition, the realisation of one further project had, at the time of the study, been deferred due to difficulties with the commissioning venue.

Alongside the tangible, quantifiable outputs, such as new work and exhibitions, the survey showed that the project awards produced a large number of qualitative outcomes. Particularly notable for this category of award were outcomes associated with:

- New relationships made possible by the project.
- Opportunities for learning, often leading to the development of new, non-creative skills.
- Additional professional opportunities or recognition, stimulated both by the project and by the fact of having gained an RHF award.

Freedom from financial constraints and having an incentive to focus on creative work were also important qualitative outcomes associated with project funding.

Although most of the project awards supported studio-based practice, a number had helped to foster creative engagement with new types of audience or participants, some of whom had become protagonists in the work. Sophie Benson, who was supported to complete a three-month residency at a heritage property, Harewood House, near Leeds, enjoyed a qualitatively different kind of relationship with her on-site audience than she had been used to. 'My practice normally is quite solitary; working on my own in my studio,' she said. 'As an artist at Harewood House, I was one worker amongst all the other people working in the house and the grounds. That was a really nice position to be in. I got to talk to people and to find things out through the process of conversation. I really valued their feedback. They picked up on connections within the work that you would only recognise if you knew the environment really well. They may not have been familiar with contemporary art, but they were very informed about the work because of their familiarity with the context to which it referred.'

In at least one case, building and negotiating relationships was the essence of the project. Simon Grennan, in partnership with Christopher Sperrandio, was supported to realise a public art project that resulted in a series of cartoon-style portraits, which were devised by residents and traders and then inscribed by a sign-writer directly on to shop windows on Wembley High Road. 'They [the residents and traders] were the hardest bunch we've worked with for ages,' said Grennan. 'That's good, that's interesting to me. Our artistic criteria are about our learning, not the public response. We think of ourselves as immature, unformed. The work is a way for us to learn about what things are like. The more we try to put things in places that they're not meant to be, the more we learn from it. The idea of public art as something focused on an object is patently untrue. The exchange isn't in the work, it's in the negotiation processes. The participants are often seduced by the unusual proposals we put to them. They become completely our allies.'

For several artists, project funding from the RHF had helped them to realise their first significant solo shows, which often involved organisational as well as creative challenges. Jennifer Godlieb, who succeeded in staging an exhibition in a space in central London, said: 'I don't think I'd previously done a solo show that I was particularly proud of. In this case it was entirely my own project; I'd raised funding, I'd found an appropriate venue, I'd got some press coverage and I was pleased with the work I'd produced. Artists are notorious for being quite bad at the coordination and the practical stuff. This enabled me to show that I could do it. It's still one of the best things on my CV.'

Derek Mawudoku's award assisted with the costs associated with *Feed Me*, a solo exhibition at the Morley Gallery, London. Gaining funding for the project meant that Mawudoku was able to exert more influence on the outcome. 'Having the funding for the framing and the catalogue meant that I could work towards a more professional presentation,' he said. 'Fifteen years after graduating from Goldsmiths College, I could at last put on a show that I was in control of. It was good for me to have that responsibility. I was able to project the work how I wanted it.'

A number of artists felt that their RHF project award had helped them to achieve positive spin-offs. Jenny West, who was funded to create a new series of drawings, believed that the fact of having the award was of value in itself. 'The award has helped me to make further successful applications for funding for large-scale site-specific drawing projects,' she said. 'I am sure that being the recipient of a Rootstein Hopkins award has made a difference. I've received two Arts Council grants since then and I've undertaken significant projects with public institutions, such as an exhibition at the Angel Row Gallery, Nottingham, and a commission for the Government Art Collection.'

For Andrew Ekins, the financial cushion created by the award proved creatively empowering and helped him to achieve a new sense of professionalism. 'It was liberating to be able to buy the materials you needed on that day, and not to have to make do, or wait to be able to do so,' recalled Ekins. 'I was able to buy new materials, investigate different kinds of materials and pay for things to be done. It put me on a more professional footing. Awareness of the importance of professional standards is something I've been able to carry on since that period.'

Barbara Loftus was one of several artists for whom a project award provided a welcome sense of focus. Loftus believed that without it she might have had to continue to work as a commercial artist in order to earn a living. 'It kept me focused as a professional artist at a time when I could have been side-tracked,' she said. A modest amount of project funding can be important, Loftus felt, to achieving a qualitatively satisfying creative outcome. 'It gives you elbow room to do the project as fully as you can,' she said. 'You don't have to cut corners so much with materials and research; you don't have to make so many compromises.'

## Travel

Between 1995 and 2002 the RHF made 13 awards, totalling £65,000, to enable artists to travel overseas for research purposes. Although all of the projects in this category were based around specific proposals for overseas travel (and each received the standard amount for an RHF travel award of £5,000), some are classified in the Foundation's records as 'project' grants.

Usually, travel projects were exploratory in nature and were not linked to a specific defined outcome, such as an exhibition. Although proposals were received in 2003, no travel award was made because the trustees were disappointed by the quality of the applications. In 2004, the RHF travel award was discontinued.

Travel was seen by a number of artists as an important way of gaining access to the new or to the unfamiliar. Travel grants tended to produce outcomes associated with learning experiences and with possibilities for forging new relationships, some of which had led on to creative or professional opportunities. In some cases, travel was associated with a sense of creative and/or personal freedom. The idea of having reached a turning-point, or an important watershed which was to have long-term consequences, also featured strongly in interviews with artists who had undertaken travel projects.

For Ian Hartless, a Liverpool-based glass-maker and conservator, two RHF-funded research trips to France to visit and observe glass workshops provided a refreshing alternative to the relatively limited professional networks that he had access to in the United Kingdom. 'There are fewer and fewer people now working with glass, so you need to be able to travel further to keep your practice fresh,' said Hartless. 'You need to find ways to remain inspired. I've exhausted the northwest; everyone knows who I am and I know everybody. I feel I need to expand; to move further afield. Travel is a really good way of seeing new ideas and new pieces of work.'

Lucille Nolan began a PhD degree months after returning from an RHF-funded visit to California, where she had gone to make links with, and to observe, scientists at the University of California at Berkeley. Nolan found that the Berkeley experience enabled her successfully to bridge the gap between two different periods of academic study. 'It provided a link between my MA [completed shortly before Nolan's RHF-funded travel project] and the PhD at a crucial formative stage,' said Nolan. 'Twelve months is too short for a Master's degree; it doesn't give you time properly to reflect on what you have done. That period in California allowed me to elaborate on ideas that were incipient at the end of the MA. I still attribute the success of my [subsequent funding] application to the AHRB [Arts and Humanities Research Board] to the research made possible by the Rootstein Hopkins award. It helped me to focus on what was relevant to my practice in those areas of overlap between artistic and scientific practices. All my professional and creative practice since that trip has been around this area of enquiry.'

Whereas for Lucille Nolan a travel grant provided the chance informally to continue her academic research, for Ishbel Myerscough, who was funded by the RHF to travel to New York just a few months after leaving the Slade School of Fine Art, it provided an opportunity to leave academia behind. 'It was a chance to do all the things I had in my head that I hadn't been able to do at the Slade,' said Myerscough.

'I wanted to escape and be someone else for a while, and not have anybody looking over my shoulder at what I was working on: not my tutors, not my dealer, not my friends. Just to be on my own to work things out. It was fantastic to be able to be anonymous in a huge city. I gained a sense of distance and freedom. I came back feeling very optimistic and enthusiastic, ready for anything.'

Travel-based projects had sometimes involved periods of solitude. Often though, they had encouraged artists to be proactive in forging new relationships and sometimes had led to an artist working in a more social way than he or she was used to. This was the case with Lucy Heyward, who was awarded a travel grant to journey to Zimbabwe, where she hired the services of a light aircraft and a cameraman in order to shoot aerial footage of the Lower Zambezi River. 'Until the Africa project,' said Heyward, 'my practice was studio-based. Being out there on location and working with people was a first. Achieving things in a team of people was quite different from sitting in a studio on my own. That was a very positive experience, and it's how I still like to work now.'

Sometimes travel projects had led to what were perceived to be positive outcomes for the local inhabitants. Yuen-Yi Lo, for example, journeyed to a remote province of China to track down and interview some of the few surviving exponents of Nushu, a language developed by and peculiar to the women of the Jiangyong region. Yuen-Yi's research had multiple outcomes: it led to the development of an artist's book and a series of exhibitions, and it provided valuable material for a PhD degree, which she completed in 2005 at what was then Wimbledon School of Art. 'The interviewees also benefited from the exchange,' said Yuen-Yi. 'It made them proud of themselves; they gained esteem from recognition. Exposure to the outside world through the book has given them encouragement to keep Nushu alive. It is helping to stimulate awareness of this lost tradition.'

The opportunity to travel in Mexico for an extended period marked a clear watershed in the creative development of the painter Frances Turner. 'Fran felt that there was a great development in her practice as a result of the Mexican visit,' said Turner's partner, Peter Gandy. 'Her palette, for example, completely opened up in response to the saturated light. All her subsequent work was influenced by her experience of Mexican culture. It was absolutely crucial to the last third of Fran's career, and without an understanding of the effect that Mexico had on her work, you can't really understand Fran as an artist.' Sadly, Frances Turner died in July 2003, shortly after returning to the United Kingdom from a trip to Belize and Guatemala.

## The broader picture

In the previous section, I have offered a brief summary of the outcomes associated with particular categories of award. In the section that follows, I will look in more detail at the outputs and outcomes that it was possible to identify and observe across the full range of projects and activities funded by the RHF.

## Outputs and outcomes – a blurred spectrum

Arts funding is usually awarded on the expectation of some kind of direct and explicit result, such as the creation of a new facility or the staging of an exhibition. However, in addition to the primary anticipated result, many secondary or indirect benefits and impacts can flow from a particular instance of arts funding. These may often go unobserved and unrecorded. The Rootstein Hopkins Fellowship research provided an opportunity to take an uncommonly holistic overview of the kinds of impacts and consequences that might be either caused or facilitated by the provision of funding.

I shall now proceed to map and to classify a considerable number of different types of outputs and outcomes that my research showed to have been associated with RHF funding, where 'outputs' are defined as measurable and concrete achievements, which can clearly be demonstrated, and 'outcomes' refer to effects or consequences that are generally less tangible. Reflecting the degree to which they can be objectively measured, outputs are described as quantitative. Outcomes, which often imply a greater degree of subjectivity in their interpretation, are described as qualitative. An exhibition of work or the creation of a digital media suite, for example, would be classified as a quantitative output, whereas the opportunity to reflect on and to re-evaluate creative and professional practice is classified as a qualitative outcome. The dividing line, however, is sometimes blurred and, for the purposes of this study, I propose that the two sets of terms, quantitative/output and qualitative/outcome, should be regarded as representing the opposite ends of a continuous spectrum.

In the most basic quantitative terms, drawing on the testimony of the interviewees (which was supported in most cases by written and/or photographic documentation), the primary outputs supported by RHF funding during the period from 1995 to 2004 can be summarised as follows:

- 40 of the 41 artists interviewed had been supported to create and/or present new bodies of art work.
- 37 of the 41 artists' projects funded had resulted in work that had been presented to a public audience (although this was not necessarily a required outcome of the funding).
- 28 of the 41 artists interviewed had had work created or supported by RHF funding featured in a solo exhibition.
- 24 of the 41 artists interviewed had had work created or supported by RHF funding featured in a group exhibition (14 had showed RHF-supported work in both solo and group exhibitions).
- 20 of the 41 artists had gained direct economic opportunities (usually sales of work) as a consequence of the activity supported by RHF funding.
- 11 of the 18 institutions interviewed had used RHF funding to support the creation and/or presentation of new art work.
- 13 of the 18 institutions interviewed had used RHF funding to deliver projects and activities that had attracted public audiences.
- 9 of the 18 institutions interviewed had used RHF funding to create or develop new facilities or resources used for public benefit (usually within a higher education context).

- 22 of the 41 artists and 7 of the 18 institutions were supported to realise projects or activities with an international dimension, which involved travel to a foreign country.

The study identified a wide range of qualitative outcomes, which were observable across a significant number of the projects funded by the RHF and which appeared to a greater or lesser degree to be related to RHF funding.

To assist interpretation and analysis of the different identified outcomes, I have classified these outcomes under six headings: *production; presentation; education; economic; personal;* and *sustainability.* Although the generalisable outcomes that could be identified from the research data were very largely positive, it was also possible to identify outcomes which, potentially at least, were more negative, which I discuss later.

## Production

The previous section, in which outputs were summarised, testifies to the large quantity of new work that was enabled by RHF funding. However, there were a number of ways in which artists' production was supported qualitatively. These were through access to resources and through creative skills development, which were often contributory factors to a perceived development within an individual's creative practice.

### Access to resources

Ten out of 41 artists (24 per cent) said that as a result of the project or activity funded by the RHF they were able to access new or additional facilities to assist in the production of their work. Seven out of 18 institutions (39 per cent) said that their project or activity had led to new facilities for production being available for use by artists or art students.

A number of art colleges had used RHF funding specifically to create new production facilities and spaces. Additionally, the availability of new and different resources for production was cited by some colleges as a useful benefit of providing students with international exchange opportunities. Chris Jones of Newcastle University (*exchange* 1997), for example, who organised a student swap with the Cleveland Institute of Arts, Ohio said: 'Some technical resources were available at Cleveland that were not at the time available here, particularly in terms of digital resources, and that was beneficial to a number of our students.'

A significant proportion of the students who had had their fees supported by the RHF (44 per cent) cited access to production resources as a particular benefit or incentive for undertaking formal study. Emma Churchill (*student fees* 2004), who was supported to undertake an MA degree at University College Falmouth, said: 'I wanted access to facilities and space that I don't have at home, and to have access to equipment such as video technology, so that I could record my experiments with drawing processes.'

Less predictably, 50 per cent of the artists funded to undertake international travel also identified access to resources or facilities for production as a significant benefit derived from their project or activity.

*Creative skills development*

Fourteen out of 41 artists (34 per cent) indicated that their projects or activities had resulted in the acquisition of new creative and/or professional skills. As might be predicted, this outcome was most prevalent in artists who had been funded to undertake formal study. Seven out of nine artists who had had support with students' fees mentioned the acquisition of new skills. These might be either the technical or technological skills necessary to the development of creative practice, or skills that were necessary to assist the research, presentation and promotion of their art work.

Eight institutions indicated that their projects had resulted in new creative or professional skills. For three institutions, the acquisition of new and additional skills was seen as a benefit of providing students with international exchange opportunities. A further five institutions indicated that their projects had provided the opportunity or stimulus for the learning of valuable new skills at an institutional level. The skills acquired by the institution, however, might not necessarily be directly linked to the production of new art work.

*Developments within creative practice*

Thirty-one out of 41 artists (76 per cent) described how the RHF-funded project or activity had enabled at least one significant new development to take place within their creative practice. The majority of artists in each category of individual award (*sabbaticals; student fees; artists' projects; and travel*) testified to important new developments in their practice at the time of the RHF award. Unsurprisingly, 100 per cent of student award winners regarded their period of study as particularly formative to their creative development.

Innovations could take a number of forms. Often they might involve the exploration of new media and techniques. Sometimes they were conceptual, perhaps involving a new approach to research. Some artists had had the opportunity to extend their practice to new types of location, or to work with different types of collaborators. Occasionally a development might be of a significant but indirect nature, as was the case with the artist Richard Talbot (*sabbatical* 2002), who made an important breakthrough in terms of the framing and presentation of his drawings during an RHF-funded sabbatical. Talbot said of his time away from teaching: 'It wasn't so much about making a new set of drawings; it was more about taking some of the drawings I had already done and getting them into a state where I felt confident about exhibiting them. It was a case of making the best of a body of work that I already had.'

Five institutions, four of whom had used RHF funding to create new technical facilities for art students, mentioned the development of the range and quality of student artists' practices as being a particularly beneficial outcome of their project.

Presentation

The principal benefits of RHF funding in terms of the presentation of new art work are summarised in the earlier section that details outputs. An important additional benefit or impact in relation to presentation, however, is the support that the RHF has given indirectly to the partners or collaborators of the recipients of its funding.

In 34 out of 41 artists' projects it was possible to identify that there had been a significant benefit to at least one organisation with which the artist had worked, either as an integral part, or as an unpredicted development, of the RHF-funded activity. Most often, an art gallery or other arts venue had benefited from the opportunity of having a new body of exhibition-quality work to present. The second most prevalent category of ancillary beneficiary was the art college. Some colleges had derived benefits of research esteem (through the Research Assessment Exercise) from the presentation of work by artist teachers who had been granted sabbaticals by the RHF. In the categories of *sabbaticals, artists' projects* and *travel* 31 of 32 projects (97 per cent) had brought benefit to at least one organisational partner or collaborator, usually for reasons connected to the presentation of work. In the category of *student fees* there was a significantly less pronounced benefit to partners, with only three out of nine projects (33 per cent) describing such a benefit.

Education

As was demonstrated earlier, the RHF has targeted a high proportion of its funding (59 per cent) at support for fine art within higher education. I wish to highlight here a range of distinct types of educational outcome (some of which are associated with higher education, but most of which are not) that emerged from the study. These are described as: artists' formal education; artist and institutional learning; and other learning.

Twelve of the 41 artists' projects (29 per cent) and 14 of the 18 institutional projects (78 per cent) funded by the RHF had a specific and beneficial impact in terms of the formal academic education of artists. In addition to the nine artists that the Foundation supported with fees, three further artists regarded the assistance they had received from the RHF as instrumental in supporting either their involvement in, or else their transition to, higher academic study, which was seen as essential to the development of their practice.

Only a small proportion of the educational impacts described by participants in the study, however, were derived from formal learning situations. Thirty-six of the 41 artists (88 per cent) and 14 of the 18 institutions (78 per cent) referred to significant learning outcomes that were in some way additional to, or exceeded, academic criteria or curricula.

In the case of artists, these learning outcomes were most often associated with approaches to researching and developing new work, or else they were related to new tasks and challenges encountered in the process of staging and presenting work. In some cases, these learning situations were linked to the development of new skills. Ian Hartless (*travel* 1997), for example, who received RHF funding to visit France to observe traditional and contemporary glass-making and conservation techniques, described how his trip provided a learning experience that brought benefits to the institution which employed him, as well as to himself. 'It gave me an extra level of education, on top of my college training and practical training at York Minster,' said Hartless. 'I learned what I was expecting to learn and brought that knowledge back to York, where I was able to introduce an awareness of new ideas; ideas that were an improvement on what was happening in Britain at that time. I brought back sample panels that helped to illustrate new techniques. It had an immediate impact on the practices of the Minster.'

In terms of the awards given to institutions, although *students' international exchange* projects were designed primarily to benefit a selective group of individual students, five of the six institutions that administered such projects saw international exchanges as a valuable opportunity for institutional learning. Exchanges, it was reported, brought in new perspectives and presented new challenges to the institution as a whole. Leo Duff, who used RHF funding to enable students at Kingston University to exchange with students at Hong Ik University in South Korea (*exchange* 2001-03), talked of the importance, in an era of increasing globalisation, of learning about unfamiliar cultures and practices. 'The point is,' said Duff, 'that a lot of people here don't know about Far Eastern thinking in art and design. When our students came back and described their experiences first-hand, it was educational for the whole institution: staff and students. And the same was true in Korea.'

In another example of institutional learning, three of the six art colleges supported to realise capital projects commented that the process of putting together an application for capital funding had in itself been of value. This process had helped them initially to identify and research, and subsequently to test, new priorities for resource allocation at an institutional level.

Twenty-four of the 41 artists' projects and 17 of the 18 institutional projects had involved learning opportunities for others, that is, individuals or groups who were neither the artists supported directly by the RHF, nor the students or staff of institutions who had received funding. In terms of artists' projects, the beneficiaries were most likely to be either people who attended educational events that were an integral part of projects delivered by artists (such as a symposium or a teachers' 'inset' day associated with a particular exhibition), or individuals who the artists had subsequently taught, drawing on new experience or knowledge gained through RHF-funded activity.

Where institutional projects had led to other learning opportunities, these were generally associated with a visit to the institution by outside groups, or individual members of the public, for learning purposes. New capital facilities in higher education colleges, for example, have presented additional opportunities for outreach activities involving new groups and audiences.

Economic impacts

Although economic impact was not a significant consideration in the allocation of RHF funding, the study showed that a large number of what could be defined as economic benefits or impacts were linked to the awards made. In addition to direct economic opportunities, such as sales of work, interviewees described benefits of leverage, competitiveness and transferable skills development.

Fourteen artists (34 per cent) and nine institutions (50 per cent) believed that funding from the RHF was important in enabling them to attract additional funding, or resources in kind. A number of artists said that having an award from a foundation made them appear more credible when they approached other funders. Jane Harris (*sabbatical* 2004) said: 'The Rootstein Hopkins grant would have helped my application for the Arts and Humanities Research Council. I applied to the AHRC before the

RHF award and was rejected but encouraged to resubmit. I did resubmit following receipt of the RHF award and was successful.'

Several institutional representatives reported that RHF funding had enabled them to test and prove the success of, or demand for, particular kinds of activity, which had led to their being able to secure further investment. Fran Lloyd, of Kingston University (*capital* 1999), described the new facilities for postgraduate students, which were made possible through RHF funding, as 'a path-finding project, which stimulated a re-evaluation of capital resource needs and persuaded the university to put major additional investment in that area.' 'It was,' said Lloyd, 'a trigger for an additional chunk of funding from the University, which probably amounted to over £1,000,000.'

Six institutions, three of which had used an RHF award to support the creation of digital technology resources in art colleges, indicated that RHF funding had helped them to increase or maintain the competitiveness of their project or institution. The Head of School at Gray's School of Art (*capital* 2001), for example, said that, because of its attractiveness to potential students, the digital suite created with RHF funding had brought the School 'significant institutional benefit in terms of maintaining its place in a competitive fine art education market place'.

The development of new skills, an outcome associated with many RHF-funded projects, has stimulated economic as well as creative benefits. This is particularly the case with capital projects focused on the provision of digital technology. The respondents for all three projects of this kind emphasised the employment benefits associated with this type of resource. Sam Ainsley of Glasgow School of Art (*capital* 1999), which used RHF funding to create a digital media suite, said: 'Employers are beneficiaries because we are equipping our students with valuable transferable skills. It [the media suite] has given career opportunities to our graduates, three of whom now work here as technicians.'

Skills and knowledge acquired through individual artists' projects have also had an impact in terms of future employability. For example, Linda Short (*travel* 2000), whose award from the RHF enabled her to visit world-renowned art galleries and museums in Vienna, Venice, Florence and Rome, regards her travel project as an important milestone in her shift towards developing a second professional role. 'While travelling in Europe, the opportunity to visit numerous art galleries and museums, and to spend a consolidated period of time studying their collections, further developed my interest in art historical research and museum practice,' she said. 'This undoubtedly contributed to my later decision to seek employment in the museums and galleries sector.' At the time of the study, Short was still a practising artist, but she earned her living as a Curatorial Assistant at the Heide Museum of Modern Art, Melbourne, Australia.

Personal outcomes

The participants in the study described a number of significant kinds of outcome which tended to be inwardly focused, often had a strong attitudinal dimension, and seemed to apply most often to individual artists rather than to institutions. They are classified here as 'personal'. These outcomes include: turning-points; self-evaluation; freedom; focus; esteem; and relationships. The first four of these categories of outcome were highly prevalent in the responses of the artists interviewed, but did not feature significantly in the interviews with institutions.

A striking statistic to emerge from the interviews with artists was that 21 out of 41 artists (51 per cent) suggested that the RHF-funded project or activity had been a major turning-point in their careers; it had represented a moment of creative or professional breakthrough or change, which had had significant and lasting consequences. Two artists, Timothy Hyman (project 1995) and Ishbel Myerscough (travel 1995), used the term 'turning-point' in their interviews. Others used related terms such as 'threshold', 'catalyst', 'watershed', 'break-point' and 'important point of shift'.

Mark Thompson (travel 1998) said of his research trip to Scandinavia: 'It was the big push for me. It was a make-or-break moment in my career.' For Thompson, who chose to give up his work and his accommodation in London in order to make the trip, the RHF-funded project had involved considerable personal sacrifice in the hope of future benefit.

For other artists, the confidence and sense of validation that comes with having an award, rather the activity that it enabled, appeared to be the catalyst for achieving an important sense of breakthrough. 'Without it,' said Emma Churchill (student fees 2004), 'I wouldn't have had the confidence to apply for the other projects, which have in turn led on to so many other things [including, for example, an opportunity to realise a project at the National Gallery, London, which was televised as part of the Big Draw event in 2004]. It set a chain of events in progress which has taken me to where I am now in my art practice. Without it, I might well have gone off into a more commercial area, just simply to pay the bills.'

Twenty artists (49 per cent) indicated that their RHF-funded project or activity had provided the stimulus or opportunity for a significant re-evaluation of their creative and/or professional practice. This was most strongly the case with recipients of sabbatical awards, where six out of ten artists spoke of the value of time out for reflection. Ray Masters (sabbatical 1997) described his period away from the University of Sunderland as: 'An opportunity to reconsider my artistic direction and the position I was in, artistically and professionally. I was fundamentally re-examining all aspects of my practice.' Masters was one of several sabbatical recipients who, as a result of the opportunity for reflective time, chose to make changes to the balance between their art practice and their involvement with teaching.

Less predictably perhaps, several artists said that the process of making an application for funding (rather than the project that the funding subsequently enabled) had offered a valuable opportunity for self-reflection. Andrew Ekins (project 1997) made this point forcefully. 'Having awards out there makes people put themselves up for them,' he said, 'and that means they have to evaluate what it is that they are doing. It gets you to look again at your work and to organise yourself in a professional way. So before you even get the money, there is tremendous value in going through that process.'

Twenty-one artists (51 per cent) described how the RHF award provided the possibility of escape or liberation from some kind of constraint. Typically, this was

associated either with time, money or education. The sense of liberation was most prevalent in artists who had gained awards to realise projects (75 per cent), or to take sabbaticals (60 per cent). For the recipients of sabbaticals, freedom from the responsibilities of teaching and the time limitations that teaching imposed on their practice was crucial. For artists awarded project funding, freedom from financial pressures tended to be the most important factor.

Brian Grassom (*student fees* 2000) offered perhaps the most succinct summary of the liberating effects associated with funding: 'Funding smoothes the way for you,' he said, 'so that you can do something that you want to do, rather than being forced by circumstances or necessity to do something.'

A significant minority of artists, 12 out of 41 (29 per cent), referred to a positive sense of focus that stemmed from having an RHF award, which usually confirmed that they had a concrete project, such as an exhibition, to work towards. This was particularly common with recipients of project funding, where seven out of 12 artists (58 per cent) mentioned a strengthened sense of focus. Timothy Hyman (*project* 1995) typifies this point of view in his comment that: 'Not very large grants given directly to artists by foundations is money very well spent. It gives that extra possibility of focus that otherwise can get distracted just by the business of living.'

The issue of focus is perhaps not unrelated to the issue of esteem, which came up in one form or another in 29 of the 41 artists' interviews (71 per cent). Alternative ways of expressing the notion of esteem included 'affirmation', 'endorsement', 'recognition' and 'validation'. The benefits of esteem, associated with having an award, featured strongly in the interviews for all categories of artists' awards, except *travel*, where it was mentioned by only three out of ten interviewees. The esteem associated with having an award was generally described as a double benefit providing, in the words of Sophie Benson (*project* 2000), 'validation, not just externally but for yourself; that is important'.

Esteem is linked to other benefits, which seemed in many instances to follow on from having an award, in particular to 'confidence' and sometimes to a renewed sense of 'energy' and/or 'enthusiasm'. As Ray Masters (*sabbatical* 1997) pointed out: 'The credibility of what I do has been reaffirmed. I now think of myself differently in relation to my practice. Getting confirmation that the work was of sufficient interest to deserve recognition was quite a powerful thing in itself. Having external endorsement gave me confidence that going back to the studio was a worthwhile thing.'

A number of artists indicated that the esteem associated with getting an award was, perhaps, more important than the financial benefit that it brought. There was a suggestion in some interviews that artists, as a professional class, feel a particular need for external or peer group recognition. Andrew Ekins (*project* 1997) was clear about the galvanising effects of such recognition. 'To get that level of endorsement was fabulous; it really did give me a good kick,' he said. 'It gave me confidence in the way I thought of myself as an artist. You have to resonate confidence to be an artist, and yet every artist I know is wracked with doubt.'

Twelve institutional representatives also mentioned the fact that their RHF award, or the activities that it had made possible, had led to benefits of esteem, which sometimes were passed on to artists. The British Museum representative, for example, referred to 'the reputational benefits' enjoyed by artists who were able to have their work purchased for the Museum's Prints and Drawings Collection because of RHF funding.

In the majority of cases, an important outcome of RHF-funded activity, for institutions as well as for artists, was that valuable new relationships were forged. These were usually professional in character and were often associated with longer-term benefits. These are summarised below in the section below which considers sustainable outcomes. Twenty-seven artists (66 per cent) and 12 institutions (66 per cent) described new, or in some cases improved, relationships that were directly related to their RHF-funded project.

Eric Snell (project 2004), whose dual site installation, *View through to the other side of the world*, involved a complex web of relationships ranged across two continents, recognises that artists today are expected to be increasingly proactive in building and managing relationships. 'You need a lot of skills these days to be an artist,' said Snell. 'You can't just be in the studio. To make a project like this happen, you've got to be a negotiator, a diplomat and a businessman.' In some instances, the new partnerships and collaborations that were enabled by RHF funding led to the development of new skills and competencies, such as those described by Snell.

In some cases, RHF-funded activity had led to unexpected benefits in terms of the personal relationships of award recipients. For example, one artist, Susan McCall (project 2001), was able to show work in an exhibition alongside her daughter Katy. Another was able because of her award to spend valuable additional time with her partner, who was diagnosed with a terminal illness shortly after the artist gained confirmation that she had been granted a sabbatical.

## Sustainability

A concern that the benefits of a particular project should be sustainable over an extended period of time was an important consideration with some kinds of awards made by the RHF. This was most notably the case in its funding of collections – the Prints and Drawings Collection at the British Museum and National Life Stories at the British Library – where it was anticipated (and in the case of the British Museum contractually agreed) that the project would produce public benefit in perpetuity. Longevity of impact was also a significant consideration in the capital awards made by the Foundation. For other awards made to institutions, however, such as awards to enable students' international exchanges, considerations of legacy or sustainability were not an explicit factor in the decision-making process. In the case of the various categories of awards to artists, artists were not required to state in their applications to the Foundation whether any sustainable benefits or impacts would result from the activities for which they sought funding.

Notwithstanding the RHF's variable expectations regarding sustainability, the study found evidence that in a very high number of projects sustainable outcomes and/or valuable types of legacy had been achieved. These different types of sustainable outcome are classified here as being related to some form of continuation, to additional quality opportunities, or to networking.

Forty of the 41 artists' projects (98 per cent) and 15 of the 18 institutional projects

(83 per cent) indicated that elements of the activity supported by RHF funding were in some significant way carried on beyond the immediate lifespan of the project. In many instances, the ramifications or developments that had been triggered continued to be of importance to the individual artist or institution concerned at the time of the study (which took place up to ten years after the date of the award).

Even though artists had been funded for a relatively short period – usually six months for sabbaticals and up to a year for artists working towards a project – in a number of instances they described the RHF-funded activity as representing a beginning, rather than marking a finite project. This was more likely to be the case where artists had identified the RHF-funded period as a 'turning-point' in their development.

Where artists (as opposed to institutions) were concerned, it was most often the development of a particular way of working – in terms of technique, subject matter, or intellectual approach – that had continued. Often material or data collected during the course of a project had continued to provide the raw material for creative work long after the envisaged lifetime of that project. This was particularly the case with artists who had been funded to travel. Julian Grater (travel 2000), who was supported to visit Alberta in Canada and Alaska in the United States, exemplifies this tendency in his comment: 'The whole trip kicked off a process of research and avenues of enquiry, which have provided the stimulation for my practice ever since.'

One important longer-term outcome of many artists' projects is that the knowledge and experience gained became incorporated into teaching practice and was therefore disseminated to a new generation of aspiring artists. This was particularly the case with artists who had been funded to undertake sabbaticals, but was also true of artists who had been funded for other purposes.

There were also instances where non-creative skills, developed during the course of certain projects (such as the ability to work in, or to lead, teams of people, or to present funding proposals), had fed usefully into the artist's professional practice at a later date. Liza Gough Daniels (project 2002), for example, described how: 'After a productive period in the studio, there came a period of project-managing other professionals and persuading them to do things for me. That experience [of working with others to find the best solutions to challenges in presenting the work] has supported subsequent commissions, principally for the Chelsea and Westminster Hospital, where I have produced a series of lightboxes for the new Day Treatment Centre.'

In some cases a more concrete form of practical legacy had resulted from RHF funding, such as a catalogue, which had a useful afterlife as a valuable aid to the artist's self-promotional activities.

With institutional projects, RHF funding had often allowed activities to be piloted or tested, which were subsequently able to be sustained or enhanced with the assistance of funding from other sources. This was particularly the case with capital projects where, on a number of occasions, external funding from the RHF had provided a catalyst for trying out something new, which would otherwise have taken longer to achieve because of the constraints associated with internal institutional bureaucracy. The Head of School at Gray's School of Art (capital 2001), sums up this

*Above:* Liza Gough Daniels

general point: 'The benefit of the Rootstein Hopkins grant,' he said, 'was that it gave us a foundation that otherwise we would have lacked. We would have had to put formal applications through the University system, which might have taken a year or more to progress. The award allowed us to establish a new media facility as a pilot, which then enabled us successfully to make our case to the University for more investment. It is increasingly difficult to expand into new areas. It is very difficult to make that kind of quantum shift, but with the help of RHF funding it was both envisaged and achieved.'

Twenty-eight artists (68 per cent) and nine institutions (50 per cent) described how the RHF-funded activity had provided a bridge, or acted as a catalyst, to subsequent high quality opportunities.

In some cases the RHF project was seen to have triggered a process of professional progression that had been sustained and qualitative. Sue Williams (*project* 2000) described how the process worked for her: 'Artistically, it was just a natural progression. It enabled me to get on and do well the work I was already being successful with. But professionally, it provided the fillip for me to jump on to another level, in terms of recognition, demand and opportunities.' Williams, who was shortlisted for the prestigious *Artes Mundi* prize in 2005, believed that her professional situation had significantly improved 'purely because of the knock-on effect of having the award; each knock-on enabled more money, funding or sales. Since then, professionally speaking, I've had a different level of projects and opportunities.'

Sometimes the ability to identify and pursue opportunities beyond the time-frame of the RHF-funded project was linked to the possibility to focus and the freedom from time constraints which were discussed in the earlier section on the personal outcomes associated with RHF funding. Richard Talbot (*sabbatical* 2002) said: 'There are lots of opportunities you can take on board once you have a clear amount of time. I looked into applying for an AHRC [Arts and Humanities Research Council] fellowship, which is what I'm doing now. I didn't get it the first year, but I was encouraged to reapply and I got it the following year. Having that time away from teaching helped to sort all that out.'

Networking is clearly related to the kind of relationship-building described in the earlier section that deals with *personal* outcomes. The distinction I make, for the purposes of this study, is that networking refers specifically to that sub-set of relationships that are concerned with *professional* development, connectedness, or advancement.

There were numerous examples in the study where professional relationships, developed during the period of RHF-funded activity, had led on to additional benefits or opportunities. In the case of individual artist's projects, relationships were often forged with other artists or artists' groups, and these had sometimes resulted in subsequent exhibition opportunities.

Sometimes RHF-funded activity was perceived to have smoothed the way for either artists or institutions to establish relationships with other funding agencies. For example, during an initial RHF-funded six-month stay in Mexico in 1999, Frances Turner (*travel* 1998) established contact with the British Council. The Council subsequently supported Frances financially on each of her several return visits.

An RHF-funded project helped at least one institution to consolidate the networking function at the heart of its mission. Soon after it had realised a successful international touring exhibition, *From the Interior*, with the help of RHF funding, the Museum of Women's Art changed its corporate identity and became the Foundation for Women's Art. 'It was decided to change the organisation,' said the Director, Monica Petzal. 'It would no longer aspire to become a building-based venue, but more a network that would organise projects. The venues that take women's projects are usually run by women. A circuit develops that follows the curators as they move between venues. The project [*From the Interior*] has helped to develop and consolidate this touring circuit. That networking function becomes very important in terms of the Foundation's aims.'

## Negative outcomes

Few of the artists or the institutional representatives who took part in the study described significant negative impacts or outcomes related to their RHF-funded activities. It is, however, possible to posit a number of such categories of outcome, including: pressure and criticism; difficult finances; failure to complete; failure to maximise; lack of resources; unsustainability; opportunity costs; difficulty of returning and destruction of art work.

Eight artists (20 per cent) and two institutions (11 per cent) described pressures associated with their project, which could be construed as negative. The examples that follow show, however, that pressure could lead to positive as well as to negative outcomes.

A particular form of pressure was academic criticism, which two of the students supported by the RHF referred to in their interviews. In both cases, having RHF funding was seen as a factor in being able to confront and deal with the criticism. Stina Harris (*student fees* 2002) reported that she had experienced negative feedback from her tutor. 'He was quite critical at times,' she said, 'and at one point I wondered whether I should carry on. One of the things that made me do so was the fact that I was being funded … I felt a sort of obligation towards my sponsors to complete the course, and I was very glad that I did so. '

Several artists referred to pressures associated with having to realise an exhibition as an outcome of their funding. As with the criticism described earlier, this kind of pressure could have both positive and negative effects. Susan McCall (*project* 2001) was unsure, in retrospect, that the pressure of having to produce an exhibition had been helpful. She felt that she could have been more confident at the time of applying to the Foundation to say: 'I just want to be working again on my art.' She described her initial plan to secure an exhibition in London as 'too difficult an objective at a time when I needed to concentrate on my work'. For McCall, the need to produce an exhibition was both a distraction and an incentive. In the end, she did succeed in securing one closer to home, at the Buxton Art Gallery in the Peak District.

Ten of the artists (25 per cent) said that at the time at which they were interviewed their financial situation was either worse, or significantly worse, than at the time of the RHF award. Although some of the artists appeared happy to accept this situation as a trade-off for either extending their academic education, or for 'downshifting' their employment in order to free up more time for their art practice, others

seemed less comfortable with their financial lot. In the case of some of the artists who had undertaken academic courses, this seemed to be in part related to a lack of vocational emphasis within their subject or institution of study. One artist said: 'I've found it immensely difficult this year to find a job. Doing sculpture is not particularly vocational. I've been surrounded by really talented artists who can't get jobs and struggle financially.' Another artist, who had also had a difficult time financially since completing an MA degree, said: 'I probably spend more on my work than I make from it. The college is very good at technique but it gives you no help at all in that area. It prepares you well artistically but not professionally.'

Six artists (15 per cent) and two institutions (10 per cent) said that there were elements of their projects which might be said to be incomplete. In the case of institutional awards, this was because students had either failed to complete their studies, or had been unable to take up an international exchange opportunity.

Where artists had failed in some way fully to complete the project described in their funding application, this was not necessarily seen as negative. Liza Gough Daniels (*project 2002*), who received RHF funding to make and exhibit a new body of work (lightboxes and paintings), had exhibited the lightboxes she had made but, despite an opportunity to do so, had not at the time of her interview shown the paintings. Gough Daniels felt positive about not having succumbed to the pressure to deliver in full the project she had described. 'I always try to take the long view of my work,' she said. 'Some things just take a long time before they come through. The important thing is to be ready for that opportunity when it comes along.'

In eight artists' projects (20 per cent) and one institutional project there was a perception that, although the activities described in the funding application had been fully realised, even more might have been made of the opportunity, or additional goals could have been achieved. Several artists mentioned that their work had not had as much public exposure as they would have liked, or had not been seen by enough people with influence within the art world. Some referred to a failure to achieve critical recognition for their project.

The planning phase of a project was identified as the point at which more focus could have been given in order to maximise the benefits. Pam Skelton (*sabbatical 1995*), said: 'I felt that there were opportunities that I hadn't really taken up, though I can't really say now what they might have been. For an artist, it's very important to forward-plan projects, and I don't think I was very good at that then.'

In the case of six artists' projects, difficulties were identified that could be said to relate to a lack of resources, including the skills, contacts and strategies needed to make the most effective use of an opportunity. One artist, who had not yet been able to exhibit the work made with RHF support, was at the time of her interview undertaking an artists' mentoring programme to help her to effect the transition of her work from the studio into the public realm. The artist, who described herself as 'very closeted', had come to realise that she needed another step in terms of professional development in order to make most of the RHF-funded opportunity – 'to make it publicly articulate'.

Another artist attributed the problems that she had had in realising her project to the failure of an institution to support the opportunity that it had offered her with appropriate resources. 'Unfortunately,' she said, 'galleries often seem to want to put very little money into artists' projects and then expect the artists to fundraise.'

Lucy Heyward (travel 1998) was funded by the RHF to undertake a particularly ambitious travel project, which involved her first attempt at film-making. 'I was quite naïve about the technical aspects of film production,' she said. 'The RHF money only covered the budget for the filming. When I came back I had to start thinking about post-production and how I would get the work shown. It took longer than I realised to make the final work.' Heyward, though, was able rise to the challenges she encountered. 'On reflection,' she said, 'it was amazing that it succeeded. But it was an interesting challenge and great to follow an ambitious idea through. If I'd had the appropriate technical support at the beginning, I could have achieved the result that I wanted a lot more easily.'

Remarkably few projects – just two artists and two institutions – reported difficulties in sustaining the type of activity that was supported by RHF funding. An example was Glasgow School of Art (exchange 1998), which had faced a recurrent problem of having to fundraise every other year to enable staff and students on its MFA course to take up a prestigious opportunity to make a research visit to Berlin at the invitation of DAAD, the German academic exchange programme. Sam Ainsley, the Head of the MFA course at Glasgow, reported that, despite the success of the 1998 trip, the DAAD visits could not easily be sustained. Following a gap of eight years, however, the 2006 cohort of MFA students took it upon themselves to fundraise so that they could take up the opportunity once again.

Seven artists and one institution described examples of what could be termed opportunity costs associated with their RHF-funded project. Sometimes these opportunity costs involved economic down-shifting in order to free up more time for art practice. Andrew Ekins (project 1997) exemplified this tendency. 'Maybe the affirmation of myself as an artist meant that other aspects of my life fell away a bit,' he said. 'My commitment to being a painter was strengthened, and that meant that I gave up some paid work. Since becoming more full-time as an artist, my financial situation has actually worsened.'

In the case of Ian Hartless (travel 1997) an opportunity for academic advancement was forfeited in order that he could complete his project. 'The trip actually stopped me from getting an MA,' Hartless said. 'Wrexham College wouldn't allow me four weeks off from the MA course to go on the second leg of the France trip.'

Alan Holmes of Manchester Metropolitan University (exchange 2004) felt that there were opportunity costs associated with students' international exchange. 'There is always a question in exchanges as to whether students gain or lose overall,' said Holmes. 'They gain by being away and having exposure to new things, but they lose in terms of the teaching they miss over here. Overall, our students reported that they felt the benefits outweighed the negatives. They did, however, express a slight sense of anxiety about coming back to resume their final year having missed some of the things that their fellow students had learned to prepare them for it.'

Difficulties associated with returning to work were described by 50 per cent of artists who had been awarded a sabbatical. These are described in the earlier 'Sabbaticals' section.

One unexpected recurrent outcome, noted in interviews with five artists, was the destruction, dismantling or working-over of art work made during the RHF-funded period. In some instances, this was done for practical reasons concerned with the storage, (un)portability or site-specificity of the work. In three cases, the destruction or working-over of work was seen as a normal, or even necessary, part of the artistic process. Paul Butler (*sabbatical* 2000), for instance, said that he had later 'destroyed quite a bit' of the work he had made on sabbatical. 'It's all part of the creative process,' said Butler. 'Making art is a hell of a lot to do with changing your mind. I often think of E.M. Forster's "how can I tell what I think till I see what I say". And sometimes when you see it, you don't like it, so you say something else. For me, it's part of the normal creative dialectic.'

## Conclusion

The testimonies of the individual artists and the representatives of institutions that had received awards (which, in most cases, were corroborated by some form of objective documentation) suggest strongly that the funding provided by the Rootstein Hopkins Foundation had resulted very substantially in the successful realisation of the projects and activities that were originally envisaged. Moreover, the activities that the funding had helped to make possible had produced, or were felt to have contributed to, a significant and diverse range of direct and indirect benefits, which were of value to the recipients of the funding and to others. The data collected from the interviews indicates that there was a very high perception of benefit, of success, and of influence associated with the activities that were enabled to happen.

There was a very strong consensus amongst recipients that RHF funding had been beneficial. Of the 58 respondents who expressed an opinion 55 (95 per cent) felt that funding had been very beneficial, two (one artist and one institution; 3.5 per cent) felt that funding had been beneficial and one (artist; 1.5 per cent) felt that it had been moderately beneficial. No respondents felt that funding had been either not very or not at all beneficial.

There was a very strong consensus amongst the institutional recipients of funding that the project or activity that had been supported by the RHF had been successful. The perception of success, although still strong, was less pronounced amongst the artists.

Out of 17 institutional respondents 15 (88 per cent) felt that the project had been very successful and two (12 per cent) felt that it had been successful. Out of 41 artist respondents 23 (56 per cent) felt that the project had been very successful, 13 (32 per cent) felt that it had been successful, two (5 per cent) felt that it had been moderately successful and three (7 per cent) felt that it had been not very successful. Two of the three artists who rated their projects not very successful nevertheless said that funding from the RHF had been very beneficial to them, which indicates a perception that significant benefits can flow from a project even when it fails fully to achieve its stated aims.

There was a strong consensus that the project or activity that RHF funding had supported had been influential in terms either of the subsequent career of an individual artist, or in terms of the practice of an institution. The perception of influence was slightly more pronounced for artists than for institutions.

Out of 16 institutional respondents nine (56.5 per cent) felt that the project had been very influential, four (25 per cent) felt that it had been influential, two (12.5 per cent) felt that it had been moderately influential and one (6 per cent) felt that it had been not very influential.

Out of 41 artist respondents 23 (56 per cent) felt that the project had been very influential to them, 12 (29 per cent) felt that it had been influential and six (15 per cent) felt that it had been moderately influential. No artist respondent felt that his or her project had been either not very, or not at all, influential. This indicates that, although grants were awarded to artists only for time-limited projects, in most cases there was a definite sense of legacy.

A potential difficulty of the impact study was that, as beneficiaries of the philanthropy of the RHF, the survey group might be inclined to talk up the benefits and gloss over any negative outcomes – particularly as the study was carried out under the auspices of the Rootstein Hopkins Research Fellowship. To mitigate this, it was made clear to interviewees that this was to be a 'warts and all' study, where frankness, not flattery, was the intention. Some negative outcomes, or potentially negative outcomes, were discernible from the testimonies of those surveyed. These, however, were perceived by the interviewees to be marginal when measured against the benefits that were felt to have accrued.

For all but the largest of the RHF's awards, the conditions and the reporting requirements attached to the offer of funding were minimal and tended generally to be quite informal. In one important respect this light-touch approach to funding, which implied an unusual degree of trust on the part of the funder, created a context in which respondents did not feel the pressure of having to prove that they had met the kind of targets that public sector funders increasingly require artists and arts organisations to specify in their applications for funding. It was clear to me that the vast majority of those interviewed welcomed the fact that some kind of stock was being taken of what had happened with the RHF's funding.

The study was also less constrained than many of the impact studies commissioned by public sector agencies in the sense that it did not have a case to make, such as to advocate for a continuation or increase in resources for a particular purpose. The findings of the study will not directly inform the future funding policy or practices of the RHF, which is in the process of 'spending out' its resources and which will cease its activities in 2008.

It is hoped that the broad range of outcomes, which this study has shown to be associated with the receipt of funding, may encourage funders, from the public as well as the independent sector, to take a more holistic view of the results that might be achieved with their support. It is hoped also that the findings of this study might encourage other researchers (or those commissioning research) to look more closely and analytically at the full range of impacts and effects that can flow from a particular instance of funding, or example of arts activity. On the evidence of this research project, it seems that value might just as equally reside in the 'soft' or qualitative outcomes of such activity as in the 'hard', quantitative outputs that are most often the principal focus of enquiry.

In the next section of this Volume, a series of thirteen 'Case Studies', which are based on the interviews conducted for the impact study, provides a more detailed and textured sense of some of the outcomes made possible with the help of RHF funding.

# LONDON COLLEGE OF FASHION, UNIVERSITY OF THE ARTS LONDON

YEAR OF AWARD
2001

AMOUNT
£500,000

INTERVIEWEE
Heather Lambert, Head of
Communications and Development

London College of Fashion (LCF) was awarded £500,000 to help meet the costs of a state-of-the-art multi-purpose facility, which is known as the Rootstein Hopkins Space. The capital project involved the conversion of a space that had not been upgraded since the LCF building, which occupies a prime location in central London, just off Oxford Street, was opened in 1963. The proposal was to create a flexible resource which could be used for exhibitions, catwalk shows, conferences, and for teaching purposes. The facility can function as one whole area or be divided up, as required. 'Users have expressed amazement at how flexible it is and how well it works in different formats,' said Heather Lambert, Head of Communications and Development at LCF.

The London Institute, which became the University of the Arts London (UAL) in 2004, had agreed to support the proposed conversion if match-funding could be found. The cost was initially estimated at £1,000,000, which meant that £500,000, the value of the Rootstein Hopkins award, was needed. The actual cost turned out to be £1,400,000, so additional match-funding had to be raised: £250,000 was secured from the London Development Agency (LDA). 'As their funding was predicated on increasing employment in the creative industries in London, the LDA were more demanding in terms of what they called "outputs",' said Lambert. 'The Rootstein Hopkins funding was more responsive to our needs and less tied to another agenda.'

The Rootstein Hopkins Space was completed on time and was ready for use in the autumn term of 2001. It has helped LCF to interface more effectively with the other colleges in the UAL (Central Saint Martins, Chelsea, Camberwell and Wimbledon Colleges of Art, and London College of Communication) and with external audiences. Until Chelsea College of Art moved to its new site at Millbank in January 2005, none of the other UAL colleges could offer a comparable facility. 'It has enhanced how LCF is perceived within the University,' said Lambert. 'The College of Fashion did not previously have a significant cross-University reputation for staging events. The Space has added to the prestige not only of LCF but also of the UAL. It has influenced both internal and external perceptions of its professionalism.'

The whole of the student community and staff of LCF enjoy use of the Rootstein Hopkins Space, as does a large proportion of the students across the UAL. Its use is mainly as a high calibre teaching facility, and as a well-appointed display area for both student and professional work. 'The Space has given us bigger and better teaching facilities than we have ever had and we're able to stage a wider range of events a lot more easily than before,' said Lambert. 'All of the students at LCF, around 4,500, will benefit from the Space while they are here, from Foundation level to PhD.'

The Rootstein Hopkins Space has also been well used for outreach projects with the wider community. The annual prize-

giving event for the Young at Art project, for example, which provides arts activities at weekends and in the holidays for schools with limited access to the arts, takes place in the Rootstein Hopkins Space. 'Lots of schoolchildren and their teachers come to that,' said Lambert. 'It has brought many people in to the College who probably would not have come here before.'

LCF invites external speakers to the Rootstein Hopkins Space to give lectures, which are open to a public audience. 'When Colin McDowell, the fashion writer for *The Sunday Times*, gave a talk,' said Lambert, 'LCF invited fashion students from the whole of the southeast.' The principal beneficiaries of such events will have an interest in fashion, but the Space has also been of benefit to the wider visual arts. CHEAD (the Council for Higher Education in Art and Design), for example, has staged several conferences there, and other not-for-profit organisations have also been able to use the facility for free, or at reduced rates.

Events held in the Rootstein Hopkins Space have attracted national and international press coverage, which has increased the external profile of LCF. This has encouraged new partnerships to be formed, resulting in further events which have attracted luminaries from the world of fashion. 'Speakers such as Tom Ford, the former American designer for Gucci, have helped to build a new audience for LCF,' said Lambert. 'He was a real attraction, drawing in top fashion people. That kind of event is more possible because we have a high quality facility that we can invite high calibre people to.'

In the evenings, the Rootstein Hopkins Space may be hired out for corporate events. This enables LCF to attract to the College new business clients with whom it can then build a relationship. Like other higher education providers, LCF is seeking to develop its income from a range of sponsors. 'This will continue to be important if we want to maintain our position at the forefront, especially in terms of equipment and technology,' said Lambert. 'We are a vocational college linked to industry, so we have to remain up to date with industry practice.'

The creation of the Rootstein Hopkins Space marked an increase in ambition at LCF. It had never attempted a capital project on such a scale before, nor had it undertaken significant fundraising. The project helped to build LCF's internal sense of capacity and it has led on to the development of further successful bids for large-scale government education funding, some of which has been used to upgrade the technology in the Space.

Beyond its impact in London, the development of such a prestigious facility has signalled an increased level of ambition for fashion as a discipline within higher education. 'It has raised the stakes both nationally and internationally,' said Lambert. One of the first major events held in the Space was the 2002 conference of the International Foundation for Fashion Technology Institutes (IFFTI), which has 25 member organisations worldwide. It was the first time the conference had been held in the United Kingdom.

The funding relationship between the Rootstein Hopkins Foundation and LCF has brought benefits to both sides. LCF is committed, by its contract with the Foundation, to preserve a Rootstein Hopkins Space for at least a hundred years. From the Foundation's point of view, part of the appeal of the LCF project was that the Rootstein name would remain in the West End, where the mannequins that had made the company's fortune had been displayed in many of its shop windows. 'The Space has succeeded in raising the profile both of the College and of the Rootstein Hopkins Foundation,' said Lambert. 'The name Rootstein Hopkins just trips off the tongue now.'

Previous and following page: The Rootstein Hopkins Space, London College of Fashion

# WIMBLEDON COLLEGE OF ART, UNIVERSITY OF THE ARTS LONDON

YEAR OF AWARD
2004

AMOUNT
£24,000

INTERVIEWEE
Professor Rod Bugg, Head of College

A capital grant was awarded to Wimbledon College of Art, which in July 2006 became one of the six specialist art colleges that together constitute the University of the Arts London, to help it to meet the costs of converting and equipping a specialist facility within the College. The proposal was to turn what had formerly been a photography studio into a new purpose-designed space, The Observatory, which could be used for teaching and for research projects focused on drawing and lens-based media.

'The original intention,' said Professor Rod Bugg, 'was to create an observatory with a raked floor so that students could work with "all things seen", using drawing, photography or film. We decided to take out the rake and retain a level floor because the idea of a floor at different levels, to enable people to work from differing points of view, was very much based on a traditional life class. It was predicated on a narrow definition of what drawing is, and it would be limiting for lens-based work. Also, we uncovered a beautiful parquet floor, which made it a much more pleasant space; in keeping with the original design.'

The Observatory is a flexible space that allows people to work on specific tasks in a purpose-built environment. Users of The Observatory tend often to work collaboratively, an approach that can be discouraged by the traditional *atelier* model of the individual artist's studio. The sharing of space changes the character of the work produced. 'It is important for colleges to think about how they can best use their limited space,' said Professor Bugg. 'Artists are using space in a more flexible, multi-purpose way than was formerly the case. The tradition of everything being divided up for personal space is being turned around, creating spaces for use by the many rather than the one. This idea is not yet fully embedded within the art school.'

The Observatory offers a new type of provision for observation-based work in the College. It comes equipped with state-of-the-art technology, which will continue to be upgraded. 'A dedicated space for observation didn't exist,' said Professor Bugg. 'The life room was always a fairly basic studio. This is a new level of facility. The kitting-out has allowed us to engage in activities using digital imaging that we couldn't have done before. The lighting rig has provided a new degree of control in terms of life drawing and photography.' The Observatory did not mark a radical change in direction; it helped to focus some of the work that was already beginning to happen in the College. It allowed things to be brought together in a way that had not previously been possible.

The use of The Observatory is wide-ranging. In addition to the community based at the College – around 900 students, teaching staff and researchers – it has been used extensively by visitors attending events designed to 'widen participation'. It has also accommodated exhibitions, such as end-of-year shows of students' work. 'Numbers are impossible to quantify,' said Professor Bugg, 'but substantially more people have benefited than we estimated. It is a well-used facility, open all the time the College is open, and it has allowed us to do things that we would not otherwise have been able to do.'

Some of the most successful use of the space has been in widening public participation; a benefit that was not predicted. Wimbledon College of Art has increasingly developed community-based projects, such as a short course in which students from local schools were able to use the facilities in The Observatory to build a portfolio of photographs. 'The Observatory was crucial to allowing that course to take place,' said Professor Bugg. 'We could have done it somewhere else, but it gave the course a professionalism that has influenced how those kids now think about art and design. That could be very important in terms of the way that one or two of them go on to develop.'

Given the priorities already identified in the 'master plan' for the College, the creation of The Observatory could not have happened without external funding. 'The award acted as a trigger,' said Professor Bugg. 'It was a statement of confidence, which allowed us to single out The Observatory as a real priority. We would probably not have continued to fundraise for that project had the Rootstein Hopkins Foundation funding not come through.'

Professor Bugg remarked upon the nature of the relationship forged between a college and a charitable foundation, which is very different to that which exists with public sector agencies. 'You are not dealing with a public body, you are dealing with a group of people,' he said. 'The difference is to do with entering into a genuine discourse. It is about the Foundation understanding the character and nature of what we do and about us understanding their intentions. It is very different from the "cold calling" that comes with a national bidding process. It becomes complementary to public funds, which you have to develop in a different way.'

Funding from independent sources, such as the Rootstein Hopkins Foundation, is of high importance to a college like Wimbledon.

'It can create an accumulator effect, triggering other funding through its initial endorsement,' said Professor Bugg. 'One can then pitch for match-funding from public sources. Matching private finance alongside public finance feels right in the current funding climate within higher education.'

Professor Bugg noted that public and private funding come with different kinds of constraints and expectations. 'Trust funding is less accountable because it is private money,' he said, 'and it allows for a degree of idiosyncratic response which can be extraordinarily positive. It can produce a result which might be lost in the public-accountability-driven bureaucratic experience. A private trust or foundation has the capacity to intervene in a way that is focused, without having to fulfil a whole set of bureaucratic criteria.'

When The Observatory was completed, the College invited the Rootstein Hopkins Foundation trustees to a special launch event. 'We wanted to make it more than a paper exercise and to demonstrate what the outcome actually was,' said Professor Bugg. 'The Observatory was a gift. We wanted to acknowledge that and to show the trust the importance and value of what had been achieved. That helps to build the relationship. The Foundation might then be inclined to come back to us and invite further applications because we had established a track record of delivery.'

## Student Exchange
# MANCHESTER METROPOLITAN UNIVERSITY (MMU)

YEARS OF AWARD
2004 to 2006

AMOUNT
£30,000 over three years (£2,500 per student, to support a total of twelve students).

INTERVIEWEES
Alan Holmes, Programme Leader, BDes (Hons) Textile Design for Fashion and Phillipa Barnett, a graduate from MMU who participated in the 2005 student exchange

MMU was given an award in 2004 to enable two second-year textiles students from the University to participate in a one-semester exchange with two students from Hong Kong Polytechnic University (HKPU). The textiles programme at MMU had previously participated in the Erasmus European international exchange scheme, but had never before organised an exchange so far afield. Following the successful completion of the first year (which fell within the ambit of the impact study), funding was confirmed for a further two years (which did not).

### The tutor's view

'We were particularly interested in the Far East and China because of what is happening there in terms of economic development,' said Alan Holmes, who co-ordinated the project for MMU. 'China is where stuff gets made; the West is where the design is said to happen. As its economy develops, China will become a consumer as well as a producer of fashion goods, so the dynamic of design and manufacture will change and China may not look so much to the West for design ideas. We wanted our students to witness what was happening there, and to visit places where manufacture was taking place.'

From an educational point of view the difference in the respective curricula was an issue, but it was considered instructive for the students to experience that difference. 'We were looking to send students who could learn skills over there that they could not learn here; skills that could then feed in to their final-year work,' said Holmes. 'The only real difficulty was to do with assessment. There are different grading systems, so credits are not directly transferable. This is quite a common problem with exchanges. The MMU students had to do exams, which scared them a little.' All four students, however, succeeded in attaining the required academic targets.

On their return, the MMU students submitted a report on their experiences and gave a talk to the textiles department. The feedback from the exchange students was very positive. 'The biggest benefit was being in another culture and finding out about different ways of doing things and working alongside different people,' said Holmes. 'There is always a question with exchanges as to whether students gain or lose overall. They gain by being away and having exposure to new things, but they lose in terms of the teaching they miss here. Our students reported that they felt the benefits outweighed the negatives and they were all able successfully to pick up the threads on their return.'

Bringing new students in to MMU also had its rewards. 'The Chinese students were assets to MMU,' said Holmes. 'They came over with a good work ethic and were very dynamic within the teaching group. It has been useful for staff here to be able to interact with and teach students from overseas.' At MMU, the entire year group was said to have benefited from the Chinese students' presence: about 50 students and 10 staff. MMU and HKPU are now looking to build on their initial collaboration.

The exchange would not have happened without the Rootstein Hopkins Foundation award. 'In the growing climate of enterprise within UK higher education, this kind of relationship with external funding will perhaps become a more normal part of what we do,' said Holmes. 'It encouraged us to do something that we could not have contemplated otherwise; it made it possible for students who couldn't find the funding themselves to have a completely new learning experience.'

### The student's view

The first student exchange took place from January to June 2005, during Phillipa Barnett's second year of studies at MMU. The change of scenery took some getting used to. 'The academic side was very different,' said Barnett. 'Over here, the course is studio-based, over there it is classroom-based. In England you're encouraged to be artistic in the way you approach design, over there it is driven by industry, but in quite a positive way.'

The MMU students found the workload at HKPU, based on a cycle of one- or two-week projects, quite intense. 'It was geared to the rhythms of industry,' said Barnett. 'We worked to industry-set briefs, which was good training for the real world.' Direct contact with industry came through organised visits to factories and discount warehouses on the Chinese mainland, in Shenzen and Shanghai. 'The workers move away from their families to work on massive complexes,' said Barnett. 'It is very different from anything you would see over here.'

While Barnett was in Hong Kong, she drew constantly, taking inspiration from the things around her. 'I was struck by the contrasts within the different environments,' she said. 'The themes of cultural difference, architecture and a kind of nostalgic memory of place became part of my creative practice.' Barnett felt that she had gained more from being in Hong Kong for that term than she would have done had she stayed at MMU. 'I came back full of ideas about the work I wanted to do in my third year and really enthusiastic to get on with it,' she said. 'Most of my final year work was influenced by the visit in some way; the written as well as the practical.' Barnett's dissertation, for example, considered whether Hong Kong, which has been through many cultural changes, including the transfer of its governance in 1997 from the United Kingdom to China, has retained its own fashion identity. 'People over there want to wear Western designer labels because they feel it increases their status,' Barnett observed. 'That's a shame because they have a lovely heritage in clothing which is in danger of being undervalued.'

The exchange was, for Barnett, one of the most important aspects of her studies at MMU. 'It gave me so much inspiration,' she said. 'There were exchange students at HKPU from all over the world and we were able to make friends with a really cosmopolitan mix of people. The exchange made me think that I would like to do an internship abroad, maybe even in Hong Kong. A lot of companies are moving over there, so there are lots of opportunities.' Barnett felt lucky to have had the opportunity to spend time in Hong Kong. 'Living in Asia for five months taught me that nothing is as scary as it might at first seem,' she said. 'I feel much more confident now in doing just about anything. I would definitely recommend a student exchange. It gets you out of the little bubble that you can find yourself in at university. It really opens your eyes.'

## Mature Student
# JULIA POLONSKI

YEAR OF AWARD
2001

AMOUNT
£2,950

Julia Polonski received an award from the Rootstein Hopkins Foundation to help with the fees for a two-year part-time MA in Drawing at Wimbledon School of Art (now Wimbledon College of Art). Polonski, who had initially trained as a graphic designer, had given up her career to raise her two sons, which she did as a single parent. The MA was the first formal education that Polonski had had in fine art. She was eager, once her sons had reached secondary school age, to resume her education and to re-establish her creative practice. 'Before I went to Wimbledon, I'd been working in isolation,' said Polonski. 'I'd never had a studio space; I worked at home. My work was dictated by the space I had available, and by financial restrictions. Wimbledon was very liberating. It gave me the opportunity to focus and to develop in an intensive environment. My work became more demanding, both mentally and physically.'

The MA required Polonski to write about her work for the first time, and to contextualise her practice. The critical theory department at Wimbledon proved particularly supportive. 'The research and the written work helped me to understand how to reflect on my practice,' said Polonski. 'If the course had just been studio-based I could easily have drifted, but the theory tutors really wanted to help you to understand and explore concepts with confidence. I found that extremely valuable. You had to use thinking to justify all aspects of your work.'

Polonski sold a portrait drawing whilst at Wimbledon. 'That drawing got completely different responses from my tutors,' she recalled. 'One was extremely supportive; the other ripped it to pieces. I think it can be very hard for students to know whether what they are producing is going to lead anywhere. I'd seen students just abandon a direction because of a fierce crit. I always made a point of showing the work to a range of tutors. As a result, I learned to trust my own judgement; to be informed by what everybody else said, but not to crumble when criticised. In some ways it was a survival course. If I had gone to Wimbledon without the affirmation of the Rootstein Hopkins Foundation award, I might have found it more difficult to retain confidence under that sort of pressure. When people have faith in you early on, it gives you confidence and is a catalyst for development.'

Polonski admits to being surprised, in a positive way, by the work that she produced at Wimbledon (which culminated in her winning the postgraduate prize for drawing) and by the progress that she made in the months leading up to her final MA show. With the body of work achieved at Wimbledon, Polonski felt confident to apply for exhibitions. Immediately after graduation, she entered the annual Open Exhibition competition at Artsway, a well-regarded Arts Council-funded gallery in the New Forest, with two of her larger drawings. Both works were accepted and Polonski was awarded the prize, which was to have a solo show, *Body: a sense of place*, at the gallery in August the following year. She has had a number of further solo exhibitions since then. 'The exhibition at Artsway showed that my work was of public interest and merit,' said Polonski. 'I really enjoy the public response to my exhibitions. I make large-scale tactile drawings – unframed and pinned to the wall – which people often want to touch; their vulnerability has become part of the work. People like the idea that such large images can be made on a wall in one's bedroom, which is how they are produced. They find it exciting that you can work in an ambitious way with the simplest of means and without a large studio.'

The MA at Wimbledon helped Polonski to regard her art as a positive part of her domestic life. 'I was anxious when I started the course that I hadn't got all the things I needed to become an artist, such as a proper studio,' said Polonski, 'but I found that actually I had. You just have to work with the restrictions that you find – lack of resources, or family commitments – because positive things can come from limitations. The restrictions become part of your working method.' The course was enriching from a family point of view. 'My children started talking about contemporary art and taking an interest in it in an excited way,' she said. 'Because I'm working in my bedroom, on the wall, my practice is actually a part of my family life.'

Gaining an MA qualification helped to revitalise Polonski's CV and it gave her the encouragement to become a self-employed artist. She was not sure that she could have done her MA without the Rootstein Hopkins Foundation's support. 'I might have been able to borrow the money from somewhere,' she said, 'but it's not just the money, it's the growth in confidence that comes with receiving an award. It was important to know that someone had faith in my potential.'

'The MA was a life-changing thing for me,' said Polonski. 'It has given me a new confidence in, and insight into, my work; it has enriched my life, my working method and my thinking. I'd drawn all my life, but I had never realised what being a professional artist meant. Previously, drawing was something I did because I loved it. Since Wimbledon, I'm aware that it's something that I can do professionally.'

## Mature Student
# STINA HARRIS

YEAR OF AWARD
2002

AMOUNT
£2,150

Stina Harris received a Rootstein Hopkins Foundation award to help with the fees and the costs of materials during her two-year part-time MA in Printmaking at Bradford College. 'I didn't have a very clear idea of what I wanted to do when I started at Bradford,' said Harris. 'I'd been fairly isolated, living in the village of Ackworth, Yorkshire, and ten years after leaving art college I felt I needed to be working with other artists, to find out what was new. My aims at the start were quite technically focused; it was an opportunity to learn new printmaking skills. There was less of an expectation about what the content of the work would be.'

The unexpected outcome of the MA was that Harris found the courage and support to confront in her art the theme of mental illness. 'Something about the culture of the MA, which was quite issue-based, led me in that direction,' said Harris. 'Other students were making confessional work about subjects that were troubling them; I felt encouraged to do that too. It seemed that I was being invited to delve deeper into myself and to give expression to something that was very deep and troublesome.'

Harris had for a long time thought about producing a book based on the experiences she had had as a patient in a mental hospital in 1981. 'But it felt like a very private and painful subject,' she said; 'not one that I would want to tackle in any sort of public space. Then when I came up with the idea, to my surprise, I was encouraged by the tutors.' Harris completed an artist's book, *Sectioned*,

during her first year at Bradford. 'It was quite cathartic for me,' she said, 'and it also seemed to speak to a lot of other people.'

The positive feedback she received encouraged Harris to explore the subject of insanity further in her second year. 'I wanted to find some form of healing through visual practice,' she said. 'I had a compelling need really to pursue this topic and I tried lots of ways to find a proper visual language. In the process I did some appalling stuff; things like printing with chocolate on underpants, inspired by people like Tracy Emin. I realised in the end that that wasn't the direction that I wanted to go in.' Harris had tried all sorts of approaches and, with only a few months to go before her MA show, she still lacked a clear sense of direction. 'In May 2004,' she said, 'I went off for two weeks on a boat trip around the Hebrides and up to St Kilda. I did lots and lots of drawings there and felt much better at the end of it.' On her return, Harris made prints and a book, *Journey around the Edge*, based on that trip. She also included her initial book, *Sectioned*, in her MA show. The two books complemented each other; they were on a similar theme, but it was approached differently.

The degree show was well received and Harris was happy with the outcome. 'People who saw the books and were touched by my work seemed to have gained something from it,' she said. 'It's surprising how many people suffer from mental illness but don't dare to talk about it. It emerged that a lot of people were glad that I was dealing it and that I was prepared to be very frank and open about my experiences. I think I'm on something of a mission in that respect. I've given talks about it to various groups, and I would like to do more. I think the arts are tremendously important in preventing mental illness and also in keeping people well.'

Harris thought that she might in future move more in the direction of teaching. 'I think the things I learned on the course would be helpful to other students,' she said. 'I might now consider developing a focus within the mental health area, which I would not previously have had the confidence to do. The MA qualification should help me.'

Harris felt that doing her MA had been a rewarding experience. 'The ripples have gone on for quite a while afterwards,' she said. 'Technically, the MA was a very explorative time; it was a great opportunity to experiment and extend my range. I was in a very different place at the end of the course to where I was at the beginning. I felt I had been broadened and enlarged. My technical abilities had been challenged, my vision of what was going on in the art world had changed, and I understood much better  how I related to the contemporary art scene. I had felt a bit of an outsider, out on a limb, before. So, I felt that I had gained tremendous riches and that there were a lot of things to develop. That is still going on.

Harris's experience at Bradford was not, however, without its travails. 'Although I was pleased with some of the work,' she said, 'I also had negative feedback from my tutor. He was quite critical at times and at one point I wondered whether I should carry on. One of the things that made me do so was the fact that I was being funded. Gaining the award was an incredible confidence boost. It was a powerful recognition of the value of what I was doing and that meant an awful lot to me. It pushed me through that very difficult period in March and April 2004. I felt a sort of obligation towards my sponsors to complete the course, and I was very glad that I did.'

'It is a tremendous boon to have funding,' Harris said. 'Most artists have to do other work to keep afloat. That gives them little time and space to experiment. Awards give artists the time, the space and the resources to flourish. My experience shows that if you can exist for a year or two without having to worry whether your work is selling, or without having to teach, it is possible to make quite a breakthrough.'

# Sabbatical
# JANE HARRIS

YEAR OF AWARD
2004

AMOUNT
£12,000

Jane Harris was awarded a sabbatical to enable her to take a six-month break from teaching at Goldsmiths College, London, from September 2004 to March 2005. She wanted to concentrate on making work for a solo exhibition at the Aldrich Contemporary Art Museum, Connecticut, USA. The exhibition, *Jane Harris: New Painting*, which ran from August 2005 until March 2006, was a significant milestone in terms of Harris's overall career. It was supported by both a catalogue and a DVD. Harris secured an additional award of £5,000 from the Arts and Humanities Research Council (AHRC), in May 2005, to support the costs of the DVD and catalogue, which give the exhibition a useful afterlife. Harris felt that having the sabbatical award would have helped her application to the AHRC. 'I applied to the AHRC before the Rootstein Hopkins Foundation [RHF] award and was rejected but encouraged to resubmit,' she said. 'I did resubmit following receipt of the RHF award and was successful.'

An international solo exhibition contributes towards a college's Research Assessment Exercise (RAE) submission. Goldsmiths was therefore happy to support Harris's sabbatical and to make up the part of her salary not covered by the Rootstein Hopkins award. 'I had the best of both worlds in that respect,' said Harris. 'I had the award, which is a very significant thing to be able to say that one has, but I also got the full salary, so I didn't have to make a financial sacrifice. I was completely untroubled by pressures of any kind.' Harris believed that the stimulation and status associated with her sabbatical would also have had a positive effect on her teaching. 'At Goldsmiths,' she said, 'I teach postgraduate students, who all have a sense of their own practice. There has been a strong move towards painting in the last few years. My position with regard to that has been reinforced by the sabbatical.'

When Harris applied to the Rootstein Hopkins Foundation, she intended only to make work for the Aldrich Museum exhibition. However, a show that had been due to take place at Hales Gallery in London was postponed. Therefore, she found herself making work, in effect, for two exhibitions. Some of her new paintings received their first exposure in the rescheduled Hales show, *Divine*, in April 2005. The exhibition at the Aldrich Museum, later in the summer, featured six large paintings, five of which were made during the sabbatical period. Harris had proposed to make ten paintings during her six-month break; she actually made eight. 'Producing eight was as much as I could do,' she said, 'and they were major paintings as far as I was concerned.'

Harris found that the freedom to focus solely on her creative practice for an extended period benefited the quality and vitality of her work. 'The great thing about the sabbatical was that I didn't feel pressurised,' she said. 'That feeling – of a lack of pressure, of not having other duties – meant that I could give the work more breathing space in my head. I could come into the studio every day and concentrate totally. There was a flow to the

*Above:* Jane Harris

work that came from the continuity which it is impossible to achieve when you are distracted by other commitments. Someone at Hales said that the paintings had a real zest. I felt they were re-energised.'

A technical development occurred in Harris's work during the sabbatical: the use of metallic paints. 'That has been a very successful development,' said Harris. 'The work didn't change fundamentally, but the use of metallic paints to add a sort of lustre was a significant shift. I was less inhibited because I had time to play with it. The way that light affects the painted surface is important in my work, and the metallic paint has made that more apparent.'

Harris felt that, following a relatively low-key period in terms of significant exhibitions, her two solo shows in 2005 had helped to put her back on the map. 'When you are working as teacher as well as doing your own work, the balance can get out of kilter,' she said. 'I've always maintained a strong commitment to practice, but it has been quite a struggle to sustain my profile as an artist.' In the 1990s Harris had quite a lot of international exposure, but as teaching commitments increased that diminished. 'Having these two significant shows has put my name back in people's minds,' she said. 'There was a two-page feature on the Hales show in the *Independent* by Tom Lubbock. It was my first big solo review in a national newspaper and it was extremely positive.' Harris's show at Hales Gallery also made it into Lubbock's Five Best Exhibitions of 2005 in the *Independent*'s 'End of Year Review'.

Harris felt that without the sabbatical award it would have been very difficult for her to have made and shown new work in two exhibitions. 'I would probably have had to postpone the Hales show and just focused on the Aldrich Museum,' she said. 'That would have been a shame because the Hales show was a good lead up in terms of building my profile.' The response Harris received from curators and other art professionals to her sabbatical period paintings was encouraging. 'There's a sense for me that there could well be other very positive things to follow,' she said. 'It's too early to evaluate the full impact, but the signs are promising. Going back to full-time academic life, I realise there is absolutely no way I could have achieved the quality and quantity of work that I did without the sabbatical. The intensity of focus achieved during that period is just not possible to sustain when one is juggling one's time with other commitments.'

Harris felt that the sabbatical, and the exhibitions that followed, could turn out to mark a turning point in her career. 'Although I do very much enjoy working with students,' she said, 'I'm considering whether it might be possible to work again as a full-time artist. That opportunity during the sabbatical to work full-time was very rewarding. That's what you set out to do as a young artist, and the potential is now there for me to do so again.'

Postscript:

Jane Harris resigned from her post at Goldsmiths College in October 2006 and has moved with her family to France to pursue her wish to become a full-time painter again. 'It is clear to me now,' said Harris, in December 2006, 'that the Rootstein Hopkins sabbatical award was the springboard for a much desired shift in my focus and my ambition for my work.'

## Sabbatical
# RICHARD TALBOT

YEAR OF AWARD
2002

AMOUNT
£6,000

Richard Talbot was awarded a sabbatical to allow him to take a six-month break from teaching, part-time, at the City and Guilds of London Art School. Talbot decided, however, to take a whole year away from teaching. A major benefit of the sabbatical was not so much the opportunity to make new drawings, but the chance to resolve an important practical issue that was impeding Talbot's work. One of the selectors of the Jerwood Drawing Prize exhibition in 2001, in which his work had featured, had remarked on the inappropriate framing of Talbot's drawings. 'The sabbatical gave me the time and space, and some money, to sort out that problem,' said Talbot. 'It can often boil down to simple things like that, which sometimes someone else needs to point out to you. I had always cut down the drawings in order to keep framing costs down. Some I would cut down and then realise I had screwed them up. That was due purely to financial constraints. So, it was a case of making the best of a body of work that I already had.'

Talbot used sometimes to pin his drawings to the walls of galleries, but that risked damage; they needed some kind of protection. 'The time off was valuable in terms of sorting out the best way to resolve this problem,' he said. 'I was able to use Perspex box frames for the first time, and to do things like source the best suppliers. That kind of thing can be difficult when you are teaching part-time.' The Perspex frames, which needed to be specially made, cost around £500 each. 'It was quite difficult to find a company who could do it well,' said Talbot. 'I had a few test ones made and then I approached Arts Council England [ACE] to raise the money to make more. It was essential to try out the frames before approaching ACE and having some Rootstein Hopkins Foundation money made that possible.'

During his year off, Talbot was nominated for the Comme Ça Art North Prize, which involved exhibiting a series of drawings in a show in Manchester in 2004. This provided an ideal opportunity to test out the new way of presenting the drawings. The Perspex frames had a positive effect. 'From the Comme Ça event,' said Talbot, 'I was offered a solo show at the Red Box gallery in Newcastle; Red Box is located within an architectural practice, which is an ideal context for my work. I showed the same drawings as at Manchester, with the new style frames. One of the drawings in the Comme Ça show was also selected for the 2004 Jerwood Drawing Prize exhibition.

The sabbatical came at a point when Talbot had begun to doubt whether his teaching in London was leading him anywhere professionally. 'There was no professional advancement in part-time teaching,' said Talbot. 'There was no career structure where I was. But it's hard to tell whether I would have taken the risk and had a year out anyway. As a part-time teacher you're always taking a risk if you have a break.' When Talbot returned to the City and Guilds of London Art School he found that his hours had been reduced. Eventually he decided that it was no longer worth his while to teach there and he left.

The sabbatical year was to mark a major change in direction for Talbot: away from teaching and towards academic-based research. During his sabbatical, Talbot had applied for a three-year Arts and Humanities Research Board (AHRB) fellowship at Newcastle University. 'I didn't get it that first year, but I was encouraged to reapply and I got it the following year,' he said. 'Having time away from teaching helped to sort all that out. There are lots of opportunities you can take on board once you have a clear amount of time. I'm still connected to education, but in a different way. I still have a small commitment to teaching, but it has to be related to my own interests. That's more satisfying than having to follow someone else's agenda.'

Talbot started to write during his sabbatical year, about the history of perspective. He had an article published by an Italian academic journal, the *NEXUS Journal of Architecture and Mathematics*, in spring 2003. The research for that article informed a new series of drawings. Talbot felt that his own education as an artist was revitalised; his academic research fed into and benefited his practice.

The sabbatical period also coincided with a commission at Westminster Abbey, which was offered to Talbot and his brother, Neil. The result, *Constant Endeavour*, a memorial for RAF Coastal Command, was unveiled by the Queen in March 2004. The commission was confirmed following Talbot's successful application to the Rootstein Hopkins Foundation and he was able to work on it during his period away from teaching. 'That allowed me to devote more time it,' said Talbot, 'which made it a more successful outcome. It was quite a big commission, involving new skills and research which have fed back into my teaching.'

'Everything slotted nicely into place,' said Talbot. 'The framing definitely helped to gain more positive feedback for my work. The period spent on academic research prepared me for the AHRB fellowship. The sabbatical gave me renewed confidence in what I was doing. It helped to open things up more. I'm working with a broader academic body of people, which is good for my practice. I'm free to pursue what I want to pursue. I feel now like I could take on lots of different things. You can get sucked into a kind of insidious reliance with part-time teaching. The balance between teaching and art practice is a difficult thing to get right. It is very different to be involved in higher education as a research fellow rather than as a teacher. I now feel more like a practicing artist, which is what I want to be.'

## Collections
# THE BRITISH MUSEUM

YEAR OF AWARD
2001

AMOUNT
£500,000

INTERVIEWEE
Antony Griffiths, Keeper,
The Department of Prints and Drawings

Founded in 1808, the Department of Prints and Drawings is one of the oldest departments in the British Museum. It is the repository for the national collection of Western prints and drawings, one of the pre-eminent collections of its kind in the world. The collection contains over 2,000,000 prints and around 50,000 drawings, which date from the beginning of the fifteenth century to the present day. It includes large holdings of works by such major artists as Dürer, Michelangelo, Raphael, Rembrandt and Goya.

Historically, the British Museum has built up its collections using funding from the government, but in the mid-1990s its budget for new acquisitions suffered a major cutback. It was against this background that, in 2001, the Rootstein Hopkins Foundation awarded the Museum an endowment of £500,000 to enable it to purchase, in perpetuity, works for the Prints and Drawings Collection by artists, living or recently deceased, who have contributed to the artistic life of the United Kingdom.

It was intended that the endowment would provide a regular annual income, and in the first two years following the award the Museum was indeed able to draw down funds to buy new work. However, a formula was built into the endowment agreement to protect the value of the capital and an unanticipated decline in the financial markets meant that, in 2003, its value fell below that threshold. There followed a two-year purchasing moratorium until the endowment recovered to its original level. Purchasing was able to begin again in April 2005, and as of December 2006, the British Museum had spent £78,136 from the fund on 76 works of art.

The Museum's policy for the use of the Rootstein Hopkins endowment is to buy works by young or emerging artists, or else by more senior artists who may previously have been overlooked. 'It is very important to be able to buy work by young artists, who may just have come out of art school and perhaps have had one or two shows, and equally by people towards the end of their careers who never made it into the Collection, or who have dropped out of sight,' said Antony Griffiths, Keeper of Prints and Drawings. 'We bought a wonderful John Hoyland watercolour from 1965. We already had one of his works from the 1980s and we were eager to add something from the 1960s. We also bought some work by Hew Lock, the first time that his work has been in the Collection. He is an emerging artist, whose work we could not have purchased in any other way.' The endowment has also been used to buy prize-winning artworks, such as Kate Davies' *Condition Blue*, which received a Jerwood Drawing Prize in 2002. The drawing was loaned back to the artist in 2005 to be the centrepiece of a solo exhibition. 'We don't normally lend to commercial exhibitions,' said Griffiths, 'but we may make an exception for an emerging artist who needs to show their important works in an early career show.'

The freedom and flexibility of the Rootstein Hopkins award is considered to be invaluable; it allows purchasing decisions to be made entirely at the discretion of the curatorial team. 'It is wonderful not having to seek the donor's approval,' said Griffiths. 'We can move very fast and make purchases when opportunities present themselves. We can buy more cost effectively that way.' Having a permanent fund dedicated to new acquisitions means that the Prints and Drawings Department can continue to build up its contemporary collection. 'There are 50,000 drawings here already, from all the Western schools of art,' said Griffiths. 'The emphasis is on the past rather than the present, but we have an obligation to continue it as a living tradition.'

Any art work that enters the Prints and Drawings Collection does so in perpetuity; the Museum is bound by an Act of Parliament not to sell its holdings. 'Evaluating a project like this after just five years is not really appropriate,' said Griffiths. 'Our success or failure will be judged in a hundred years, when it will be possible to assess whether what we have bought is seen to be of value by future generations. When you work in museums your timescales are pretty long. Nothing we do is for the short-term; the benefit racks up over the centuries.'

Public benefit arises from the use of the Collection. The art works are permanently available to be viewed on request, and free of charge, in the Print Room, which receives around 500 visitors every month. 'We don't audit who visitors are, or what their study purposes might be,' said Griffiths, 'though there are some formal study groups, taught in front of objects.' Lecturers from art schools are regular users of the Collection, for research and for teaching purposes. Some of the first works to be purchased using the Rootstein Hopkins endowment were exhibited in *Paper Assets*, a public exhibition which showcased acquisitions from the period 1996 to 2001. The works may also potentially be used for exhibitions staged by other museums and galleries; around 1,200 items a year are loaned from the Prints and Drawings Collection to outside institutions.

Artists derive both financial and reputational benefit when their work is purchased for the Collection. 'To have work in the British Museum Collection on your CV means quite a lot,' said Griffiths. 'Some artists will try to present us with work, just to be able say that they are in the British Museum. To say "no, thank you very much" is one of the trickier diplomatic aspects of our job.' The Rootstein Hopkins Foundation endowment has had a positive impact on the Museum's ability to attract donations. For example, several of the artists whose work was purchased using the endowment have subsequently donated additional artworks. 'Collectors will take an interest in what we buy, and that in due course will, we hope, lead to further gifts and bequests,' said Griffiths. 'People are happy to bequeath things to institutions that they feel they can trust to look after their works. The more we buy well, the more people will trust us.'

Griffiths observed that there had been a significant shift in his Department's balance of funding in recent years. 'When I joined, in 1976,' he said, 'there was no outside funding; now we are heavily dependent on outside funds. We are doing more things because the world has changed, but there has also been a drop in public funding. Trying to raise money can take up a lot of time and the one thing we don't have in this Department is time.' Without the Rootstein Hopkins Foundation endowment, Griffiths felt that it would have been a struggle for the Department to continue to purchase contemporary work in a significant way. 'Any public collection wishing to acquire work by relatively new artists is very circumscribed these days,' he said. 'So, the purchases made possible by the Rootstein Hopkins Foundation award are actually quite a serious part of what is currently being bought in terms of works on paper. In this sense, the award is of real national importance.'

# NATIONAL LIFE STORIES (NLS)

YEARS OF AWARDS
2001; 2004; 2006

AMOUNT
£8,000; £10,000; £400,000 & £26,930

INTERVIEWEE
Cathy Courtney,
*Artists' Lives* Project Officer

National Life Stories (formerly the National Life Story Collection) was set up in 1987 'to record first-hand experiences of as wide a cross-section of present-day society as possible'. It is an independent charity located within the Oral History section of the British Library Sound Archive. NLS has since its inception initiated a number of oral history interviewing projects, each of which has focused on a particular category of person within society, such as workers in the steel industry. The result is a series of subject-specific collections made up of audio-recorded interviews, which can be accessed free of charge by visitors to the British Library. Some academic institutions are also able to access sections of the collections on-line. Each life story interview lasts for a number of hours and covers the subject's family background, childhood, education, work, leisure and later life.

*Artists' Lives* is one specific collection within the overall National Life Stories collection. Its first recordings were made in 1990 and, on average, approximately 15 new recordings per year have been added since. They offer listeners a privileged and intimate contact with the artist, which most people could not achieve by other means. The collection includes such significant names as Elisabeth Frink, Ian Hamilton Finlay, Eduardo Paolozzi and Anthony Caro.

Traditionally, oral history has provided a platform for the voice of the disenfranchised. Given that many artists already have documentation from other sources, justification was needed when *Artists' Lives* was set up as to why artists should be represented in this way. Cathy Courtney, who initiated the project said: 'I was always aware that the language of artists was very different to that of art historians and I felt that it would be a tragedy for artists not to be represented for posterity in their own words, in addition to how they were presented by academics.'

The Rootstein Hopkins Foundation has developed an ongoing funding relationship with *Artists' Lives*. During the period covered by the impact study it made two awards, in 2001 and in 2004, to support a minimum of nine new recordings. In 2006, a major endowment and a capital award followed, to provide funding for at least four recordings per year for the foreseeable future and to enable NLS to purchase new digital recording equipment.

More than the agreed nine recordings were produced using the first two instalments of funding. 'Given the number of urgent candidates for interview,' said Courtney, 'we decided we would do a larger number of recordings, rather than a few recordings supported by transcriptions. At the time of the first award, there were a number of individuals who we knew we were likely to lose.' Eleven recordings were made using the first award of £8,000: Evelyn Williams, Alexander Mackenzie, Monica Sjoo, Deanna Petherbridge, Karl Weschke, Mary Kelly, Jane Dowling, Joanna Drew, Pat Whiteread, Catherine Lampert and Daphne Casdagli. Four of these interviewees have since died.

'We are fantastically glad that we had that money to rescue their words for posterity,' said Courtney.

The funding awarded in 2004 enabled recordings to be made with John Hoyland and John Ward. Two additional artists had been targeted but, as of May 2006, had yet to begin their recordings. At that point in time, the Rootstein Hopkins Foundation had funded around five per cent of the total number of *Artists' Lives* recordings: 13 out of 230. The Advisory Committee, which determines the priorities for interview, has a 'wish list' of around 300 potential subjects. 'We have never had enough money to do all the recordings that we want to do,' said Courtney. 'It is a tussle between artists who are recognised now to be important and those who are underrepresented and who lack other kinds of documentation.'

Artists benefit from having made their recordings in the sense that the listener hears their account direct, without an intermediary. 'It matters that an artist should be able to represent him or herself for posterity rather than be represented by other people,' said Courtney. 'The project has gained respect for the way artists use language to describe what they do. They have been given a platform that previously had been denied them, and they have risen to fill that space. One of the most rewarding things is when an artist says, "I hadn't realised that before". That's very exciting; when something they may have known subconsciously, but hadn't articulated before, comes to light. One artist said that, prior to making the recording, he had never fully understood how interwoven his life was with his work. It was an important moment of self discovery.'

A primary target audience for *Artists' Lives* is one with a specialist interest in art, which would include art historians, biographers, critics and researchers, as well as students. Various monographs, books and obituaries have used material from the recordings. The oral histories also appeal to the general listener. 'A complex tapestry of cross-references has built up within the body of recordings,' said Courtney. 'You may have artists talking about one another, or talking about the same piece of work or event from different perspectives. It becomes social history, a lot broader than just the art world. People without an interest in art might find our artists' recordings interesting for totally different reasons. The entire world, potentially, has access to the British Library.'

With no ongoing source of revenue funding, *Artists' Lives* has been sustained almost entirely through sponsorship (most steadily from the Henry Moore Foundation) and through voluntary effort. Oral history is a low visibility activity, which makes fundraising difficult. Many trusts and foundations have guidelines that exclude it. 'Ours is a particularly hard project to fund,' said Courtney. 'We are not eligible for heritage lottery funding, for example, and it is difficult to get commercial sponsorship because of the relative invisibility of the project. It is vital that there are trusts whose guidelines are more open and who can recognise the value of what we do and support it.'

The financial support from the Rootstein Hopkins Foundation has helped to unlock additional resources. 'We got a grant from the Calouste Gulbenkian Foundation to do a subsection of *Artists' Lives* called Art Professionals,' said Courtney. 'It certainly helped us when making that application to be able to say that we already had Joanna Drew' [a former Director of Arts at the Arts Council, whose recording was funded through the first Rootstein Hopkins award].

In 2006 the Rootstein Hopkins Foundation gave Artists' Lives an expendable endowment of £400,000 to enable it to overcome the stressful position of having to survive hand to mouth, from one recording to the next. 'We can now plan at least a year ahead, which is totally different to how we worked previously,' said Courtney. 'I will still need to fundraise for other interviews, but it gives us the flexibility to move quickly when an artist suddenly becomes vulnerable. We will also be able to make transcriptions, where we feel it is valuable. It will allow the project to operate at its maximum level of quality.' The first cohort of artists who were able to be interviewed using funding from the endowment included Lubaina Himid, Balraj Khanna, Geoffrey Clarke and Gwilym Pritchard.

Sustaining *Artists' Lives* has required an enormous amount of unpaid commitment; the endowment provides a welcome breathing space. 'We were reaching the point of burn out,' said Courtney. 'Getting the endowment felt like an important ratification of the project; like someone was saying, "this has been worthwhile, and will continue to be worthwhile". That was enormously important psychologically. It really felt as though someone had taken notice of what we had done.' Although *Artists' Lives* is already beginning to be well used, it represents a significant resource for the future. 'The surface has only been scratched,' said Courtney. 'The recordings will be re-assessed by each subsequent generation and will have as many lives as there are centuries to come.'

# Project
## ERIC SNELL

YEAR OF AWARD
2004

AMOUNT
£6,000

Eric Snell was awarded a grant to help him to realise an ambitious international project, *View through to the other side of the world*. Snell's proposal was to dig two holes, one at the art college in Guernsey, the Channel Islands, where Snell is a tutor, and one at the Judith Wright Centre of Contemporary Arts in Brisbane, Australia. Through the use of video cameras and digital communications technology, the illusion could be created of having drilled right through the centre of the earth. The idea came to Snell during an Arts Council England fellowship, which took him to Brisbane in 2002. 'I had no personal connection with Australia at that time,' said Snell; 'only the story told to me as a child, and repeated the world over, that if you dig a hole and keep digging you will arrive at the other side of the world. That was the origin of the project.'

The proposal could not be realised during Snell's Arts Council fellowship because time was limited and the technology required – broadband – was still in its infancy. 'It needed a lot of testing, commitment and sponsorship to make it happen,' said Snell. 'Everybody liked the idea, but realising it presented a major challenge. Without the Rootstein Hopkins Foundation's support, the project might not have happened. It was a close run thing. You have to be incredibly single-minded to develop such a project; it was important to remain focused and not to get deflected into just trying to raise funds.'

*View through* was linked to the Brisbane Festival in September 2004. In Australia, the installation was in a public space: a foyer in a multi-purpose cultural centre, which had a busy night-time programme. That meant that, allowing for the 10-hour time difference in the Channel Islands, there would be a simultaneous audience. The timing also coincided with the late tourist season and the beginning of the academic term in Guernsey. The project was opened simultaneously by the Lieutenant Governor in Guernsey and by an aboriginal elder in Brisbane, which helped to gain immediate public interest.

In Australia, the project attracted nation-wide television coverage. This was partly negative – 'a big black hole sponsored by government funding' – but it helped to bring in a different audience for contemporary art. As a result of the publicity, families arranged to visit 'the hole' to see each other from opposite sides of the world. 'Families became an important component of the work,' said Snell. 'As there was no audio link, people took to writing and holding up messages, and kids did drawings to communicate with the audience at the other end. That created a new visual level, which we hadn't anticipated.'

Originally scheduled to run from September to October 2004, *View through* was extended until Christmas because of its success in both sites. As a small island, Guernsey is quite isolated culturally; debate and discussion of contemporary art is limited. 'The project drew in a lot of people who were uncertain about art,' said Snell. 'It engaged and opened the doors for people who may not have walked into a museum to

look at work. It created a positive profile for contemporary art where previously there had not been one.' After Christmas, the venue in Guernsey reverted to a space for international artists' residencies. The Australian venue, however, would like to make the work a permanent installation. 'I need now to find a new site in Guernsey, or the wider UK,' said Snell. 'I had talks with officials about doing it at the new airport in Guernsey – a site symbolic of international exchange – but I couldn't get permission to dig a hole there.'

The project was more ambitious than anything that Snell had previously attempted. 'I like the challenge of making difficult ideas a reality,' he said. 'It was a simple concept, but there were lots of issues to resolve. It's the negotiations that go on behind the scenes – the resistance of some public officials, people who come with their prejudices, ready to put a block on it – that take up one's time and energy. You have to be open to negotiation and be ready to solve problems that you hadn't even considered when you started.' One of the biggest problems was connecting the technology. All was in place, but nothing was working. A young IT wiz-kid called Zach agreed to bring along an obscure modem to assist the project in Australia. 'This 19-year-old guy arrived with a box under his arm,' recalled Snell. 'There were just hours to go and things were looking pretty bleak until Zach figured out that if we just changed the IP number by one digit the whole thing would bounce into action. He and everybody else did a great job. From admin staff, to construction team, to sponsors, it was a real team effort.'

The project seemed to work on many levels and feedback from both audiences and collaborators was positive. 'It tested the capacities of the venues and the technologists – even of the workmen who made the holes,' said Snell. 'One of the sponsors, DHL, who are in the business of communication and exchange, said: "This is fantastic, it's just the sort of project we should be involved in." Families got reunited. Schoolchildren used it. The smiles showed that it was well received just at the level of simple public enjoyment.'

In Guernsey, the educational potential of the project – 'a cross-cultural marriage of science and technology and art' – was seized upon. Events were organised for schoolchildren and Snell also gave lectures on professional practice to students at the art college. 'It's better if you can relate it to a real event. I was able to reveal the whole machinery behind it,' said Snell. 'You need a lot of skills these days to be an artist. You can't just be in the studio. To make a project like this happen, you've got to be a negotiator, a diplomat and a businessman.'

Snell feels a professional responsibility to promote the visual arts in Guernsey and *View through* helped him to achieve that. In recognition of the project's profile-raising success, Snell was awarded the Ambassador of the Year award in 2005. The award, which is selected by a cross-section of the public, based on nominations to the local newspaper, is given annually to a Guernsey resident who has successfully promoted the island overseas. 'For the first time in the award's 20-year history an artist was nominated, and won,' said Snell. 'This represents a milestone in terms of public recognition for the arts in Guernsey.'

As the Channel Islands do not usually qualify for Arts Council England or European funding, support from trusts and foundations is, perhaps, more important for artists based in Guernsey than in other parts of the United Kingdom. 'It's not just the money,' said Snell, 'having the Rootstein Hopkins Foundation attached to the project gave it credibility, a seal of approval. There are a lot of artists who wouldn't be able to pull off their ideas unless there were people out there willing to back higher risk projects. Backing "blue-skies", perhaps controversial, concepts is important; having the foresight to support such a transient project, well that's just brilliant.'

# Project
## SUE WILLIAMS

YEAR OF AWARD
2000

AMOUNT
£2,510

Sue Williams received an award from the Rootstein Hopkins Foundation to help her to make work, during 2000, for three different projects: *Ysbryd/Spirit Wales*, an exhibition of paintings in Wrexham and Gwent; *Site-ations*, a site-specific project at a former industrial building in Cardiff; and a multi-disciplinary collaborative project, *Striking Attitudes*. 'In total, I am looking to complete 24 large-scale paintings over the year,' stated Williams in her proposal.

The year 2000 turned out to be a productive and pivotal year for Williams, who believed that she had completed 'at least' the 24 works referred to in her application. Two of the three projects happened as scheduled; the third, *Striking Attitudes*, was delayed because of funding issues, but eventually took place in November 2005. The exhibition *Ysbryd/Spirit Wales*, which was self-organised by a group of painters, toured to galleries in France as well as to the venues in Wales. *Site-ations* took place in 2001, on Staten Island, New York, as well as in Cardiff. It was a site-specific project in which artists took over various derelict buildings. Williams made work for a space in Cardiff docks. She also participated in several exhibitions in addition to those mentioned in her application. Some of the work made with Rootstein Hopkins Foundation support was exhibited in Sweden, after it had been seen by two curators from Avesta, near Stockholm. Williams was one of four Welsh artists invited to take part in a show of contemporary British art, *Ung – Young – Jung*, at the Avesta biennale late in 2000.

'It is not easy to define a beginning and an end to the project,' said Williams. 'It was the start of a very busy and productive period, which has continued ever since.' Williams felt she had achieved what she had intended with the Rootstein Hopkins Foundation funding and was pleased with the standard of the work produced. 'I was very short of money during that period, so the award helped a lot at a crucial time,' she said. 'It spared me from having to worry about the cost and quality of the materials I was using and it allowed me to work to a high level. The award certainly had an impact, and the opportunities that have followed on from it are definitely linked.'

Williams felt that since 2000 she had enjoyed an improved level of professional opportunities. 'Things have moved on very fast for me since that year,' she said. A period of unprecedented commercial success was triggered when Williams won the Gold Medal at the National Eisteddfod in 2000, partly for work produced during the Rootstein Hopkins-funded period. 'The Gold Medal was an indirect outcome of the Rootstein Hopkins award,' she said. 'And because of the Gold Medal, the Welsh Assembly and the National Museum of Wales bought some of the work made with Rootstein Hopkins' support for their collections. The Contemporary Art Society also bought my work, and after the Eisteddfod success I was able to sell work through Sotheby's two years' running. The demand from private collectors used to be intermittent, and for smaller works, but collectors are now increasingly interested in the larger paintings.'

Williams' work has also received critical recognition. In 2005, she was one of 300 artists worldwide to be nominated for the prestigious *Artes Mundi* prize, and was the only British artist to be included on the final shortlist of seven. *Artes Mundi* concluded with a major exhibition at the National Museum in Cardiff in spring 2006, in which Williams was able to present a significant display of new work. One of the two international selectors of the *Artes Mundi* shortlist, the Brazilian curator Ivo Mesquita, subsequently wrote an essay for the catalogue to Williams' touring exhibition, *Small Talk, High Heels*, which opened at the Glynn Vivian Gallery in Swansea, in May 2006. It is her most important solo show to date. 'That exhibition is a further example of how much my career has progressed since the time of the Rootstein Hopkins award,' said Williams. 'Profile-raising opportunities, increased sales, international exhibitions and positive media coverage have all been triggered by the work that was supported by the award.'

Since 2000, Williams had enjoyed greater success in terms both of commercial sales and in being able to secure public funding to support her work. She gained her largest grant to date, £13,000 from the Arts Council of Wales, in 2005 towards her touring exhibition *Small Talk, High Heels*. Subsidies and sales had helped to improve Williams' financial situation and to reduce, to some extent, her reliance upon teaching, which she contin-

ued to do on a sessional basis at colleges in Swansea, Cardiff and Exeter.

Williams felt that there had been a huge progression in her career since 2000. The Rootstein Hopkins Foundation award came at a crucial time for her, when she was in straitened circumstances financially. 'Getting the letter confirming the award was incredible,' she said. 'When somebody shows faith and trust in you it can give you the kick that you need to move on. Artistically, it has just seemed a natural progression: the award enabled me to get on and to do well the work I was already beginning to be successful with. But professionally, it provided the fillip for me to jump to a higher level.'

Without the Rootstein Hopkins award, Williams felt that, purely for financial reasons, she would not have been able to produce the work that she made during that period. 'I simply didn't have the money to spare,' she said. 'I was helping my son through college at that time and there was no way that I could have justified spending money on my art, instead of on his education. The Rootstein Hopkins award was the only funding that I applied for at that time. I was fortunate to stumble across it just at the point when I was wondering what on earth I could do next. I took a chance and it paid off, and I haven't looked back since.'

Williams felt that there was a need for more awards for artists, to encourage them to produce ambitious work without financial worry. The endorsement that comes with an award is, perhaps, as important as the

funding. 'There is a stage at the beginning of a career when an artist needs that confidence boost,' she said, 'and when a body such as the Rootstein Hopkins Foundation offers an artist funding, it can generate a huge leap in confidence. The money is important, but the confidence that comes with it is probably even more so.'

## Travel

# JULIAN GRATER

YEAR OF AWARD
2000

AMOUNT
£5,000

Julian Grater was supported by the Rootstein Hopkins Foundation to travel to Fairbanks in Alaska, United States, and to the Banff Centre for the Arts in Alberta, Canada, where he wanted to take further some research that he had begun during a visit to the west of Canada in 1998. When Grater arrived at Banff, however, things did not turn out quite as he had planned. 'One of the first things I did, which was not part of my proposal,' said Grater, 'was to link up with a team of palae-ontologists and hike up to Walcott's quarry and the Burgess Shale.' The Burgess Shale, a UNESCO World Heritage Site, is a cache of fossils located 8,000 feet up in the Canadian Rockies, in Yoho National Park, British Columbia. Grater knew of it through Stephen Jay Gould's celebrated 1989 book *Wonderful Life: The Burgess Shale and the Nature of History*. 'I didn't realise until I got to the Banff Centre how proximate the site was,' said Grater. 'You can't gain access without proper authorisation, so I contacted the Burgess Shale Foundation, which controls access to the site, and they were enormously helpful.'

Grater also collected pine resins in the forests of Alberta, as he had initially intended to do, which fed in to a series of explora-tory drawings. These were soon abandoned, however, because of a compulsion to work with the fossils. 'The Burgess Shale absolutely got its hooks in to me,' said Grater. 'Much of my activity at Banff was planning how this new project might pan out.' After six weeks at Banff, Grater flew up to the University of Alaska in Fairbanks, where he stayed for

a further four weeks at the Faculty of Fine Art. Grater chose Fairbanks because it was the perfect site for observing the Aurora Borealis, or the Northern Lights. 'During the day,' he said, 'I continued the drawings I'd begun in Banff. At night, I went out to photograph the Northern Lights. It was a mesmerising and powerful experience. The Aurora is an extraordinary, visually spectacular phenom-enon; it has an alien, other-worldly kind of feeling.' Whilst in Alaska, Grater amassed a huge photographic archive, which has informed a series of paintings that he was continuing to work on five years later.

When Grater returned to England, in October 2000, he was suffering from pneumonia. 'Because of the intensity of the experience, I pushed myself a little too hard,' he said. 'I think I just burnt myself out. I had quite a serious bout of illness, which would not have been helped by spending fantasti-cally long periods in sub-zero temperatures photographing the Northern Lights.'

It took Grater many months following his return to get to grips with the material he had amassed, to distil from it what was most important. 'The experience of a site or location always comes first – in my case, usually somewhere geographically remote,' he said. 'The practical work often only matures gradually, with hindsight.' Grater's trip to Canada and the United States triggered a process of creative enquiry which has fed into his drawings and paintings ever since. 'The work generated from that trip has been pivotal and enduring,' he said, 'much more so than in previous phases of my career.'

The Burgess Shale is an exquisitely preserved, fossilised time capsule, which provides a visual record of one of the Earth's earliest-known mass extinction events, following what is assumed to be an asteroid impact. Many of Grater's works from the Rootstein Hopkins-funded period were small, rapidly executed drawings, based on fossil specimens shown to him by Burgess Shale palaeontologists. Some were made at the site, with a meteorite on silicon carbide paper. Rendering images of fossils using the means of their extinction – that is, fragments of meteorite – marked a new departure in Grater's work. 'A correspondence is forged between the subject matter and the material in which it is made,' he said. 'It imbues the work with a kind of geological authenticity, framed by a carefully conceived conceptual rigour.'

Whilst Grater is interested in geology and in the natural sciences, he is keen that this work should not be regarded simply as illustration. 'The fossils are the starting point for a much more Romantic and philosophical enquiry,' he said. 'They are visually remarkable in themselves, but I want to create a level of ambiguity in the work that alludes to notions of horror or entropy, shot through with additional ideas linked to extinction and catastrophe.'

It was several years before Grater had produced from his source material a body of work that he felt fully ready to exhibit. That was achieved with the exhibition *Biomarkers*, which took place at Oxford University Museum of Natural History in autumn 2005. It was important for Grater to be able to contextualise his work against the Museum's collection. 'Ideally,' he said, 'I'd like to show the work at some point at the Natural History Museum in London, where I could present a much larger body of work, alongside the earth sciences and palaeontology archive.' In 2005, the series of Biomarkers drawings and paintings numbered about 100, and was still in progress.

The success of Grater's initial residency at the Banff Centre, which is renowned for its international artists' exchange programme, led to an invitation to return in 2002 for a supported residency, *SloMo*. On this occasion, he worked alongside 38 other visual artists to explore notions of time. Grater returned to Banff for two further residencies, funded by Arts Council England, in 2004 and 2006. 'To get back into a supportive setting like the Banff Centre has been really important for my professional development,' said Grater. 'There, you are very much part of a community of artists, who are committed to exploring, exchanging and debating new and emergent ideas.' The later residencies at Banff enabled Grater to take further the ideas he had developed during the Rootstein Hopkins-funded trip. Some of the work in his *Biomarkers* exhibition, for example, had been started during *SloMo* in 2002.

Without the Rootstein Hopkins Foundation award, Grater did not think that he could have travelled to North America in 2000. 'Travel awards are absolutely invaluable for an artist like me,' he said. 'Artists who are interested in the experience of landscape, particularly of an extreme kind, find it very difficult to fund their research. Visiting remote locations can be expensive and will always require funding. Sourcing opportunities has become a necessary and significant part of what artists now have to do, alongside the nuts and bolts of actually making work. Although I consider myself to have been extremely fortunate in recent years, in a broader sense, there just isn't enough suitable funding out there.'

*Travel*
# MARK THOMPSON

YEAR OF AWARD
1998

AMOUNT
£5,000

The Rootstein Hopkins Foundation gave Mark Thompson an award to travel through Scandinavia. Thompson said in his proposal that he wished to study 'water, ice and snow and their effect on both the landscape and its people'. It was to be Thompson's first visit to mainland Scandinavia. He had travelled the previous year, 1997, to Iceland, following his graduation from the Slade School of Fine Art. The trip to Scandinavia reinforced a move into landscape painting, which had started during Thompson's final year at the Slade. 'In college,' he said, 'as much as we like to think we're working for ourselves, there are tutors to please and other students to compete with. When you leave college, all those motivations are taken away. In some ways, the travel scholarship consolidated my reason for making paintings. You have to find that reason for yourself again after college.'

Thompson travelled for six months, from July 1998 to January 1999. He began in Helsinki, from where he flew to Oslo and then travelled the length of Norway to Nordkapp, the most northerly point on the European mainland. From there he journeyed through Lapland – a conceptual rather than geographical place, populated by the Sami, the indigenous people of the north – and then back through Finland to Helsinki. 'I didn't make it to Denmark,' said Thompson. 'I had so much in my head already that getting back into the studio seemed much the better option.'

There were a number of cultural highlights within the itinerary: going to see Anselm Keifer's sculpture *High Priestess* in Oslo, for example, and visiting Alta in the north of Norway to see 5,000-year-old rock carvings littered across a stretch of coastline. 'I realised that to keep myself engaged in either landscape or culture, there had to be a sense of both at each stage of the trip,' said Thompson. 'I was camping for four of the six months and you can very quickly become a kind of hermetic mountain man. Stepping back into cities and culturally reinserting yourself was an essential part of the balance.'

It was the landscape, however, that Thompson was most attuned to. 'The whole of Finland was extraordinarily interesting,' he said, 'as were the regions north of the Arctic Circle. Norway is quite claustrophobic in a way, full of valleys that never see the sun. You never get a sense of distance, or of where you are. The mountains above the treeline tend to be more shaped and separate because the climate is so much harsher. The people also change as the landscape changes; as the population becomes sparser.' Thompson camped in his one-man tent until quite late into the year. 'I realised it was probably time to stop when the tent froze and I couldn't get out in the morning,' he said. 'That was in the northernmost town in Finland, Utsjoki, in November. It got down to about -10 degrees one night, so I decided it was time to start using hostels and hotels.'

Halfway through the trip, Thompson secured a teaching residency in the north of Finland. He contacted the British Council in Helsinki, which gave him details of colleges to approach. 'I decided it would be a great way to punctuate the trip,' said Thompson. 'It was important for me to be able to meet people; travel can be a solitary experience. They gave me a studio at an arts college – Kuusamo Kansanopisto, in Kuusamo – for a month, and I made about 200 drawings. I taught some drawing while I was there, but mainly they wanted a living, breathing artist in their midst. After being on my own for four months, it was extraordinary to be thrust as a teacher into that group of 18- to 20-year-olds from all over Finland.'

Thompson filled many sketchbooks during his journey, but his diary turned out to be an equally important accessory. 'The diary notes of my state of mind and verbal descriptions of places became more vivid than the drawings,' he said. 'I started to realise that the filter of memory would be a profound aspect of the studio practice that would come later.' Thompson also became 'trigger happy' with the camera. 'My relationship with photography changed,' he said. 'Before, it was a visual record of things and places that could feed into the paintings. After that trip, landscape could survive purely as photographs rather than having to become the subject matter for painting. Photography and painting are now very much two separate strands to my practice.'

By the end of the journey, Thompson found that he had become more open as a person. 'I'd gone from living in London, where you close yourself off a lot, to months of being totally immersed in the elements,' he said. 'There was a sense of having been completely opened up; of having the blinkers taken off. It's something I'm still working with really; it becomes a part of your life experience. You don't often get a chance to spend six months out of civilisation. In one way or another it has had an extraordinary long-term benefit. Talking about it now makes me realise how much it is still there.'

Thompson had an exhibition lined up, at the Proud Galleries in London for November 1999. On his return from Scandinavia, he had just ten months in which to make a body of new work. 'I made 20 paintings during those ten months,' said Thompson, 'which was extraordinary. All the works were directly based on that trip. When you spend six months looking at and absorbing a foreign landscape without letting it out, it really builds up. Then, back home, you can squeeze out all you have soaked up, like water from a sponge.'

The exhibition, *The Luckless Land of the North* – a title derived from the Finnish national epic poem, the *Kalevala* – featured the full series of 20 paintings. 'It seemed to touch a lot of nerves,' said Thompson. 'That came through in comments in the visitors' book: things like, "thank you for putting me back in touch with memories from my childhood".' All 20 of the paintings in the exhibition were sold.

The journey through Scandinavia reinforced Thompson's desire for travel, which has been an important part of his art practice ever since. He has made further trips to Norway and Sweden, as well as to Alaska, the southwest of America and Japan. 'It is a necessary part of my research process,' he said. 'I try and do a little bit every year. If your practice is studio-based, you have to inform it with something, otherwise you would end up painting the corner of your studio.'

For Thompson, the opportunity to travel to Scandinavia involved an element of risk. 'It was a make or break moment in my career,' he said. 'I left my studio, my flat and my jobs to make the trip. It involved a lot of sacrifice at the time, but frankly I was quite happy to sacrifice those things.' The body of paintings made during 1999 gave Thompson his first major commercial success. Since then, the mainstay of his professional work has been painting, which he has been able to pursue full-time since 2003.

'The trip was extraordinary in terms of my education as an artist,' Thompson said. 'I'm not sure where my path would have led had I not taken the trip, but it was a life-changing moment. When you leave college, you can be a bit lost. I didn't feel like doing a postgraduate course, so in some ways the trip was my post-grad, but out in the world. As an artist, it is easy to become insular and not really to see anything outside of yourself, so it is extraordinary to be thrust into another world. Travel is absolutely one of the best ways of achieving that. You don't know what the next day will bring. It is one of the few times in life when your comfort zones are shot to bits.'

# SPEND OUT OR LEGACY?

*by Professor Rod Bugg*

The term 'spend out' sounds profligate, more akin to an expensive Bond Street outing or a supermarket dash than the careful and effective allocation of resources which the trustees of the Rootstein Hopkins Foundation (RHF) sought to achieve when they planned, in keeping with the wishes of the late Rick Hopkins, to wind up the charity after a little over a decade of grant-making activity. It would be more accurate to consider this final charitable act – the spend out – as a transfer of assets from the Foundation to the selected beneficiaries, and to regard the beneficiaries as the collective custodians of the Foundation's objectives, charged in their different ways with taking forward its values and ambitions. With these significant donations, the Foundation's legacy will continue to nourish and support the visual arts, the lives of those who create them and those who study and enjoy them.

The intention with the spend out – large grants made to a limited number of institutions – was to consolidate and build upon the awards made by the RHF in the earlier years of its history and to channel its funds in a way which was fully consistent with the terms under which the Foundation was created. The spend out grants were to be linked to the resources of the recipients, and used for sustainable projects with an extended life and an expectation of engaging a large audience of artists, students, scholars and the broader interested public.

After a great deal of consideration, investigation, reporting and debate, the RHF trustees decided that the spend out funds would be distributed among twelve projects and that the selected institutions – ranging geographically from Edinburgh in the north to Portsmouth in the south – would be Aspex Visual Art Trust, BALTIC Centre for Contemporary Art, the Little Sparta Trust, the National Gallery, National Life Stories at the British Library Sound Archive, the Royal Institute of British Architects (RIBA), Sir John Soane's Museum, Spike Island, the University of the Arts London, the Victoria and Albert Museum (V&A) and Wimbledon College of Art. A series of intersecting themes underlies the spend out decisions, with four primary concerns most easily identified: the wish to support the artist as an individual; the desire to promote the importance of drawing; an interest in and understanding of the needs of art education; the protection of valuable and vulnerable archives and their dissemination to the public.

The wish to support the individual artist has been at the heart of the RHF's brief from the outset, and is here expressed most overtly in the grant to the National

Gallery's Associate Artist scheme. An artist-in-residence programme has been part of the culture at the National Gallery for over ten years; with the RHF's funds, there will now be an open selection process, establishing a democratic and long-term future for the scheme which allows each chosen artist the use of a studio within the Gallery, privileged access to its unrivalled holdings for a period of two years and the opportunity to exhibit at the culmination of each residency. The National Gallery sees this initiative as a means of bridging the worlds of its spectacular historic collection and that of the contemporary practitioner.

In its award to Spike Island, an organisation dedicated to supporting the development of artists and others working within the visual arts, the RHF has made possible both the completion of a capital project to improve and extend research and development facilities and the creation of a new dedicated gallery space. The grant also makes provision for six years for the costs of an open submission, annual Rootstein Hopkins Award, to be made to an artist selected by Spike Island and an appointed panel.

In Portsmouth, the RHF grant to Aspex Visual Art Trust also contributed to the fabric of a building, enabling the completion of the redevelopment of the Trust's new home in the Vulcan Building on Gunwharf Quay, including a ground floor area named the Rootstein Hopkins Education Space. The remaining funds will enable Aspex to appoint a co-ordinator, and to make strategic developments over the coming five years for its Artists' Resource Centre (ARC). This facility – which makes available, amongst other things, one-to-one advice surgeries, professional development seminars and critique groups – has been renamed ARC+ as it will be extended across a wider region of the south, south east and south west.

In the north east, at BALTIC Centre for Contemporary Art in Gateshead, the RHF funds will bring together the Centre's educational and public programming facilities in a unified, upgraded and fully accessible space at the heart of the building. In addition, the RHF funds will support the freshly created post of Learning Co-ordinator for a three-year period and a major training programme for the twenty staff known as 'the B crew'. The latter are artists who work part-time in the gallery as invigilators and information providers, and the training will transform their role to that of proactive artist-educators.

The largest of the grants which the RHF has directed towards an educational institution goes to the University of the Arts London to create a new public space on the Parade Ground at Chelsea College of Art, adjacent to Tate Britain at Millbank. Here, the Foundation identified a rare opportunity to support a development of long-term significance for all its communities of interest. The Parade Ground will be refurbished to provide a sympathetic and flexible outdoor venue for exhibitions, events and student engagement from the whole University and for wide public access.

At Wimbledon College of Art, the RHF has been crucial in making possible the refurbishment of it's theatre space, which was originally conceived by the late Richard Negri, an early head of the theatre department at Wimbledon (and also the designer of the Manchester Royal Exchange Theatre). The refurbishment will allow the College to meet the needs of the highest standards for contemporary performance and design education, linking theatre, film and television facilities. In a separate grant, the RHF has also provided resources to house at the College over 4,000 drawings from the

*Above, left and previous page:* Little Sparta, Ian Hamilton Finlay's garden in Lanarkshire

archive of the late Jocelyn Herbert. Herbert, who worked at the Royal Court between 1956 and 1970 and later at the National Theatre and the Metropolitan Opera House amongst other venues, was responsible for the designs of many plays that are now considered twentieth-century classics. Alongside her collection of drawings is an archive of correspondence of considerable interest to researchers, and the RHF grant will enable both to be conserved, digitised and disseminated to staff and students of Wimbledon College of Art and to the wider research community.

Near contemporaries of Herbert, Sir Hugh Casson and his wife, Margaret McDonald Casson, left between them an archive of drawings, texts and photographs which cover their overlapping careers as architects, designers and artists. Their joint archive has been bought for the nation with the aid of an RHF grant that also enables the V&A to preserve the material and make it available to users. Due to the presence of the RIBA study centre within the Museum, the V&A is twice a beneficiary of the RHF spend out, the second instance being through the trustees' support for the purchase from private ownership of the Codex Stosch, a portfolio of sixteenth-century architectural drawings by Giovanni Battista da Sangallo (1496-1548), a member of Raphael's circle in Rome, which, through the RIBA, will be made available to scholars. The RHF's commitment to architectural drawing was further confirmed with a grant to Sir John Soane's Museum for furniture to display its comprehensive collection of Adam drawings in the new Robert Adam Study Room. The specially made cabinets will be a modern interpretation of the furniture Adam had in his own office.

Far in miles and in spirit from the grandeur of London's museums, the tiny home of the late Ian Hamilton Finlay in the heart of his famous garden, Little Sparta, in Lanarkshire is no less an important recipient of the RHF spend out. The Foundation's aid has enabled the Little Sparta Trust to purchase and preserve the building whose appearance – external and internal – is so expressive of Hamilton Finlay's philosophy as a private individual and as an artist, and to conserve its contents, including the library from which the artist drew inspiration. Whilst the garden is open to the public annually for a season, it is hoped that the privacy of the house will provide an intimate study centre for those engaged on research into Finlay's unique output.

Between 1993 and 1997 Ian Hamilton Finlay was recorded for *Artists' Lives*, an oral history project run by National Life Stories (NLS) at the British Library Sound Archive (his recording will become available to public access in 2012). This project provides an opportunity for artists to document their lives and careers in their own words, allowing contemporary listeners and those in the centuries to come to hear firsthand the testimony of each individual without the mediation of a critic or art historian. *Artists' Lives* was first supported by the RHF with a small grant in 2001 and, in recognition of the value of its work and in the knowledge of the hand-to-mouth nature of its finances, the trustees decided to furnish NLS with a grant to assure its stability and to allow the steady forward planning of its future. Extracts from two of the recordings funded by the RHF, made by John Ward and Lubaina Himid, follow this essay alongside a written piece by Timothy Hyman, an artist who benefited from one of the Foundation's first project grants. It seemed only right to end this Volume of the book with the voice of the artist, the central focus of the Rootstein Hopkins Foundation throughout its existence.

# THE ARTIST'S VOICE

The artist and the making of art have been central to the Rootstein Hopkins Foundation story. It seems fitting, therefore, that the last word in this Volume should be given to the artist: through extracts from two National Life Stories recordings at the British Library's Sound Archive; and through an eloquent essay by an early Rootstein Hopkins grant recipient, the painter Timothy Hyman.

### Two Voices from *Artists' Lives*

John Ward and Lubaina Himid's extensive contributions to National Life Stories' (NLS) oral history project, *Artists' Lives*, were amongst those supported by the Rootstein Hopkins Foundation. Both graduates of the Royal College of Art, nearly forty years separate their dates of birth (Ward b.1917, d.2007; Himid b.1954); although their practices have been immensely different, their careers co-existed for several decades in the multiplicity of energies which make up the British art world.

The primary material of NLS's recordings is the spoken word. The transcribed and edited extracts reproduced here, with the permission of the artists, represent a fraction of the testimony contained in these two life stories, which were completed between 2005 and 2006 (Ward), and 2006 and 2007 (Himid). Ward's extract is drawn from several recording sessions, Himid's from a single section; each has been edited to retain the conversational character of the encounter. Anna Dyke conducted both recordings on behalf of NLS.

*Above:* John Ward

# VOICES FROM *ARTISTS' LIVES*

John Ward

I was born in Hereford on the tenth of October 1917. Both sides of the family dealt in antiques. They were both London families, driven down to Hereford by the First World War. My father went and worked in a large furniture shop in Hereford and then opened his own shop where he sold antiques and restored pictures in Church Street, which is a narrow street of shops which led up to Hereford cathedral.

The shop was always exciting. Inside would be portfolios, bit of furniture, stacks of canvases, chests of drawers full of objects, and pictures hung round the walls. There was a constant drift of all sorts of odd things that had come in from sales, bunches of spears or model boats or bundles of prints and drawings. Ancestors' portraits were the regular things, cleaning and restoring the country families' ancestors. The people who employed my father and my brothers - because both brothers went into the business - were country families, so if I'd been a good boy they'd take me with them when they delivered pictures or whatever, then I caught a glimpse of the great country families which I thought was so splendid a life than any political destruction of such a way of life would be too awful. I remember reading Ruskin about it, that although he never wanted to live in a castle, he would feel very deprived if he couldn't see one from his cottage window.

My father did a bit of painting and would paint the odd picture to go in the shop window for Christmas. Flowers, kittens, dogs, horses, copied a Constable, that sort of thing. He would have talked about painters. One of the painters I remember we mutually enjoyed was Franz Hals. *The Laughing Cavalier* used to be on the cover of the drawing books which I used to buy from Boots - Boots in those days not only ran a library, they sold artists' materials. I drew horses all day. There were lots of very good engravings by Herring, a horse painter, and by Landseer. I adored drawing horses and of course there were a lot around. I grew up amongst smells of varnish and paints. It was magic. I loved it.

Come the age of fifteen I left school and was pretty feeble and useless, and the fine headmaster said I must go to the art school, a Regency building perched on the River Wye, and on the other side was the Castle Green, a beautiful green with an handsome monument to Nelson in the centre where the children played. I thought the art school was absolute heaven. I wanted to be a famous painter. The school was only open three days a week, you made the most of it, but you did learn to work on your own. There was a man, Thomas Vaughan Milligan, who'd spent five years at the Royal College of Art and who I suspected was more interested in the inside of the engine of his motor car than he was in art, and a woman who'd been trained at Glasgow School of Art: that was the staff. The man taught architecture, antique drawing, perspective, life drawing and jewellery. The woman taught pottery, still-life in watercolour, embroidery and leatherwork. And a bit of etching.

And then there were the visiting teachers, a man who taught building construction, a man who taught wood carving and one who was very important to me, a signwriter, who was the first practising artist I ever came across. His name was Fred Lofts. He adored posters and posters in those days were outstandingly good. They were on every hoarding, railway and shipping posters. I was never neat enough to manage anything worthwhile but I learnt to appreciate good lettering. It was he who talked about earning a living, otherwise there was never any mention of how you were ever going to earn a living. He lettered on vans and all that sort of thing, with these beautiful long-haired sable brushes.

You were taught the construction of a figure. There was a skeleton in the room, there were anatomy books. You got the hang of the figure from drawing from casts. One also did solid geometry. And perspective of course, very fascinating. It was all done on the blackboard. It's fundamentally that all parallel lines vanish to a point on the eyelevel. But then you got problems like an umbrella in a puddle so that you got reflections and shadows - you worked out shadows from where the light was. There was no oil painting, oil paints were too expensive. There was a very good magazine called *The Studio* and the library subscribed to a thing called the Vasari Society and through that I came across the three masters I've admired all my life: Stubbs' *Anatomy of the Horse*, the drawings which he made which are in the Royal Academy; Rossetti's drawings of his wife, Elizabeth Siddal; and Botticelli's *Illustrations to Dante*, which is the greatest series of illustrations ever made.

I came to architecture through the art school, it was something I resented having to do because I wasn't going to be an architect. But it was compulsory. You had to learn the orders off by heart, you had to be able to draw them exactly with a T-square and a set square and compass. Doric, Ionic, Corinthian capitals and perhaps some of the Roman orders. It was believed that they were the basis of good proportion, right down to the smallest detail. The smallest detail was related to the largest measurement. One caught a glimpse of what art really was when you set out a classical order, served no purpose other than it should be beautiful. It's a perfect example of how often a student is better off if he's not given his own choice.

The only exam, which in fact no-one had taken until I and about four other students decided we would take it, was the National Drawing Exam, and for that you had to study architecture, perspective, composition, life drawing and architecture. The examination papers were sent down and that was the only exam I ever took.

I wrote to the Principal of the Royal College of Art, Sir William Rothenstein, who'd been a friend of Whistler's and Degas and Pissarro, and he wrote back and said 'send me your work'. They were probably drawings of heads and things, dogs. Hands. I'd read that hands were very difficult to draw so I had a mirror and set out to master drawing hands, and I did.

I can still remember my first day in the still life room at the Royal College. Still life was taught by a very fine painter and designer called Barnett Freedman. He was Jewish and short and tubby and very fierce. I got out my watercolours and he said, 'What are those?' and I said, 'Well, those are my watercolours.' He said, 'They're old lady's things, we don't use those here. Where are your oil paints?' I said, 'I haven't got any.' 'Well,' he said, 'go out this minute and buy some.' The only shop I knew which sold oil paints was a shop underneath the Ritz so I went all the way up there and brought 'em back and he said where did I get these? I explained and he said, 'Well, you're either a very rich man or a great fool.' And he set up a still life and spent the rest of the day painting it for me. 'There you are,' he said. I've still got it. Beautiful painting.

I thought the Royal College was depressing. The subject matter most admired was anything to do with working class conditions. The prize student painted dustbins and I thought that was incredibly dreary but that was what they liked. I remember the Principal - Rothenstein had retired and a man called Jowett had taken over - said to me one day, 'You're very skilled, but what have you to say?' and I couldn't think. Say? What's he mean? Painting's not about saying anything. It's about delight. But these people were all ardent leftwing and to me that didn't enter painting, it had nothing to do with painting as far as I was concerned. Painters always make a poor fist of politics. There were ardent communists when communist was obviously as bad as fascists. But they were like hens, led by the beak. One should have the courage of one's cowardice. That wasn't my subject. I like pretty subjects.

There had grown up through the Slade the idea that an artist should be untrammelled, that he was only good if he could follow his own bent entirely. Well this is a very, very recent idea. In the past what was wanted from an artist was laid down very clearly and severely.

# VOICES FROM *ARTISTS'* LIVES

Lubaina Himid

*Would you describe yourself as a political artist these days?*

Yes, I think so. In a way I kind of try not to be because it's exhausting. I think of myself as somebody who'd just like to make a series of just lovely things, but what happens to me is I think, "well if you can make a lovely thing, think of what you could get it to say" [laughs] - you know, by seducing people into looking at it and then saying something that they perhaps didn't expect or that they have to bring their own thoughts or opinions to. So yes, I think I am an artist, I do think that, but I suspect that I don't actually make art. I think I probably make politics. I probably make something that isn't really art in that kind of accepted sense of the word. Which I think is maybe the good thing about it and sometimes the challenging thing about it for people, but it can't just sit there, it just has to be saying something and having an opinion and inviting you to have an opinion. So yes, I think I am even now. Which surprises me really because I thought that after making *Naming the Money* I just wouldn't do that any more. I thought I would quietly make things that I liked to look at and nobody would particularly want to show or talk about, it's just, it didn't really work like that. I started to make things that talked about what it is to be British even, juxtaposing African patterns and British patterns and British plants and plant structures and all sorts of things, getting them to kind of cross over and mix and juxtapose.

*Is this the current work that you're talking about?*

Well, as usual I'm working on two things at once in that I'm working on a set of paintings, small paintings and paper works that are dealing with some of those funny and peculiar things like that the patterns and the cloths for East African kangas and West African cloths were designed and made here and then shipped to West and East Africa and obviously lots of the patterns are plant patterns and making lots of draw-ings of the inner structure of British wild flowers, so the seeds and the petals and the leaves and the bits and pieces inside, sort of thing and how strangely kind of alien and peculiar and from out of space they look so that the African patterns look very kind of pleasant and pretty and the English plant structures look rather frightening and odd, trying to see what happens when you put those two things together. So that's what I call my 'kanga project'. Eventually I'm hoping there'll be lots of long, thin, patterned paintings that work a bit like a cartoon in a way that they move along the surface and keep repeating and appearing in a different guise and being interwoven with other patterns.

*Are they paintings on canvas?*

Yes, yes. Some are small, sort of ten by eight size canvasses and some are tiny, three by four inch canvases and some are maybe about six foot long by fifteen inch high canvases. I quite like that small but long and thin format. Although that isn't the shape and size of a kanga, a kanga is probably about six foot wide and about four foot high and has a sort of border and a pattern in the middle and round the border is another pattern and across it is a text, sometimes a Swahili text and sometimes an English text, that's a kind of proverb. And some of the proverbs are very funny and mostly, all these kangas are worn by women and so they're kind of women's talking clothes. So you could wear one half of a kanga round your waist as a kind of skirt and the other half round your top half and they could both have the same texts, which would be, you know, I don't know, something like 'Stealing other people's husbands is wrong' [laughs] or something like that. Or, 'The only good lover is a rich lover' and all sorts of very amusing kind of texts to make women laugh and men feel kept in their place. Or you could wear two different kangas; one with one text and one with another. Or ones with political things about praise to the President, you know. So I'm quite interested in making a whole show that examines all that, about myself really.

But I've been asked by Lancashire Museums to make a show for the commemoration, the 200 years since the Act of Parliament to abolish the slave trade, for the Judges' Lodgings in Lancaster. And that's one of these lovely small town museums. But it was like a lot of towns up there, had a Judges' Lodgings and the judges would go from town to town meting our their punishment and then moving to the next lodgings and stay there the night, or a few nights and be waited on hand and foot. And there were lovely airy rooms, beautiful fireplaces, lovely furniture. And this particular Judges' Lodgings houses a lot of Gillows' furniture which is mahogany furniture. And Gillow was one of the important people from Lancaster who also owned ships, slave ships and along with a lot of the other Lancaster merchants at the time had part ownership of ships, took goods to the west coast of Africa, picked up slaves. And they ran quite a, sort of small ships, not particularly tightly packed but you know, a few, quite a few hundred people at a time they'd take them across the Atlantic and sell them quite a lot in South Carolina and then pick up mahogany, take that back to Lancaster. Gillows particularly took back mahogany and made this fantastic furniture. So one of the tables in the Judges' Lodgings is a beautiful mahogany table so I've made a – well I'm in the process of – collecting old or second-hand cheap, but quite particular, plates, tureens, bowls to make up a dinner service to display on this table in the kitchen of the Judges' Lodgings and in the butler's pantry. And each of the plates will be either painted with people who were these ship owners, being kind of rather upset and sick that abolition has, you know, come about. Or paintings of slave servants themselves or there'll be paintings of the ships on other ones, parts of buildings in Lancaster, plant life that would have been growing in Lancaster at the time and is still growing in the streets and in the cracks in the pavement and walls today. Bits of buildings – I've taken lots of photographs of some of the buildings that remain. It's a very elegant city and its elegance directly comes from those people accruing that sort of wealth. Some of them were even Quakers, so you had Quakers who were ship owners and Quakers who were abolitionists, eventually – needless to say, the Quakers that were ship owners, you know, repented as they had to. But, so I'm trying to get the whole complexity in the town in there and to show that it isn't really just such a black and white story, it's quite complicated.

*Is that project linked to what you were talking about yesterday with the Gillray cartoons?*
Yes, I've always been rather in love with Gillray and Cruickshank and I think actually Gillray more than Cruickshank as rather more kind of scruffy somehow than Cruickshank. And I've... being trained as a theatre designer, that's all about being a magpie and stealing visuals and images from everywhere else. I'm also very interested in comics, *Beanos* and *Dandys* and all that sort of comic, so I've lifted some of the gestures and especially people throwing up, from Beano and Dandy comics and mixed it with Gillray cartoons of people, political people, you know, looking rather pained at some new legislation that's come in or royalty in some kind of compromising situation. Mostly those were kind of mocking, juxtaposing the sort of mocking royal mistresses with kind of unholy alliances with, you know, European nations and whatever. So I'm mixing and taking things from two or three sets of cartoons at once and turning them into Lancaster toffs really.

*Above:* Timothy Hyman

# ORKNEY AND AFTER:
# A MIDLIFE TURNING POINT

*by Timothy Hyman*

*It really is possible for a single grant to make an enormous difference to an artist's life. And perhaps especially – as in my own case – to an artist's midlife. What follows is an account of how, as I approached fifty, my own increasingly difficult circumstances were unexpectedly turned around, by what seemed at the time an almost miraculous event.*

## Desperate remedies

Early in January 1995, I arrived with my wife Judith at Rousay in the Orkney Islands, where we'd been lent a house for the winter months; not for 'travel' or 'holiday' but because of a need far more intense: to escape the terrible sense of entrapment that had come to poison both our lives in London. Over the previous year, I'd watched myself becoming more lethargic, sleeping badly, consumed with self-distaste. It must have been from the midst of that entrapment (which involved many ingredients: family and finance; ideology and 'career') that I'd spoken in autumn 1994 to a chance-met fellow-artist, Jackie Morreau, who happened also to be a Rootstein Hopkins Foundation trustee, and she had urged me to apply to the Foundation. By then, the tickets to Orkney were already purchased; our desperate remedy was in place.

Rousay is an island of some 200 scattered inhabitants, roughly eight miles around; our house, Fealquoy, was set in the remote upper-west corner. The Orkney Islands are a long way north – nearer to Bergen than to Edinburgh – and getting there, whichever way you make the journey, always entails a hefty fare. We'd rented out our London flat for the next few months at a low rate – just enough to cover expenses. We'd burnt our boats.

One purpose in venturing to Orkney was to set aside several months for undistracted work. I'd carried from London various artists' materials (including a few half-begun images) as well as several writing projects. The only fixed deadline was to complete a text on a painter I'd long admired, the Indian artist Bhupen Khakhar. But in general, I wanted to lay myself open to whatever creative impulse might occur. Quite soon – almost from the moment of our arrival – it became evident to both of us that our experience would be dominated by the immediacy of seeing: by this astonishing panorama of treeless green hills, floating above dark, metallic-blue waters, with further islands glimpsed on every horizon, which unfolded from our windows, and never failed to startle us out of any inward thought as soon as we stepped out into it. My eyes had never opened to so bright and clean a light as Orkney's winter sky.

That utterly unfamiliar landscape was inescapable; today, when I read my Orkney journal, it seems to consist mainly of skies and walks. Most frequently I headed due north, battling the wind, to our nearest beach, which was constantly reconfigured by each storm-tide, and always deserted, except for the seals. Sometimes I'd count as many as thirty, basking out on the rocks; and I got into a routine of singing in a high, pantomime-dame falsetto, which they seemed to love, lolloping into the waves and bobbing close to shore, their doglike heads staring out, alert, inquisitive. Or more ambitiously, if the day was fine, we might aim for one of Rousay's many prehistoric monuments, such as the great broch and tomb at West Howe, set opposite Einhallow above a wave-torn shelf, glistening black, and slated like a roof. The tomb was immense, a kind of dormitory-barrow with rows of beds to either side. Dated to 3,500 BC, it lay protected within a modern hangar, yet somehow retained its atmosphere of menace. One day, close to the broch, we stumbled across a dead sheep, lying face down in a puddle; as we dashed through, we felt spooked; intruders among the dead.

By the second week I was already noting in my journal a fateful interaction between painting, writing and seeing: how a catalogue of fifteenth-century Sienese art was feeding me with new ideas for pictures; and how the work of the Indian painter, Bhupen, owed much to Sienese imagery. While outside, Orkney's treeless hills had a surprising affinity to the Sienese Crete, the rolling clay hills so often depicted in the small 'predella' paintings commonly found at the foot of Tuscan altarpieces. It was all merging together.

Yet any attempt at some exalted *vita contemplativa* was constantly being punctured by our practical difficulties. Each morning I spent hours battling with the mysteries of the ancient, treacherous Rayburn stove. Then, about ten days in, we suddenly lost our water and with no Yellow Pages with which to buy our way out of trouble, it meant wrestling in the mud with a neighbour's Air Compressor (a gigantic, heavy wheelbarrow contraption) and spanners and extension leads and gushing water, in which I sat, close to weeping. Judith felt this calamity helped us to bond with the house, with the island, with the elemental. Until, in late January, we woke to find overnight gales had ripped a heavy steel door off its hinges, tossing it into an outbuilding, only narrowly missing the geese. Were we out of our depth? Could we cope?

I was over a month deep into this weird adventure, so poised between idyll and ordeal, when, on the evening of 7 February, at about nine o'clock (with Judith already gone up to bed), the telephone rang. It was Jackie Morreau. The island-survival course had put a big space between present and past: I hadn't thought once of my Rootstein Hopkins application. So it was with absolute astonishment – open-mouthed, gaping disbelief – that I now heard Jackie's message: the grant had been granted. My first action on putting down the phone was to swallow a tranquilliser. The next morning we woke to thick snow. Housebound, I had plenty of time to ponder over the circumstances of my application – to brood upon all the travails of those past few years.

Five troubles

The facts could be easily summarised:

*Money-trouble* I had difficulty earning enough from painting, my chief source of income. In the late 1980s, I'd been fortunate to receive a stipend from a dealer, Austin/Desmond. But in 1991, in the art-market collapse that followed the first Gulf War, Willie Desmond was among several artworld suicides, and the gallery was now barely functioning.

*Family-trouble* My father, at eighty-five, was slipping into dementia; my mother into diabetes: gangrenous ulcers, the threat of amputation, blindness. I visited as often as possible, coming away each time overwhelmed by a sense of inadequacy. They were helpless, dependent for income mostly on their four children. But with two now ship-wrecked, only my twin brother and I remained to make up the missing thousands.

*Ideology-trouble* All this was happening about fifteen years into Thatcherism, and the worldwide collapse of the Left. The long-held hopes and convictions (Gandhian, libertarian) that had partly fuelled my art, seemed now exposed as fatuous pie-in-the-sky.

*Art-trouble* The kind of art I'd often espoused and sometimes practised, which might be characterised as a 'Return to History Painting', now sounded an unconvincing gospel. To a new, hard, postmodern generation, painting itself was, in Rosalind Krauss's phrase, 'that etiolated pursuit'. Painters who'd become prominent in the 1980s were disgraced; stained with the consumerism of those years.

Yet none of these woes was quite sufficient, even when cumulative and interlinked, to account for the deeper, more-or-less metaphysical loss-of-footing that I'd experienced as I turned forty-six. It was as though I had to begin the whole of life over again, to rebuild every aspect of my beliefs and awareness. But this rebuilding had to be accomplished even as I was still falling. What was this void, this unseen darkness that leaked like some paralysing gas into every moment? Probably the heading here should read: *Mortality-trouble*. Not just my parents' but my own, grasped for the first time as an urgent reality.

### 'We Grow Accustomed to the Dark'
Although baffled and fearful, I'd remained quite active both as a painter and polemicist. My own 'career' had begun in the mid-1970s, almost ten years after leaving the Slade, when I began to show paintings, as well as to publish and teach. In 1979 I curated a controversial touring exhibition, *Narrative Paintings*, which came to the ICA in London in 1980. For a decade or so, I'd felt linked to a loose confederation of like-minded painters. In the early 1990s I taught part-time in the painting studios at both the Royal College of Art and the Slade, where I also delivered a lecture series on pictorial humour, *A Carnival Sense of the World*. I published quite vigorously in art journals as well as in *The Times Literary Supplement*. In 1993 I'd enjoyed a solo exhibition, featuring more than fifty works, in a large artist-run space in Manchester; and the following year I'd showed both in Bombay and in London, at the Flowers East gallery, as well as in several mixed exhibitions. Some of these endeavours were definitely not futile, and

would later bear fruit. But the overall sense was of becoming dispersed, in sporadic (and ill-paid) roles. A fundamental change was needed.

On Rousay, as I set out on my quasi-allegorical walks, my head full of Sienese painting, I'd found new relevance in Dante's first-person narrative, and especially in his opening lines to the *Inferno*:

*In the middle of the journey of our life*
*I came to myself in a dark wood*
*Where the straight way was lost.*

In much the same vein, I responded with new recognition to a poem by Emily Dickinson, beginning 'We grow accustomed to the Dark'. The poem describes how, initially, as we grope our way, we're bound to bump our foreheads walking slap into the trees (a comic variant on Dante's 'dark wood'). But somehow we do learn to 'fit our vision to the dark':

*Either the Darkness alters —*
*Or something in the sight —*
*Adjusts itself to Midnight*
*And Life steps almost straight.*

The Orkney episode had been undertaken as something of a midlife purgatory-journey. With the grant offering a new security, perhaps I could confront my predicament less fearfully over the year ahead.

'What Remains'

With hindsight, I think two parallel developments were taking place in my painting. One emphasised the ephemeral moment, a sudden 'seeing' or epiphany; the other took the predicament of midlife, and made an image out of it. The first tended to be more modest in scale, the second larger and more ambitious. But in both, the crucial element was in the depiction of self; and the way that, in order to paint 'in the first-person', the *me* would need to become *he*. In the sudden 'given' perception, however fugitive, one's identity is reaffirmed — it is, after all, I who sees. And again, in finding some image as a metaphor of the uncertainty and doubt attendant on midlife, one experiences also some release. That was — as I see it — the basis of the new body of work to which I wanted to devote myself while sequestered in Orkney. Free of teaching and opportunities for sociability, I might find a necessary distance, as well as a fresh seeing.

On Rousay, I could not embark on any large-scale images, but my painting did flourish — not only such Orkney-based images as *Singing to the Seals* and *On the Egilsay Road*, but more surprisingly, pictures founded on drawings and on memory. One of the few actually begun and completed on the island was a little work on paper, *Afternoon Circus, Ahmedabad*, that obsessed me for several days; it recreated an experience, two years before, in the Indian city of Ahmedabad, of a half-deserted circus tent. Soon after my return, that work was purchased by the Government Art Collection. Orkney also supplied new perspectives on London, which I explored in a series of map-like images, conceptualising the city as a distant globe. These images were painted in oil on canvas-backed, folding maps of colonial India, picked up at a local jumble sale just before I left. Their language (based partly on Sienese imagery) was unfamiliar to me and I could not quite sustain it; after a week or so, I folded them away. They were not to be completed until several years later, and most of them were exhibited for the first time only in 2006.

As the second month became the third, I became conscious of just how cut-off we were. Even to reach the nearest town, Kirkwall, entailed an expedition by car, boat and bus. Meanwhile, in distant London, calamities still rained down: Judith's aunt suddenly died; my sister, back from Japan, was diagnosed with breast cancer, while her husband was caught up in the Kobe earthquake; and my parents almost perished in a kitchen fire, leaving their flat damaged and uninsured. But, with guilt spurring me on, the final weeks proved the most fertile for painting, and the Bhupen text was also completed.

We both returned to our London existence with a new energy. Back in the Dalston studio that summer, I worked on a sequence of altarpiece-scale canvases, each allegorising the midlife theme within a London setting. The largest had a two-part title, incorporating Dante's opening line: *Nel mezzo del cammin (Midlife: Pentonville Road)*; it showed me setting out from my front door, passing through the skeletal terrors. Another, *Midriver: The Bearer*, was a retelling of the Saint Christopher story, with me wading through the midlife filth of the Thames. And in a complex, divided image I tried to embody my ideological paralysis, taking my title from the East German writer, Christa Wolf – *What Remains*. It was through these and other compositions, first conceived between 1995 and 1996, that I would eventually gain a renewed sense of identity as a painter; and these works also provided the basis of four key exhibitions: at Austin/Desmond, London (2000, 2003, 2006) and at the Museum of London (2004).

To rediscover a sense of pilgrimage
At the end of November 1995 Judith and I set out again, on the last leg of what I now thought of as 'The Rootstein Hopkins Journey'. The Bombay gallery where I'd shown work the previous year, asked me to exhibit in a group show alongside several of the painters I felt closest to; and I also delivered the Bhupen Khakhar text to the publisher in India (the monograph was published in 1998). In the weeks that followed, I joined a chaotic 'Artists' Camp' north of Bombay, where I began another midlife allegory: a painting, *Gandhian Ark*, where the vessel floated mid-sea between a drowning city and the coast of Utopia. Early in January 1996, Judith and I fluked into the extraordinary Green Hotel, which had recently opened in a former film studio on the outskirts of Mysore and was still almost empty of guests. The hotel cleared a studio area, where I began several new images, including *Midday Stillness* and *Imagining Plato's Cave*. Three meals on the lawn and a simple room worked out at five pounds each per day; we ended by staying five wonderful, healing weeks, before returning to the rough-and-tumble of Bombay, and then on to London.

The road ahead concealed many pitfalls before we reached the millennium: Judith was diagnosed with Parkinson's disease; both of my parents died, and then my twin brother. But if I still persist in recalling those years as a time of recovery, rather than of disaster, it is because I never entirely lost the impetus triggered by that unexpected respite. I had, in the words of a friend, 'rediscovered a sense of pilgrimage', both as painter and as writer. In 1998 Thames and Hudson published my monograph on Pierre Bonnard, a book whose first-person affirmations could be read as my riposte to midlife self-obliteration. Later, in another Thames and Hudson book, *Sienese Painting* (2003), I tried to explore the interchange between art and utopian aspiration.

In Britain, a contemporary artist's career often has a very odd shape. After the enthralling initial take-off, one might assume a steadily rising parabola. But quite soon, probably within ten years, the rocket ceases to rise; it wobbles, and begins to drop. Maybe it will rise again; but in the meantime, even if the internal motor still seems to be running strongly, it stays close to the ground, almost invisible. This trajectory results, in part, from the machinery of our art world, set up mostly since the Second World War: the vast art bureaucracy, whose task it is to exhibit the new and exciting – and therefore, almost inevitably, younger – talents.

I got help when I most needed it, when I was no longer 'emerging' or 'promising'. The Rootstein Hopkins Foundation has been admirable in giving its awards so directly to artists, without involving us in all that agonising form-filling; those contrived mission-statements, couched in approved Art-Speak, that are demanded by most current sources of arts funding. I still look back upon that award as one of the most fortunate turning points of my entire life.

# THE ROOTSTEIN HOPKINS FOUNDATION
## A Timeline of Significant Moments

| | |
|---|---|
| 1984 | The idea of a Rootstein Hopkins charitable trust is first mooted, in correspondence from the legal advisors of Rick and Adel Hopkins. |
| 25 OCTOBER 1990 | The RHF is established with the signing of the trust deed at the first meeting of the trustees, who comprised: Rick and Adel Hopkins, Graham Feldman (the inaugural Chair), Michael Southgate and Professor Bernard Cohen. The primary object of the trust is 'to establish a school of fine art'. |
| 12 DECEMBER 1990 | The RHF gains charitable status. |
| 10 JANUARY 1992 | The freehold of Shawfield House, the head office and showroom of the Rootstein Hopkins Group, is gifted to the RHF. This becomes the Foundation's principal asset and source of income. The RHF grants a 10-year lease back to the Rootstein Hopkins Group, at a rent of £116,000 per year. A lease for life, for a studio space within Shawfield House, is granted to Adel Hopkins for a one-off payment of £80,000. |
| JULY 1992 | Adel Hopkins graduates from the Slade School of Fine Art with a BA degree in Fine Art. |
| 20 SEPTEMBER 1992 | Adel Hopkins dies. |
| 10 FEBRUARY 1993 | The artist Jacqueline Morreau is appointed as a trustee. |
| APRIL 1993 | The trustees 'unanimously agree' that the RHF should plan 'to occupy and develop Shawfield House as studios and a gallery immediately upon expiry of the current lease' (i.e. in January 2002). |
| JULY 1994 | The trustees agree to offer 'a number of bursaries and scholarships, initially for one year only': a travel scholarship for emerging artists (to be awarded in conjunction with the Boise committee at the Slade); an international exchange programme award for students; a sabbatical for art teachers in higher education; an artists' support grant 'for talented artists in need of financial assistance'. |

| | |
|---|---|
| APRIL 1995 | The first series of RHF awards is confirmed. |
| JULY 1996 | The RHF makes its first mature student award, to enable Helen Slater to attend the Slade School of Fine Art. It is decided that, in future, grants for individual artists will be by open application and not, as formerly, by nomination. |
| DECEMBER 1996 | Rick Hopkins retires as Managing Director of the Rootstein Hopkins Group. |
| 1 JANUARY 1997 | Maureen Fawsitt is appointed Secretary of the RHF. |
| 23 JANUARY 1997 | Rick Hopkins takes over as RHF Chair. |
| 1 MAY 1997 | Jane Hartwell, the Exhibitions Organiser at the Morley Gallery, London, is appointed as a trustee. |
| OCTOBER 1997 | A feasibility study, commissioned to ascertain the viability of setting up an art school at Shawfield House, concludes that 'it will be impossible to gain public funds' and advises against the idea. |
| FEBRUARY 1998 | Professor Cohen resigns as a trustee. |
| APRIL 1998 | Rick Hopkins expresses a concern that 'if others became involved, the trust might not be administered in a way that reflects the intentions and spirit of the founders'. |
| OCTOBER 1998 | The trustees extend the Rootstein Hopkins Group's lease on Shawfield House to December 2006. |
| 16 DECEMBER 1998 | The RHF trust deed is amended to remove the original commitment 'to establish a school of fine art'. From now on, the focus of the Foundation is on grant-giving to support 'research and practice of art in all its branches, but in particular painting, drawing, sculpture, photography, fine and applied art'. |
| MAY 1999 | The first capital grant is approved: £30,000 for a creative technology suite at Glasgow School of Art. |
| NOVEMBER 1999 | The trustees agree that the Foundation should be wound up within ten years of Rick Hopkins' death. |
| 4 JUNE 2000 | Rick Hopkins dies. |
| JULY 2000 | Michael Southgate takes over as Chair of the RHF. The trustees agree a strategy to end the Foundation 'in about 10 years'. |

| | |
|---|---|
| SEPTEMBER 2000 | In accordance with a wish expressed in Rick Hopkins' will, Deirdre Hopkins is appointed as a trustee. |
| MARCH 2001 | Two 'special awards' of £500,000 are confirmed: to London College of Fashion, to create a new facility, the Rootstein Hopkins Space; and to the British Museum, to create an endowment with which to buy contemporary work for the Prints and Drawings Collection. |
| 11 JULY TO 7 AUGUST 2002 | The RHF stages an exhibition, *Chosen*, at the Rootstein Hopkins Space. It features the work of eight past winners of RHF awards. |
| MARCH 2003 | Jane Hartwell resigns as a trustee. |
| 3 JULY 2003 | Professor Eileen Hogan and Ian Cole are appointed as trustees. |
| MARCH 2004 | The RHF travel grant is discontinued due to the disappointing standard of applications. |
| APRIL 2005 | The trustees confirm their intention to sell Shawfield House. 'Upon receipt of the funds from the sale of the property, the trustees will take steps to distribute the funds and wind up the Foundation during the next few years.' Also, the Rootstein Hopkins Research Fellowship begins at Wimbledon College of Art. |
| JUNE 2005 | The sale of Shawfield House, for £6,200,000, is completed. Maureen Fawsitt retires as Secretary of the RHF. Tony Barlow is appointed in her place. |
| AUGUST 2005 | The process of 'spending out' begins with major awards to: National Life Stories (£400,000); the Little Sparta Trust (£185,000); the Jocelyn Herbert Archive (£100,000); the Sir John Soane's Museum (£99,470). |
| APRIL TO AUGUST 2006 | Further major awards are confirmed: University of the Arts London (£1,500,000); Wimbledon College of Art (£501,000); the National Gallery (£600,000); BALTIC (£500,000); Aspex Visual Arts Trust (£400,000); Spike Island (£350,000); the Royal Institute of British Architects (£110,000); the Hugh Casson and Margaret MacDonald archive at the Victoria & Albert Museum (£40,000). |
| APRIL 2007 | The Rootstein Hopkins Research Fellowship ends. |
| 2008 | The RHF winds up its affairs. |

# THE ROOTSTEIN HOPKINS FOUNDATION
## Calendar of Awards 1995-2006

During the twelve-year period from January 1995 to December 2006 the Rootstein Hopkins Foundation made the following awards, worth a total of £6,459,993.

### 1995

LONDON COLLEGE OF PRINTING AND DISTRIBUTIVE TRADES (AND THE FASHION INSTITUTE OF DESIGN AND MERCHANDISING, LOS ANGELES, USA)
Student Exchange – £8,121

HELEN SLATER
Student Fees – £2,430

PAM SKELTON (CENTRAL SAINT MARTINS COLLEGE OF ART AND DESIGN, LONDON)
Sabbatical – £12,000

TIMOTHY HYMAN
Project – £5,000

ISHBEL MYERSCOUGH
Travel – £5,000

### 1996

MUSEUM OF WOMEN'S ART, LONDON
Project – £7,500

RACHEL WITHERS
Travel – £5,000

### 1997

LONDON COLLEGE OF FASHION (AND THE FASHION INSTITUTE OF TECHNOLOGY, NEW YORK, USA)
Student Exchange – £24,000 (1997-1999)

NEWCASTLE UNIVERSITY (AND THE CLEVELAND INSTITUTE OF ART, OHIO, USA)
Student Exchange – £8,000

ROYAL COLLEGE OF ART, LONDON
Student Fees – £71,262 (1997-2004)

SHANTI THOMAS
Student Fees – £2,500

RAY MASTERS (UNIVERSITY OF SUNDERLAND)
Sabbatical – £6,000

CHRIS JONES (NEWCASTLE UNIVERSITY)
Sabbatical – £6,000

ANDREW EKINS
Project – £5,000

JENNIFER COMLEY
Travel – £5,000

IAN HARTLESS
Travel – £5,000

### 1998

GLASGOW SCHOOL OF ART
Student Exchange – £8,000

JANE HARRIS
Student Fees – £2,500

JAYNE PARKER (GOLDSMITHS COLLEGE AND THE SLADE SCHOOL OF FINE ART, LONDON)
Sabbatical – £12,000

MARK THOMPSON
Travel – £5,000

LUCY HEYWARD
Travel – £5,000

FRANCES TURNER
Travel – £5,000

### 1999

LYNNE ROBERTSON
Student Fees – £1,025

PAUL BUTLER
(SURREY INSTITUTE OF ART AND DESIGN)
Sabbatical – £12,000

BARBARA LOFTUS
Pro ject – £3,750

JENNIFER GODLIEB
Project – £2,000

CAI YUAN
Travel – £5,000

GLASGOW SCHOOL OF ART
Capital Project – £30,000

KINGSTON UNIVERSITY
Capital Project – £30,000 (1997-2000)

### 2000

BRIAN GRASSOM
Student Fees – £2,500

DUNCAN NEWTON (NORTHUMBRIA UNIVERSITY)
Sabbatical – £12,000

SOPHIE BENSON
Project – £2,500

SUE WILLIAMS
Project – £2,510

LUCILLE NOLAN
Travel – £5,000

LINDA SHORT
Travel – £5,000

JULIAN GRATER
Travel – £5,000

### 2001

KINGSTON UNIVERSITY
(AND HONG IK UNIVERSITY, SEOUL)
Student Exchange – £10,000 (2001 - 2003)

SRINIVAS SURTI
Student Fees – £1,550

JULIA POLONSKI
Student Fees – £2,950

VIRGINIA BODMAN
(UNIVERSITY OF SUNDERLAND)
Sabbatical – £12,000

SUSAN MCCALL
Project – £3,000

DEREK MAWUDOKU
Project – £4,000

MORLEY GALLERY, LONDON
Project – £12,000

FASHION AND TEXTILES MUSEUM, LONDON
Project – £3,000

SUSAN MILLER
Travel – £5,000

GRAY'S SCHOOL OF ART,
THE ROBERT GORDON UNIVERSITY, ABERDEEN
Capital Project – £30,000

LONDON COLLEGE OF FASHION,
UNIVERSITY OF THE ARTS LONDON
Capital Project – £500,000

BRITISH MUSEUM, PRINTS AND DRAWINGS
DEPARTMENT
Collection – £500,000

NATIONAL LIFE STORIES, *ARTISTS' LIVES*
Collection – £444,930 (2001-2006)

CHELTENHAM AND GLOUCESTER COLLEGE OF
HIGHER EDUCATION
Student Prize – £5,000 (2001-2005)

2002

STINA HARRIS
Student Fees – £2,150

KAREN COLLEY
Student Fees – £2,950

JUNE TRAFFORD
Student Fees – £2,200

RICHARD TALBOT
(CITY AND GUILDS OF LONDON ART SCHOOL)
Sabbatical – £6,000

LIZA GOUGH DANIELS
Project – £6,000

YUEN-YI LO
Travel – £5,000

LONDON COLLEGE OF COMMUNICATION,
UNIVERSITY OF THE ARTS LONDON
Capital Project – £30,000

2003

EMMA CHURCHILL
Student Fees – £2,500

EMMA STIBBON
Student Fees – £1,000

JANINE BARRACLOUGH
Student Fees – £2,500

SUE SPARK (NORTHUMBRIA UNIVERSITY)
Sabbatical – £12,000

SIMON GRENNAN
Project – £6,000

2004

MANCHESTER METROPOLITAN UNIVERSITY
(AND HONG KONG POLYTECHNIC UNIVERSITY)
Student Exchange – £30,000 (2004-2006)

PAULA GARCIA STONE
Student Fees – £2,940

JANE HARRIS (GOLDSMITHS COLLEGE, LONDON)
Sabbatical – £12,000

ERIC SNELL
Project – £6,000

JENNY WEST
Project – £6,000

WIMBLEDON SCHOOL OF ART
Capital Project – £24,000

2005

VANESSA BULLICK
Student Fees – £6,000

HELEN BAKER (NORTHUMBRIA UNIVERSITY)
Sabbatical – £12,000

FRANCES BORDEN
Project – £6,000

SIR JOHN SOANE'S MUSEUM, LONDON
Capital Project – £99,470

LITTLE SPARTA TRUST, LANARK
Capital Project – £185,000

VICTORIA & ALBERT MUSEUM, LONDON
Archive – £40,000

WIMBLEDON COLLEGE OF ART,
UNIVERSITY OF THE ARTS LONDON
Archive – £100,000

2006

KATE GENEVER
Student Fees – £6,000

ANDY CRANSTON (GRAY'S SCHOOL OF ART)
Sabbatical – £12,000

MIMI JOUNG
Project – £6,000

ASPEX VISUAL ARTS TRUST, PORTSMOUTH
Capital Project – £400,000

BALTIC CENTRE FOR CONTEMPORARY ART,
GATESHEAD
Capital Project – £500,000

UNIVERSITY OF THE ARTS LONDON
Capital Project – £1,500,000

SPIKE ISLAND ARTSPACE LIMITED, BRISTOL
Capital Project – £350,000

WIMBLEDON COLLEGE OF ART,
UNIVERSITY OF THE ARTS LONDON
Capital Project – £501,255

ROYAL INSTITUTE OF BRITISH
ARCHITECTS, LONDON
Collection – £110,000

THE NATIONAL GALLERY, LONDON
Associate Artists scheme – £600,000

# TRUSTEES' BIOGRAPHIES

### Ian Cole

Since 2001 Ian Cole has undertaken consultancy work in the field of visual arts education and practice on behalf of galleries, museums, schools, universities, youth arts agencies, funding agencies and local authorities. From 1988 to 2001 he was Head of Education and Public Programmes at the Museum of Modern Art Oxford (now Modern Art Oxford). From 1972 to 1988 he taught art, design and art history in secondary schools in Oxfordshire.

### Eileen Hogan

Eileen Hogan is a painter who has exhibited extensively in the United Kingdom and the United States. Since 1980 she has been represented by and had regular solo shows at The Fine Art Society, London. Hogan studied at Camberwell School of Arts and Crafts, the British School at Athens and the Royal College of Art. From 1989 to 1997 she was Dean at Camberwell College of Arts, where she established The Camberwell Press, of which she was Director from 1984 to 1997. Hogan was also a founding member of the Wellcome Trust committee which inaugurated the Sciart Awards. She is currently a professor of the University of the Arts London.

### Graham Feldman

Graham Feldman is a chartered accountant living and working in Israel. He is a founder trustee of the Rootstein Hopkins Foundation. He was an independent financial and tax advisor to the Rootstein Hopkins Group until the early 1990s and his association with the company's staff continues via his role as Chairman of the RH Pension Scheme. Feldman is currently a partner in a successful accounting practice based in Jerusalem, the director of two consultancy companies and the chief finance officer of a technology company. Prior to emigrating to Israel in 1981, he was a partner in a chartered accountants' practice based in London.

Deirdre Hopkins

Following an early career in retail design, Deirdre Hopkins spent twenty-six years teaching at London College of Fashion, London College of Communication and the Roehampton Institute. She has an MSc in Education Management, a BA in the History of Art, Design and Architecture and is a Fellow of the University of the Arts London.

Jacqueline Morreau

Jacqueline Morreau is an artist who has exhibited her prints, drawings and paintings widely. Her work is held in many public and private collections, in Britain and in the United States, including the British Museum and the Arts Council collections. She has been a visiting lecturer at the Royal College of Art and has written extensively on contemporary women artists.

Michael Southgate

Michael Southgate was a freelance designer for Adel Rootstein Limited from the formation of the business in the mid-1950s until 1976, when he was asked to relocate to New York as Executive Vice-President of the American company Adel Rootstein Inc. In 1978 he was made Creative Director of the parent company. After Adel Rootstein's death in 1992, he returned to the United Kingdom to run operations with Rick Hopkins until the latter retired in 1995. From 1995 until his own retirement Southgate was Managing Director. He became Chair of the Trustees of the Rootstein Hopkins Foundation in July 2000 following the death of Rick Hopkins.

# GOOD FOUNDATIONS
Author: Paul Glinkowski

# GOOD FOUNDATIONS

Trusts & Foundations and the Arts in the United Kingdom

Author: Paul Glinkowski

VOLUME II

*An Overview*

# CONTENTS

# THE GIFT: A PREFACE

by *Professor Mel Gooding*

'*The gift must always move.*'
Lewis Hyde

Diverse are the ways in which charitable trusts and foundations begin, proceed and evolve. Complex or simple in its institution, having resources great or small, each constitutes the continuation of a cycle of gifts. Each is concerned with the exchange and dissemination of good things, with a widening augmentation of value. Each embodies a dynamic generosity that seeks through its operation to keep in flow that which will enhance the quality and richness of social life as a whole and individual lives within it. Every trust and foundation is then part of a living process, its procedures – however constrained by changing law and custom – being of a kind that can be traced to the beginnings of human culture, and which shape the coherence of interests that is at the heart of social meaning.

Since the publication in 1924 of Marcel Mauss's *The Gift*, his pioneering study of gift exchange in archaic societies, there has been an ever-increasing awareness of the significance of the gift as a social and moral agency. The idea of the gift that must be honoured by a reciprocation of value is at the centre of social and political culture as a whole, and when it is diminished and derided in practice then the culture suffers and human exchange is reduced to mere utility. Introducing Mauss's classic essay, the anthropologist Mary Douglas wrote: '… the whole idea of the free gift is based on a misunderstanding. There should not be any free gifts. What is wrong with the so-called free gift is the donor's intention to be exempt from return gifts coming from the recipient. Refusing requital puts the act of giving outside any mutual ties.' Without any such mutuality, the gift, in a manner of speaking, dies; the flow of living connections is stopped, a circle is left uncompleted. But there are many ways in which the necessary requital may be enacted and in which the value of the gift may be acknowledged and in some manner returned to the common wealth.

The institution of the gift is also a crucial component of that special exchange of experience and value that is art. This is because the exchanges of art are neither of material things (that is, within the domain of economics) nor of the exercise of power and conferral of status (that is, within the domain of politics), but of things of the spirit, within a domain of experience not subject to the workings of political prestige or commodity value. We reciprocate the gift that is a work of art by responding to it, by giving to it our attention and concentration; by making it our own – through visual contemplation, reading, listening – we give it a continuing life within our personal being and then, by extension, within our social culture. The artist has, in his or her turn, responded to what we properly call his or her gift or talent, giving time and energy in the exercise of the imagination that goes into the making of the work.

It is easier to see this gift exchange in action in the performing arts, where the work is not portable, and the work of the work is effected in a given time and space for an appreciative audience. But what of those works of imagination, of art or design or craft – paintings, books of poems or novels, clothes, pottery – which are also commodities that can be carried away and sold on? It remains true that its work as a work, which is to say, the effect of increase it has on the mind, the feelings and the spirit of the receiver, is no less intangible for all that. It has a value of another kind, separable from that which it commands in the market place. That inestimable value may be described as its gift to its readers and viewers, and while conditions make it possible – while it is accessible to a public – that gift is by definition a public good, albeit of a kind that cannot be measured.

Joseph Conrad understood perfectly this complex of interlocking values, personal and social, which is made manifest as the gift. Distinguishing the artist from the scientist and the thinker he wrote: 'The changing wisdom of successive generations discards ideas, questions facts, demolishes theories. But the artist appeals to that part of our being which is not dependent on wisdom; to that which is a gift and not an acquisition – and, therefore, more permanently enduring. He speaks to our capacity for delight and wonder, to the sense of mystery surrounding our lives; to our sense of pity, and beauty, and pain; to the latent fellowship with all creation – and to the subtle but invincible conviction of solidarity that knits together the loneliness of innumerable hearts, to the solidarity in dreams, in joy, in aspirations, in illusions, in hope, in fear, which binds all men to each other, which binds together all humanity – the dead to the living and the living to the unborn.'

It is the personal element in their formation that distinguishes charitable trusts and foundations from those agencies created by governments to fund and utilise the arts in our society for a certain perceived social value. It is not that those in government, who have responsibility for the arts and culture, and their advisors and their employees, are necessarily lacking in vision; it is that they operate within narrow constraints determined by changing party policies, by unpredictable financial and fiscal imperatives, and by the requirement to answer to an electorate that may not share their view of the value of the arts as a public good.

Such initiatives as emerge from government agencies are inevitably subject, among other exigencies, to changing conditions of operation, lack of continuity and consistency in funding, changing fashions which affect political approval and disapproval, and the different enthusiasms of successive ministers. This is not to mention the various means, foul and fair, by which governments of all kinds – totalitarian, authoritarian or democratic – may directly favour some kinds of art, prohibit or inhibit others, or exercise more or less subtle forms of influence over the creation and dissemination of the arts in general.

I believe, as many do, that a modern democratic government has a duty, to the people as a whole and to the future, to encourage and support the arts; to facilitate – and at times to commission – the creation, publication and performance of works of art, works that by definition 'appeal to that part of our being which is not dependent on wisdom; to that which is a gift and not an acquisition – and, therefore, more permanently enduring'. I believe, also, that we must be vigilant of any government whose uses of funding and patronage hides an agenda whose objectives are less enduring than those of art itself.

Those who set up trusts and foundations for the arts begin with an independent vision, and the terms and conditions of their benefactions are shaped, develop and evolve in accord with that vision, free to a large extent from the political constraints that often hobble and cripple initiatives for the arts that originate in government funding. Neither are they continuously susceptible to the kinds of criticism – whether principled or populist – that can deflect them from their initiating purposes. There may be trusts and foundations whose philosophies and principles we may find objectionable, or aspects of whose policies we might disagree with, or consider misguided, or wish were different, but there are few – and none mentioned in the present study – whose beneficence will not have done something of the good that defines that word. There will be others which we will find totally admirable, and which we will feel have been invaluable to art and artists in our time.

The differing emphases that have characterised those trusts and foundations whose greatest concern has been with funding and supporting the arts inevitably reflect the personalities, passions and predilections of their founders. *Vive la difference!* Even as I advocate government support for the arts, exercised through independent agencies that can act free of political interference in collaboration with artists, writers, curators and creative entrepreneurs, I rejoice in the glories of a mixed economy within which diverse trusts and foundations make the gift that demands in requital nothing more – or less – than the exercise of creativity by those to whom it is given. The individual sabbatical, the travel grant, the funding of exhibition, publication, performance and documentation, the endowment to a school of art, to a museum or collection, the institution of spaces for exhibition and performance: all of these are crucial to the increase of what is good and necessary to the health of our artistic culture, to Conrad's beautiful 'solidarity … which binds together all humanity – the dead to the living and the living to the unborn.'

In the current climate for philanthropy, diversity of intent and purpose, and of organisation and practice, are alike encouraged. The diversities and specificities are described in close detail and analysed with great intellectual clarity and elegance by Paul Glinkowski in these volumes, which uniquely combine presentations of his ground-breaking research, and his intriguing history of one remarkable foundation, with personal testimonies and case studies which provide vivid insights into the dynamic of the gift in creative action. The gift is circulated, the gift moves, there is a living flow. These accounts are supplemented by provocative and revealing essays by Marjorie Allthorpe-Guyton and Timothy Llewellyn. Having both recently stepped down from their leadership respectively of the principal public and private funding bodies for the visual arts in the United Kingdom, they are better placed than most to speak as they find of the current situation in the funding of the arts. What they have to say is salutary, and gives added salt and savour to a publication that is a powerful and timely contribution to the vital discourse on the funding of the arts at this complex moment of our modernity.

# REFLECTIONS ON 21ST-CENTURY PHILANTHROPY AND ON THE ROLE OF TRUSTS AND FOUNDATIONS IN SUPPORTING THE ARTS IN THE UNITED KINGDOM

*by Paul Glinkowski*

## Introduction

The purpose of this essay, in conjunction with those that follow it, is to begin to map and to analyse the bigger picture within which support is given to the arts in the United Kingdom by independent grant-making trusts and foundations. Drawing on the literature and data available from a wide range of sources, augmented by interviews with experts and practitioners in the field of arts funding and philanthropy, I will consider, with a particular focus on the visual arts, the following questions: What is the current state of the funding economy for the arts in the United Kingdom? Where do trusts and foundations sit within this overall funding economy? What is the present climate for philanthropy and for grant-making trusts in Britain, and for private giving to the arts? What are the key issues that the independent grant-making sector currently faces?

I will conclude this essay by offering some reflections on how a number of grant-making trusts and foundations which support the arts are positioned in relation to some of the important questions and debates that seem currently to be preoccupying the independent funding sector; questions such as: Should the arts be funded primarily for art's sake? And, to what extent should trusts and foundations adopt a developmental rather than simply a reactive role? I shall also give brief consideration to the small but significant niche occupied within this sector by the artist-initiated trust. With a constant turnover of grant programmes and priorities, and with new trusts and foundations starting up whilst others wind down, the independent grant-making sector is highly fluid and idiosyncratic. What follows will therefore necessarily offer only a selective, and ephemeral, snapshot of the total picture.

*Ladies and gentlemen, the Golden Age is, I believe, happening right here, right now.*[1]
Sir Christopher Frayling, Chair, Arts Council England (ACE)

An optimistic consensus has recently been promulgated by the custodians of our culture – the leaders of the major arts venues and their paymasters in the Arts Council and government – that the arts have 'never had it so good'. The advent of National Lottery funding for arts building projects in 1994, followed by a major uplift in government funding for the arts via ACE's grant-in-aid 'settlement' in 2000[2], has undoubtedly provided a welcome boost to the economy and landscape of the arts in this country.

Fears have been expressed, however, that for some organisations the recent boom enjoyed by the arts sector could eventually turn to bust. The ACE *Turning Point* report, for example, which proposes a ten-year strategy for the contemporary visual arts in England concludes: 'The UK leads Europe in the status of its artists and the economic value of its art market … [but] our collective investment in the contemporary visual arts sector has not kept pace with the expansion in audiences and participants or the expansion in artistic practice. The growth of the last ten years and the exceptional contribution that the visual arts make is unsustainable.'[3] The report notes a recent shift in the funding base for the visual arts sector. 'Arts Council England subsidy,' it says, 'has dropped from 45% in 2000/01 to 42%. Earned income was up 23%, against 4% in Arts Council subsidy. Local authority subsidy to art galleries alone fell by 4%.'[4]

A decline in local authority spending across all areas of the arts was confirmed by the findings of the 2006 annual survey of the National Association of Local Government Arts Officers (nalgao). An article in *Arts Professional* (Issue 130, 25 September 2006), reported these findings: '38% of local authority arts services,' it says, 'are operating under smaller budgets than in the previous year … With inflation taken into account, three quarters of authorities have experienced cuts in arts budgets.' At central government level, too, cuts are feared. It is widely anticipated that the three-year allocation to the Arts Council announced in autumn 2007 will fail to keep pace with inflation. The spectre of the 2012 Olympics also looms. At the end of March 2007 ACE made a dramatic announcement that its 2007/08 budget for the arts from National Lottery revenues would be cut by a swingeing 35 per cent, from £83 million to £54 million. 'There is currently a view in Whitehall and Westminster that the arts sector can absorb the impact of the Olympics raid on lottery funding without visible impact. This is not true,' said ACE Chief Executive, Peter Hewitt.[5] Within this context of diminishing public subsidy, the role of private investment in the arts, which includes funding from trusts and foundations, becomes increasingly significant.

Arts & Business (A&B) estimates that arts funding from private sources is at record levels and is continuing to grow. Its *Private Investment Benchmarking Survey 2005/06* found that the total figure for private sector support for culture had reached £529.5 million; more than a 2.2 per cent increase compared to 2003/04. This figure, it says, 'compares favourably to the main public funders of Arts and Heritage in the UK. For instance,

ACE receives on average more than £410 million in parliamentary grant-in-aid and distributes over £150 million from National Lottery Funding ... This places businesses, individuals and trusts and foundations as key players in the cultural funding landscape, complementing the crucial role of the public sector.'[6] However, according to A&B: 'The issues surrounding funding for the arts remain serious. The arts have not done particularly well in recent spending reviews and the future looks uncertain ... For many, the lottery created an environment of underfunded expansion; there are many artistic mouths to feed, all needing more funding than ever to survive ... arts organisations will only survive in a mixed economy ... We need a combined effort to ensure that the structures and resources required to support this work can adapt to the political, social and economic climate.'[7]

A&B's *Benchmarking Survey* breaks down private investment by three sources: business, individuals, and trusts and foundations. The 2004/05 survey found that whilst funding from business and from individuals was up markedly from the previous year, by 6 per cent and 10 per cent respectively, trust and foundation investment had decreased by 15 per cent (from £104 million to £88 million). This finding, says A&B, reflects 'the mercurial nature of this investment stream which is strongly influenced by large one-off awards'[8]. The remainder of this essay is devoted to shedding some light on the mercurial world of trusts and foundations. I will consider first the general situation of, and climate for, philanthropic trusts and foundations in this country.

## The Climate for Philanthropy

*We make a living by what we get; we make a life by what we give.*[9]
Winston Churchill

### A new zeitgeist for giving

Before 2000, little systematic attention had been paid to the promotion of philanthropy in the United Kingdom. The formation of new charitable foundations had been sporadic, with times of growth tending to coincide with periods when the national economy was strong and worthwhile tax incentives were available. According to Beth Breeze, the Deputy Director of the Institute for Philanthropy, Britain's first truly significant charity-friendly budget was in 1986, when the Chancellor of the Exchequer, Nigel Lawson, offered tax relief on payroll giving. In 1990, his successor, John Major, introduced Gift Aid, through which charities can reclaim the basic rate income tax paid on all individual charitable donations. In the Labour government's budget in 2000, Gordon Brown went further by removing the upper and lower thresholds that had previously applied to payroll giving and Gift Aid. Income tax relief is now available on every cash donation made by taxpayers in the United Kingdom.

In the first decade of the new millennium, the Labour government has proactively developed instruments (such as the more generous and easy to use tax mechanisms described above) and supported endeavours that are designed to stimulate a more dynamic culture of giving in the United Kingdom. This is, in part, a response to changing patterns of wealth, which offer the potential for the emergence of a new generation of philanthropists. The fast-growing finance and digital media and communications industries, for example, have over the last two decades produced a sizeable crop of new wealthy individuals. Beth Breeze claims that: 'There are, on one measure, now more millionaires than teachers in Britain.'[10]

Along with a growth in new rich entrepreneurs, the prospect of an impending intergenerational transfer of wealth is also attracting the interest of governments across Europe and in North America, where it is hoped that the estate planning of an aging population of wealthy people will lead to more charitable giving. According to the findings of *A Review of Charitable Giving Vehicles and Their Use in the US and Canada*, produced for A&B by AEA Consulting in 2004: 'The coming transfer of wealth between generations is expected to be the largest in history, as years of accumulated wealth in both Europe and the United States changes hands with the dying off of the post-War generation.'[11] The report estimates that the value of this transfer will be between $41 trillion and $136 trillion.

Alongside a recognition that the historical circumstances might be favourable for attracting more private funds to support public causes, an additional motivation for the step change in the British government's interest in encouraging philanthropy is the realisation that the country's aging population will increasingly put a strain on the public purse as the government faces pressure to meet rising health and retirement costs. An increase in the combined amount of public and private funds available to support areas of public life that currently rely on subsidy, such as the arts, could help to alleviate some of the burden shouldered by government.

At around the turn of the millennium, policy makers recognised that both the new wealthy and those seeking to leave a legacy would benefit from encouragement and guidance to assist them to use part of their fortune for the public good. In order to stimulate and support potential donors, and to provide clear information and advice to help them make best use of their funds, a number of campaigns and initiatives were set up. In 2000, the Institute for Philanthropy, which was initially based within the Law faculty at University College London, was established, with a mission 'to develop a greater understanding of philanthropy and its place in modern society' and 'to promote the profile and practice of all types and levels of philanthropy'. In July 2001, supported by government funding, a three-year Giving Campaign was launched to encourage charitable giving at all levels. The trusts and foundations sector, too, was eager to play its part in nurturing a new climate for giving. In April 2001, the Association of Charitable Foundations (ACF) – with funding support from the Esmée Fairbairn Foundation, the Gatsby Charitable Foundation and the Lloyds TSB Foundation for England & Wales – set up Philanthropy UK, a three-year project, which has recently been extended, 'to promote new philanthropy, particularly among the wealthy'.

Theresa Lloyd, the former Director of Philanthropy UK and author of the book *Why Rich People Give*, recognises that a millennial zeitgeist seemed to develop around this mission, with a number of interested parties beginning simultaneously to seek solutions to the same sort of questions. According to Lloyd, the salient questions included: How can we maximise the benefit from Gift Aid? What can be done to nurture the 'dot com generation' of millionaires? Why is there more of a culture of giving in the United States? Should the new transatlantic phenomenon of 'venture philanthropy' be promoted and encouraged? The response was a raft of initiatives, including those described earlier, concerned with researching, encouraging, celebrating and providing information about giving. 'There is a need in this country,' says Lloyd, 'to recognise and to celebrate philanthropy; more than is currently the case.' A gradual progressive shift in attitude is signalled by events like the annual Beacon Fellowship awards, announced at a high-profile ceremony at 11 Downing Street, which recognise and reward philanthropy and help to fuel a receptive culture for giving.

Beth Breeze believes that, although progress is being made, for those with a mission to create a new culture of giving in the United Kingdom there is still a significant way to go. 'After a trough in donations during the late 1990s,' she observes, 'individual giving is returning to levels last seen in 1995. Yet private giving in Britain is still disappointingly low – £7.3 billion in 2002 (less than 1 per cent of GDP).'[12]

*The United States versus the United Kingdom: different cultures of giving*

Breeze is one of a number of commentators to observe a marked differential in attitudes towards, and in the practice of, philanthropy in Britain as compared to the United States, where a significantly higher proportion of GDP (just over 2 per cent) is donated for charitable purposes. Part of the reason is pragmatic – 'Britain has enjoyed a fiscal regime that encourages philanthropy since 1986,' Breeze notes, 'but charitable giving in America has attracted tax relief since the eighteenth century' – yet most of the explanation lies in profound differences of culture. 'Britain invented modern philanthropy,' says Breeze, 'but in the twentieth century an important strand of British opinion, mainly on the left, came to see charity as a poor alternative to state-funded provision; Americans have had no such qualms ... Americans' scepticism of bureaucracy and lack of faith in the effectiveness of the state have made charitable donations seem preferable to taxes.'[13]

Theresa Lloyd concurs with Breeze's analysis. 'Philanthropy in the US is a social institution that takes on meaning in a culture of individualism and private initiative and in the absence of a comprehensive welfare state,' says Lloyd. 'It operates in an environment which is resistant to the idea that the state has a very prominent role to play. In the US, philanthropy is not just an option which wealth provides, it is a defining characteristic of the elite. In this respect the US differs markedly from the UK.'[14]

For Breeze, 'Philanthropy is a British virtue which dares not speak its name, unlike American philanthropy which is a proud element of elite culture.' In the United States, charitable giving does not carry the same 'poor relief' connotations as in Britain. Wealthy Americans often support charities from which they benefit personally, such as arts organisations, universities, or organisations that promote the interests of their own ethnic or religious group. There can often be a competitive edge to North American philanthropy, which manifests itself in, for example, a rivalry for places on the boards of high-profile charities, such as the leading museums and opera companies. There is also a far greater incidence of 'naming', via plaques in honour of donors for example, as a public reward for donations. By comparison, wealthy people in this country tend to conduct their giving in a more understated way. What Breeze calls 'donor payback' is a much less conspicuous feature of philanthropy in the United Kingdom.

### The impact of Gift Aid

Another difference between philanthropy in Britain as compared to the United States is that charitable gifts in the United States tend to be planned, while British donations are largely responsive; a spontaneous reaction, for example, to media-based appeals following disasters such as the Asian tsunami of Christmas 2004. 'Shifting donors from spontaneous to planned giving is the holy grail of British fundraising,' says Breeze, not least because this will ensure that the maximum advantage can be gained from tax relief.

What is not yet clear is whether the introduction of Gift Aid has discouraged wealthy donors from organising their giving through the vehicle of the charitable trust or foundation. Prior to the introduction of Gift Aid, in order to get tax relief it was necessary to set up either a charitable trust or a long-term covenant. Tax relief for one-off gifts through the Gift Aid option has created a user-friendly alternative that offers a number of advantages: it does not require a long term commitment; it allows the donor to preserve their anonymity (which some prefer to do); and it is relatively easy to administer.

Although the simplicity and flexibility of Gift Aid offers clear benefits to the would-be philanthropist, it has a potential downside from the point of view of nurturing a culture of sustained philanthropy. The setting up of a trust or foundation implies an ongoing obligation to charitable giving and to supporting a particular cause (or portfolio of causes), and it has often helped to establish what has become a dynastic culture of giving within a family. The option of no longer having to adopt this mechanism to get tax relief has created, in the view of some commentators, a disincentive to developing a sustained and engaged commitment to philanthropy.

In the process of researching her book *Why Rich People Give*, Theresa Lloyd interviewed one hundred wealthy individuals.[15] She found that many of her interviewees used more than one mechanism for their giving. Prominent amongst these were both charitable trusts and Gift Aid. Just over half had set up a charitable trust and on the whole recognised its benefits; they cited, in particular, the tax advantages and the fact that having a trust enabled them to involve the whole family. However, Lloyd's research also discovered that some interviewees had 'serious reservations' concerning aspects of the charitable trust option. Lloyd lists these as: 'the bureaucracy associated with the mechanism, the investment advice, monitoring by the Charity Commission, the lack of privacy, inconsistency of government policy to allocation of company shares to trusts, and criticism by the Directory of Social Change.'[16]

There are not yet any publicly available statistics to indicate whether the rate of foundation formation has been affected by the availability of Gift Aid, but the consensus amongst the commentators whom I interviewed for my research was that the availability of Gift Aid could well, in time, lead to a reduction in the creation of new charitable foundations.

*Engaged philanthropy*

In his introduction to *The business of giving: a survey of wealth and philanthropy*, published by *The Economist* in February 2006, Matthew Bishop writes: 'Giving away money has never been so fashionable among the rich and famous. Bill Gates, today's pre-eminent philanthropist, has already handed over an unprecedented $31 billion to the Bill and Melinda Gates Foundation, mostly to tackle the health problems of the world's poor.'[17] Bishop points to a newly awakened interest in philanthropy amongst the world's entrepreneurial elite, many of whom have rapidly accumulated fortunes of unprecedented proportions; according to the 'rich list' published by Forbes magazine in 2005, there are now 691 dollar billionaires (388 of them 'self made', and 350 based outside the United States) compared with 423 in 1996.

Many of the world's new super rich philanthropists are, like the Gateses, still comparatively young. Ambitious to replicate the success they have achieved in the commercial sphere, they are importing into their charitable endeavours attitudes and approaches learned in the 21st-century business world. 'A generational shift is under-way,' states Bishop, 'from the old wealthy, who tended to practice traditional charity, to the new wealthy, who are open to more entrepreneurial approaches. The need for philanthropy to become more like the 'for profit' capital markets is a common theme among the new philanthropists.'[18]

This new approach to philanthropy has been called 'philanthrocapitalism' or, more commonly, 'venture philanthropy'. Where the traditional model of philanthropy is based on gift-giving, the new model implies a more active form of engagement in which the philanthropist develops a more hands-on relationship with the recipient of his or her funding (which is often referred to as 'investment'). The resources deployed by the new breed of philanthropist may include time, expertise and social capital as well as money. Terms such as 'social investing', 'social entrepreneurship' and 'high engagement' have been imported from the business world into the lexicon of 21st-century philanthropy.

Although the concept, ethos and practices of venture philanthropy were largely developed in the United States, a recently formed European Venture Philanthropy Association (EVPA) suggests that its influence is making itself felt on this continent too. In the United Kingdom, an example of this new model of charitable foundation is ARK (Absolute Return for Kids). Set up by a group of hedge fund managers from the City of London, it has committed several millions to support charities working to alleviate child poverty in Britain and in Eastern Europe. ARK trustee Jennifer Moses, a former Managing Director at Goldman Sachs, has said that: 'The grants feel more like private investments. Recipients have to define what success is and they only continue to receive funding if they can show they are achieving what they want to accomplish' ('Trust Deeds', the *Guardian*, 27 November 2002).

At the 2006 Beacon Fellowship celebrations of philanthropy in the United Kingdom, ARK's Managing Director, Paul Bernstein, explained its approach further. 'The philosophy,' he said, 'is about identifying the need, building up programmes around an evidence base, filling gaps in existing services, and then targeting what is delivered ... at ARK we place great emphasis on a genuine two-way process by setting up and managing key programmes ourselves: it is the partnership between the venture philanthropist and the entrepreneur who runs the programme, and how the two of them work together in a way that delivers something very different from what each of them would do alone ... we view our relationships as investments: we make a social investment for a social return. And that is the essence of why measurability is important to how we operate, because it enables us to say, first of all, what the donors' money will do, and, second, what it has done. It is creating a link between funding and performance.'[19] The 'Absolute Return' of ARK's name is a hedge-fund term, describing a determination to improve results year-on-year.

'The trend,' predicts David Emerson, the Director of the ACF, 'will be less and less hands-off funding. There will be a greater emphasis on wanting to know more from recipients about how the money was used. In terms of good grant-making practice, it seems a sensible thing to ask what your resources achieved. If things didn't go well, you want to know why. It gives the option for more direct, active involvement.'[20]

Whilst the focus of venture philanthropy has, to date, largely been on the social welfare sphere, the potential exists for the methods and philosophy of this emerging form of engaged philanthropy to be applied to the arts sector. Later in this essay, I shall show that elements of this new approach are already evident in some of the developmental work pursued by, for example, the Louise T Blouin Foundation, a recently formed charitable foundation whose focus is on the arts and creativity.

## Trusts and Foundations and the Arts in the United Kingdom: Current Issues

*What are trusts and foundations? What is the independent grant-making sector like in the United Kingdom?*
A charitable trust or foundation is a tax-exempt legal entity that enables charitable giving to be conducted in a planned and systematic way. Most trusts and foundations derive their income from an endowment given by the donor. The donor sets out the aims in a trust deed, which lays down the framework within which the trustees must operate. The charitable purposes must be for public benefit within the broad range of activities permitted by charity law. Trusts are totally independent of government. The only outside supervision comes from the Charity Commission.

No two trusts or foundations are alike, their motivations and priorities vary greatly. Some give funds for general charitable purposes, others are restricted to a particular area of benefit, such as the arts, or to a specific beneficiary group, such as young people; some trusts give nationally or internationally, and some restrict their giving within a local or regional geographic area. In general, trusts and foundations prefer to fund what government does not fund: that is, activity that would be hard to finance through conventional fundraising.

The Association of Charitable Foundations (ACF) estimates that there are around 9,000 grant-making trusts and foundations in the United Kingdom. According to the Charities Aid Foundation (CAF), they give away about £2 billion in grants each year. CAF estimates that around 70 per cent of trusts and foundations support health and social welfare; 30 per cent give to the arts and recreation. Information is lacking on the proportion of this 30 per cent that gives specifically to the arts, but the findings of A&B's *Private Investment Benchmarking Survey 2004/05* suggest that only 4.4 per cent (£88 million) of the estimated £2 billion given annually benefits the arts.

*Private investment in the arts: a focus on the individual donor*

Within the area of what A&B calls 'private investment' in the arts, recent research and development work has been focused on understanding, and working out how better to solicit and to encourage, giving by individuals, particularly in the form of major donations. This reflects the fact that of the three categories that together constitute the private giving sector for the arts (business, individual, and trusts and foundations) 'individuals' is identified as the most significant source of funding. According to the A&B *Private Investment Benchmarking Survey 2004/05*, 'individuals' contributed £244 million out of a total of £452 million of private investment, or 54 per cent; by comparison, 'trusts and foundations' contributed £88 million, or 19 per cent. Moreover, for the reasons I have described earlier (which include the availability of user-friendly tax relief mechanisms such as Gift Aid), 'individuals' are seen to offer the greatest prospect for growing the income available for the arts. This would appear to be borne out by the A&B statistics on individual giving for the financial year 2004/05, which show an increase over the previous year of 10 per cent.

Responding to this trend, in 2004 A&B launched The Maecenas Initiative. Named after Gaius Maecenas, a renowned philanthropist in ancient Rome, this three-year project was set up to encourage a higher level of donations to the arts through the promotion of debate and awareness about individual giving, and by equipping arts professionals with the skills and knowledge needed to capitalise more effectively on this particular income stream. It echoed and complemented the generic initiatives introduced to stimulate charitable giving in Britain, which are described earlier, such as the Giving Campaign and Philanthropy UK.

By comparison with the work recently undertaken on individual giving, very little research appears to have been done to date on the role of charitable grant-making foundations in supporting the arts. The most useful and comprehensive report that takes a view across a range of trusts and foundations is *Corporate Foundations and the Not For Profit Arts Sector*, a report produced for A&B in 2005. Compiled by David Carrington, it looks at the attitudes and practices of a specific type of grant-making foundation, the corporate foundation, towards funding the arts.

*Corporate foundations and the arts*

The Carrington report was prompted by a 2003 document, *Corporate Foundations; building a sustainable foundation for corporate giving*, published by Business in the Community (BiTC), which stated that 53 of the 101 corporate foundations that it was able to identify had been set up since 1990. A&B wanted to understand what the implications of this apparent recent growth in corporate foundations might be for the arts. For the purposes of Carrington's research, a corporate foundation is defined by two key features: firstly, it receives all of its income from a company, either as an annual donation agreed by the company's board, or by some profit-related formula; and secondly, the power to appoint all or most of the trustees is vested in the company from which the foundation derives its income. The power to appoint trustees does not, however, mean that the company has the authority to dictate what the trustees of the corporate foundation should do with their assets.

The central aims of Carrington's report were: to understand the current range and scale of corporate foundation support for the arts in the United Kingdom; and to understand the approaches of a range of different companies to supporting the arts through a corporate foundation. On the first aim, the report concluded: 'It is likely that there has been a steady growth in the number of new corporate foundations, but this has not been spectacular and may not be continuing. It does not seem to have led to substantial new funds becoming available to the non-profit sector – or, within that, to the arts.'[21]

Regarding the second aim, Carrington's report unearthed a number of findings that shed light on practices and attitudes which, as my own research has confirmed, seem to apply across the independent grant-giving sector, not just to the corporate side. It found, for example, that: 'Few corporate foundations have grant programmes targeted specifically at support for the arts – but that is also true of independent non-corporate foundations. One corporate foundation interviewee reported: "A lot of what we do for the arts falls under other priorities and it gets hidden. For instance, it's directed through our education and training priorities."'[22]

Many of the charitable foundations that fund arts activities, be they corporate or non-corporate, do not describe or even think of themselves as arts funders because their support is focused on projects and activities whose primary aim is to meet other social priorities (such as the provision of healthcare, or education), and which just happen to use the arts as a means to that end. This situation leads to data problems for researchers in this area because expenditure on arts activity is often classified within other categories, such as education, social welfare, regeneration or health.

Carrington found a resistance to funding some kinds of arts work based on the erroneous perception that it did not constitute charitable activity. 'This question came up repeatedly throughout the consultations,' says Carrington, 'and is clearly a cause of confusion within the corporate sector.' Funding visual arts exhibitions, for example, or commissioning new opera or dance productions, were thought by some interviewees only to be possible if done as business sponsorship, and must thus be routed through the company per se, rather than through the corporate foundation. '"High art is not charitable" was how this was described to us by one interviewee,' says Carrington. 'An orthodoxy exists within some parts of the corporate sector that the funding of the arts with charitable funds can only be possible when it is done within an educational or community programme. There would "always be some benefit to the company from providing such support and how could that be a charitable outcome?"'[23]

Alongside the erroneous belief that an illegitimate benefit to the associated company might accrue from the funding of certain types of arts activities, Carrington found an additional attitudinal barrier to corporate foundation funding being given for cultural purposes: some trustees of corporate foundations appeared uncomfortable with the perceived elitism of the arts. Carrington reports that one corporate foundation manager 'had to describe all arts-related applications as "creative activities" to avoid immediate rejection by the trustees; another had to "hide the art" because the committee members who make the grant decisions "do not believe in supporting art for art's sake activities, they have to be educational and not about creating new art forms (they see the arts as elitist). So I have to sell these projects as social cohesion, access projects."'[24]

Although these findings refer to interviews with representatives of corporate foundations, they tally with some of my conversations with the managers of non-corporate trusts and foundations which have been quite significant funders of arts activity but which have charitable objects that focus primarily on areas of social welfare. The new Charities Act, which came into force in November 2006, includes, for the first time, 'the advancement of the arts, heritage or science' as one of its explicitly defined, charitable purposes. This should strengthen the perception across the independent grant-giving sector that all kinds of arts activity can, in principle, legitimately be viewed as charitable so long as they can demonstrate 'public benefit'.

*The influence of the Corporate Social Responsibility (CSR) agenda*

Although the Charities Act 2006 has reinforced the charitable status of the arts, there are concerns that the growth within the British business community of a culture of Corporate Social Responsibility (CSR) could have detrimental consequences for the arts. It is feared that the CSR focus on social welfare issues might impede the ability of the arts to attract income from all corporate sources: business sponsorship, as well as corporate foundation funding. Carrington's report notes an anxiety amongst arts fundraisers that 'companies would switch funding for the arts to activities which would have solely social objectives … We did find some indications of this; not, however, restricted to companies with corporate foundations – it seems more to be part of how a CSR focus is changing the nature of business support for the arts.'[25]

The experience of a leading authority on arts philanthropy, whom I interviewed for my research, corroborates this finding: 'The head of corporate communications at a major company told me proudly that "we don't do arts funding any more, though we did lots in the 1990s",' my interviewee disclosed. 'It is to do with government-influenced priorities for CSR. From a corporate perspective, supporting an orchestra is now seen as bad, that is, elitist, whereas supporting a school in Tower Hamlets to work with an orchestra is seen as good. After a promising start, this government has given out the message that the arts are elitist.'

The Carrington report identifies three specific factors that might lead to a reduction in funding to the arts from corporate foundations: changes in senior staff or board members; difficulties in demonstrating the 'return' from supporting arts activities; and changes to CSR policies that result in more emphasis being given to employee-determined priorities.

The first factor, which can equally be true of non-corporate foundations, illustrates that, where the charitable purposes of a trust or foundation are broadly defined, a willingness to fund the arts may often be linked to the tastes and enthusiasms of the individuals who happen to control the assets of the trust at a given time. The second factor reflects a growing emphasis – which can be observed currently in all types of funder, public sector as well as private – on measuring and accounting for the value achieved from a particular grant or award. The report notes 'a common concern that demonstrating such a return from a company's support for arts activities was especially difficult'. The third factor reflects a shift in the locus of policy-making control over corporate philanthropic giving: from a coterie of executives to a broader representation of staff. Carrington notes that one company reported: 'The staff now decide what should be our priorities for charitable gifts; and they choose disabled children, not the arts'. Another executive of a corporate foundation was quoted as saying that the causes supported 'reflect employees' interests, and our employees aren't involved with arts based projects ... it really reflects staff demographics'.[26]

Trusts and Foundations: Examples and Observations

*A Foundation, unless it has narrowly confined objects, will always reflect the thoughts and preferences and the vision of those charged with the task of running it ... No two groups of people would reach the same decisions. What a dull world it would be if it were so.*
Sir Charles Whishaw, former trustee of the Calouste Gulbenkian Foundation[27]

*Preamble*

In the remainder of this essay, I will highlight and discuss a number of the salient themes and issues that have emerged from my research into the practices of a range of trusts and foundations which have a major focus on, or else give significant sums of money to, the arts. The trusts I have looked at do not constitute a comprehensive sample, rather they were chosen because they represent a broad spectrum of the kinds and characteristics of the current crop of independent grant-making charities: some are well known to have a specific focus on the arts (and I have looked in particular at funders which, in some way, have prioritised the visual arts) others are major trusts whose predominant remit is to support non-arts activity; some are new or emergent organisations, others are long established; some give millions to the arts each year, others may give only a few thousands; some are corporate, most are non-corporate; some have a remit to fund regionally, others fund nationally, or internationally; some just give grants, others also operate arts programmes of their own; some have a living donor who is an active participant in their affairs, others are now several generations removed from the donor.

As the independent grant-making sector is such a fluid entity – where funding priorities and schemes are constantly being reconsidered and redrawn, and where new players enter as others leave the stage – it would not make sense to attempt to map in detail what every trust and foundation is currently up to; the map would no sooner have been drawn than the boundaries would have shifted, rendering the picture obsolete. Instead, my approach is to draw together issues that link in some way the various conversations that I have had with practitioners in the field, and which reflect the philosophies and activities that trusts and foundations describe in the material which they have put into the public domain. The themes, which I formulate as a series of four questions, are: 'Autonomy or instrumentalism?', in which I consider the distinction between funding to support the arts per se, or funding which aims to achieve some other good; 'Catalysts or reactors?', in which I look at the question of whether contemporary charitable foundations should undertake an active, developmental role; 'How do trusts evolve?', which raises issues concerning the life-cycles of foundations; and 'Artist-initiated trusts and foundations: purposes and distinctions', which asks: why have some artists set up charitable trusts, and what purposes do they serve?

*Autonomy or instrumentalism?*

*The distance between the Arts Council and government is narrowing. While it was the Conservative government of the 1980s that first introduced the mantra 'culture should serve the economy', since 1997 New Labour has added a whole new list of priorities – still on the basis of instrumental outcomes.*
Sir Christopher Frayling, Chair, Arts Council England[28]

A dominant concern within cultural policy debates over the last two decades has been the degree to which the arts in this country should be supported by the public authorities (i.e. central and local government and 'non-departmental public bodies', such as Arts Council England) for the value they can bring to priority areas of social policy – such as the regeneration of towns, cities or neighbourhoods, or the improvement of health and well being – as opposed to being supported for the value that they might represent in themselves. Using or promoting art as a way of addressing wider social issues is referred to here as instrumentalism; art that seeks to represent a value in itself is described as autonomous.

The consensus view amongst commentators on the arts and amongst those who work in them is that, in the subsidised sector at least, the instrumentalist tendency has steadily been gaining ground; the 'arm's length principle' that has historically prevented government from seeking too directly to interfere in the arts is being eroded. In Sir Christopher Frayling's words, 'the length of the arm has become very short indeed, almost Venus de Milo length'.[29] How, then, has the independent grant-making sector responded to this trend?

In broad terms, it appears that the circumstances could be favourable for a 'win win' situation to develop. At one end of the spectrum, amongst grant-making trusts and foundations which exist primarily to meet social welfare objectives, it is possible that the current climate, in which the arts are increasingly viewed and talked about as a potential palliative for society's problems, will encourage more funding to be made available to support utilitarian, community-focused examples of arts work; so long as its ameliorating effects can be persuasively demonstrated. At the opposite end of the spectrum, amongst foundations which have always regarded the arts as an important, or even primary, part of their funding remit, there is evidence of a hardening of support; a new urgency to fund art purely for art's sake is becoming apparent.

In 2002, the arts programme manager of one major foundation, which includes the arts as one amongst several funding priorities, conducted an informal survey of 35 charities which were at that time funding the arts. It was found that 57 per cent of them preferred to fund work where the beneficiaries were children and young people, and that a high proportion would only engage with arts activity that was concerned with what is now referred to as 'arts and social inclusion'. 'There were very few funders,' the programme manager discovered, 'who would say "we just want to fund this piece of art", or "we believe that improving the living standards of artists, who are very poorly paid, is our mission".'

'Our foundation's mission statement,' my interviewee continued, 'stresses that we want to fund the "hard to fund", and what counts as "hard to fund' will change over time. As the landscape and economy for the arts shifts, so should the funding priorities of trusts and foundations. For example, education has, over time, become a core part of what arts organisations are expected to do. Where in the past it relied heavily on the independent sector for support, it should now be underpinned by core funding.' Having surveyed what others were doing, this foundation was able to articulate more clearly what made it distinct as a funder, and that meant a move away from 'art and social inclusion' and towards 'art for art's sake'.

Another representative of a charity with a strong history of funding the arts told me: 'We have always been committed to art for art's sake, but we have become more vehement about that as others elsewhere have become increasingly focused on art's role in the community.' A third described the stance that some trusts appear to be adopting against the instrumentalisation of art as being the natural response of the independent funder. 'All this "arts for social engineering" makes me very perverse,' s/he said. 'It makes me say "no, I don't believe in this at all, we're just going to do art." You feel that you ought to be a bit contrary to keep the balance. We did masses and masses in our history – of community arts, and of arts for re-energising neighbourhoods – but you can go too far that way. And now that the government is interested in that, we're saying "no, art for art's sake is important." It's a healthy perversity, really, that you tend to want to keep.'

It could be argued that some of the most innovative and forward-thinking support for arts activity and development in the United Kingdom is currently coming from trusts and foundations. At a structural and strategic level, the independent sector has used its influence and resources to spark and to seed-fund initiatives that aim to equip the arts sector as a whole with new managerial ideas and competencies, which will help it to meet the challenges of the 21st century. The Clore Duffield Foundation, for example, created the Clore Leadership Programme in 2003 to fill a gap that it had identified in the provision of professional training for cultural leaders. A cohort of around 20 Clore Fellows is selected each year to follow an individually tailored, year-long course of training. The Programme became a separate charity in August 2005, but the Clore Duffield Foundation maintains a significant financial commitment, which helps to draw in funds from other sources.

The Clore Fellows have been contributors to a complementary project initiated by another charitable foundation with a strong focus on the arts. Mission, Money, Models is a three-year national research programme and campaign, developed by the Jerwood Charitable Foundation in partnership with a coalition of leaders from the arts and cultural sector, which is committed to 'improving current practice and exploring radically different conceptions of how the sector might operate in the future'. It aims to promote new approaches to key issues that affect sustainability in the arts and to explore new business models and ways of funding. Roanne Dods, Director of the Jerwood Charitable Foundation and a Co-Director of Mission, Money, Models, says that this initiative arose out of 'a need to find new ways of operating, particularly when it became clear that there was not going to be more public funding available for the arts. It's about finding new practice and next practice, at home and abroad.'[30] The pre-eminence given within this campaign to 'mission' is significant. It proposes that arts organisations and activities must be more mission-focused, rather than funder-led – which can be an unfortunate outcome when arts organisations are drawn down the path of trying to meet social rather than artistic objectives.

Whilst some arts-focused independent funders have sought to address managerial issues as part of their overall portfolio of support for the arts, others have targeted their resources at supporting autonomous arts practice. An example is the Moose Foundation. One of several new foundations with a strong arts focus that have emerged in the first years of this century – others include the Foyle Foundation and the Louise T Blouin Foundation – the Moose Foundation has a remit specifically to support the arts in London. The Moose Foundation website carries an explicit statement that it is unlikely to support art projects which describe their benefit in terms of 'social inclusion'.

The Moose Foundation's Director, Paul Hobson, has a clear sense of focus. 'We believe,' he says, 'that art as a domain is most exciting when it is a free interplay between objects and ideas; where it resists the tendency to become either useful or to be applied in a certain way. Otherwise, why work with an artist? Why not work with a social worker, or a teacher or a social engineer? Artists are exceptional in their capacity to introduce a charge into a situation which is very dynamic, and that's what we're interested in.'[31] Following extensive informal discussion with arts practitioners in London, the Moose Foundation decided to deploy its relatively modest resources, about £150,000 a year, in support of new, experimental work which often operates at the intersection of different creative disciplines. 'The feedback from artists and organisations was that there was absolutely no funding for new work,' says Hobson. 'It was very difficult to commission new work that didn't sit within policy directives such as cultural diversity or social inclusion, things that whilst terrifically important were in some ways precluding or shaping work that artists were doing in a way that artists weren't choosing or collaborating with.'

'There is a sense,' says Hobson, 'that there aren't enough spaces in London where artists can collaborate across disciplines away from the pressures and expectations of audience; where the emphasis is entirely on process, and that that in itself is an output. Investing in the free exchange and interplay that art is all about is, in a way, a type of active resistance to the thing that most arts organisations do when they have an engagement with an artist, which is to commodify that process: to make it something that has to have an audience, and has to have an education programme around it, and has to have a merchandising opportunity, and can be something that people can acquire.'

For the Moose Foundation, the challenge is to fund artists to find a space where they can experiment and create outside the constraints both of instrumentalism and of the market. For Hobson, the pressing question facing the autonomous arts today is: 'Are there new ways of producing and funding cultural product that don't put artists in a situation where they are being owned or being consumed, where they are not transactional? One would imagine that there are other models that aren't so consumerist about the presentation and creation of new culture; foundations have some role to play in that, I think. What is the purpose of engaging with the arts unless you are thinking out of the box?'

Independent funders of the arts, such as the Moose Foundation and the Elephant Trust (which I will discuss in the upcoming section on artist-initiated foundations), which tailor their practice specifically to meet the needs of artists, are a rarity. Most prefer to balance support for practitioners with support for a more publicly embedded idea of the arts; to embrace, as it were, both the autonomous and the instrumentalist strands within arts practice.

An example of a funder that might be said to have adopted this Janus-faced approach is the Paul Hamlyn Foundation, which has developed two distinct but parallel streams of support for the arts. The majority of its arts funding in 2005/06 (which exceeded £3 million), was targeted at projects that were concerned in some way with inclusion and education. For example, a strand within its arts programme called Increasing Access to the Arts supported arts initiatives that addressed 'inequality of access and opportunity, particularly among young people, including those "at risk" and young offenders'; a strand called Arts and Learning prioritised 'partnership projects which aim to develop the arts within formal education'. Since 1993, however, the Foundation has also run the Awards for Artists scheme, which provides direct support to a small number of individual artists at a key moment in their career. Five artists are chosen annually, each receiving £30,000 spread over three years. The awards are decided on the basis of 'talent, promise and need, as well as achievement'.[32]

The Awards for Artists scheme has focused since 1998 on the visual arts. Katherine Standing, who runs the scheme, emphasised its 'blue skies' philosophy. 'Our Awards for Artists acknowledge that the practical facts of life can sometimes get in the way of focused artistic production,' she said. 'They offer no strings funding, drip fed over a period of three years, to make studio practice without pressure more possible.'[33] The outcomes of the Awards are not tracked. 'There are no stipulations about how money is to be used,' said the Paul Hamlyn Foundation's Director, Robert Dufton, 'therefore, it would not be possible for us to measure results against expectations.'[34]

The Paul Hamlyn Foundation, which is one of a number of independent funders with an arts focus that have experienced a significant increase in their expendable resources in recent years (the Esmée Fairbairn Foundation and the Jerwood Charitable Foundation are others) was, at the time of my research, considering its future spending priorities and strategy for the arts. 'We do want to maintain our approach of broadening access, enabling opportunity and combating disadvantage,' said Robert Dufton, 'but we may put a little more emphasis on art for art's sake than we currently do.'

The Northern Rock Foundation, a major corporate foundation which has a remit to fund in a specific geographic region, also undertook a review of its programmes and priorities during the period of my research. It, too, emerged from the process with a more explicit emphasis on art for art's sake. The overall objectives of the Northern Rock Foundation are 'to tackle disadvantage and to improve the quality of life in North East England and Cumbria'. Within this, the Foundation's embrace of art and culture appears to be linked to the culture-led regeneration policy that has helped in recent years to transform the North East's major urban centre, Newcastle-Gateshead. Major arts capital projects funded by the National Lottery – the BALTIC Centre for Contemporary Art, The Sage music centre and Antony Gormley's landmark public art work *Angel of the North* – have, over the last decade, helped to foster a positive reputation and profile for culture in the region that the Northern Rock Foundation is eager to help sustain.

A 'reflective paper', produced during the Northern Rock Foundation's review process to assist the decision-making of the trustees, illustrates how the strategies of independent funders may often be informed by a sense of the bigger picture. 'The role of culture in development is becoming better recognised because cultural routes have been shown to offer an effective way of achieving social and economic goals,' the paper notes. 'However, there is currently a lively debate in the cultural sector that suggests that too much emphasis has been put on culture as a tool for social and economic change. Not enough attention or research has been devoted to valuing culture for its own sake.'[35]

Following the review, in 2006 the Northern Rock Foundation introduced a Culture and Heritage programme. This replaced a more broad-ranging programme called Aspiration, which funded projects concerned with the environment and sport as well as the arts. In explaining the new programme on its website, the Foundation notes that: 'There are many funders who are interested in supporting creative activities connected with education, health, tourism or regeneration. Few, however, concentrate on the broad benefits of high-profile cultural programmes, or support professional development in the sector. We have chosen to make a long-term commitment to culture as a way of demonstrating the creative talent in our region. We are not seeking directly to tackle disadvantage in this programme, nor for applicants to demonstrate a direct link with economic regeneration. Rather we invest in organisations that provide enjoyable and stimulating activities of the highest quality to the widest population.'[36]

The Paul Hamlyn Foundation and the Northern Rock Foundation are examples of major independent funders that seek to maintain a deliberate and conscious balance between support for social welfare and support for the arts, recognising that the respective areas will sometimes overlap, but that there are points at which they necessarily diverge. Where social welfare concerns constitute a foundation's primary motivation for funding, however, it can be difficult even to trace what money is being directed to the arts. A foundation might not have a dedicated arts funding programme, or even an arts budget line in its accounts, but it might fund arts activities to a significant degree without necessarily recording the fact. An example cited by one expert on trusts and foundations was some funding given to support a component of the high-profile arts project at the Chelsea and Westminster Hospital, which appeared in the records of the foundation as expenditure against its 'health' remit. Conversely, another interviewee told me that: 'Asking a foundation what money goes to the arts would not necessarily be useful as the funding might be tagged "arts" but benefit other priorities, such as health or education.'

An additional difficulty in estimating the degree of support given to the arts by social welfare-focused trusts is that such funding may not be made too publicly explicit because of a concern that expenditure on the arts might not be construed as legitimate. One expert told me that: 'Where the remit of the trust is firmly in the area of social welfare and combating deprivation, some trusts won't tell you what they give to the arts partly out of a fear that it might be viewed by outside observers as an improper cause.'

For these reasons, it is not currently possible, beyond the ballpark statistics provided by the recipient-focused *A&B Private Investment Benchmarking Survey*, accurately to speculate on the amount, range and motivations of funding given to the arts in the United Kingdom by independent trusts and foundations. In 2004, a number of trusts and foundations which have a specific focus on environmental issues pooled resources to commission a piece of research to look at how and with what amount of money the independent funding sector supports environmental projects. The research resulted in a report called *Where the Green Grants Went*, which detailed which trusts and foundations gave to which projects and causes in that year. As a contribution to the general pattern of enquiry into existing and potential sources of funding for the arts sector that is happening at the moment, signalled by initiatives such as Mission, Money, Models, a research project looking at Where the Arts Grants Went would be a timely undertaking.

*Catalysts or reactors?*

In parallel with the debate on whether to fund art 'for art's sake', or in order to contribute to wider social agendas, there is currently a lively discussion in the trusts and foundations sector focused on the question of whether independent funders should actively seek to shape priorities and activity in their chosen area of giving, or whether their role is more properly to respond, with funding, to the projects and priorities brought to them by other charities operating within their field of interest. Couched in terms of the question 'Cash Machines or Development Agencies?', this was the central theme of the Association of Charitable Foundation's biennial conference in 2005. It is also a seminal concern of Helmut Anheier's and Diana Leat's 2006 publication *Creative Philanthropy*. I shall attempt to give a sense here of some of the arguments through which this debate has been formulated, and of how it is currently being played out in practice by a number of trusts and foundations that have a commitment to support the arts.

As with the 'art for art's sake? or art for society's sake?' debate, there is a wide spectrum of opinions and practices concerning this issue, with most foundations seeming to position themselves somewhere towards the middle: probably running responsive programmes, whilst also looking out for gaps that appear to need filling, and possibly using some of their resources to stimulate activity and/or new thinking that otherwise might not occur. There is a powerful argument, propounded by Anheier and Leat and others, that trusts and foundations are uniquely placed to take on the mantle of development agency, particularly in the realm of ideas. As one of my interviewees observed: 'Some of the most innovative funding today is coming from trusts and foundations.' Three reasons were given as to why this might be the case: 'They are not hidebound by any government agenda, they may have very imaginative and knowledgeable staff and trustees, and they are able to take risks that others might not be prepared to because it is private money.'

This analysis carries echoes of Anheier and Leat, who argue that the unique value of foundations in a democracy resides 'not in their assets or their charitable expenditure *per se*', but in the freedom afforded to them by their privileged and independent status. 'The key,' they argue, 'is that foundation resources are "free" relative to both governments and markets. Foundations enjoy the luxury of freedom from market and political constraints and constituencies ... Foundations have sufficient resources and "space" to allow them to think, to be truly innovative, to take risks, to fail, and to take the longer-term view.'[37]

Anheier and Leat doubt, however, that the majority of trusts and foundations are currently exercising their unique freedom with the strategic awareness, creative energy and democratic intent that they consider ought to be the case. 'Foundations,' they say, 'have been described as "warehouses of wealth" or as pots of money with, or in search of, a purpose ... At worst, foundations are little more than tax shelters that allow the privileged to pursue some "favoured' cause or charity. There are foundations that serve the privileged few, with no apparent net benefit added to society as a whole.'[38]

Even if they genuinely aspire to serve the public good, Anheier and Leat caution that the capacity for foundations, as a sector, to achieve positive change is circumscribed by the relative paucity of the resources that they have at their disposal. 'Foundations' financial resources pale into insignificance when compared with government spending or even the nonprofit sector as a whole,' they say. 'Thus, judged solely in terms of their financial resources, foundations have little scope for making a widespread and sustainable impact.'[39]

From Anheier and Leat's perspective, however, 'foundations are about much more than money'. The model, 'creative' foundation, which they would seek to encourage would exercise its unique freedoms and deploy its limited resources judiciously to help society to 'think the unthinkable'. 'Foundations need to spend more time and money,' they argue, 'on projects that have the promise of changing how an issue is viewed or handled. We refer to this as "creative grant-making".'[40]

As far as the arts in this country is concerned, intervening in a strategic and creative way to spur on the development of new ideas and to influence both public and governmental perceptions of an issue would not be a new undertaking for independent trusts and foundations. In the recent publication *Experience and Experiment: the UK Branch of the Calouste Gulbenkian Foundation 1956–2006*, the cultural analysts Robert Hewison and John Holden chart the not inconsiderable impact that one particular foundation has had in shaping the landscape of the arts in Britain over the past half a century. According to Hewison and Holden, the Gulbenkian Foundation has utilised its influence and its resources to play a significant creative and developmental role across a number of areas of public life, including the arts. 'Since 1956,' they assert, 'the Foundation has made interventions in the arts and culture, in social welfare and in education that have had profound and long-lasting effects ... Politicians have been prodded into action; seminal publications have injected intellectual rigour and fresh thinking into the national debate; and the Foundation has created a forum for important discussions that have helped to shape the future of the public realm.'[41] Hewison and Holden pinpoint some of the strategies by which this influence has been achieved. 'The Foundation,' they say, 'has always acted as a catalyst, a provoker of ideas, and it uses often quite small grants to launch schemes that, once proven, become part of mainstream thinking and are then taken up by organisations with deeper pockets and longer-term responsibilities for financial support.' They point to 'a well-established pattern of funding projects for a limited period, often publishing reports into the potential for new ways of working and entering into discussions with other agencies … to develop further new streams of support and promotion.'[42]

The development model is one that the Gulbenkian managed successfully to adopt at a very early stage of its evolution. Hewison and Holden describe how the UK Branch 'found its direction in 1959 with the publication of its own specially commissioned report *Help for the Arts*, remembered as the Bridges Report.' Commissioned to advise the Foundation on the needs of the arts in post-war Britain, the Bridges Report became the first of a series of highly influential reports on cultural policy that the Gulbenkian Foundation either commissioned or co-funded. According to Hewison and Holden, the Bridges Report 'set a pattern by which it would bring together a team of experts to investigate an issue, draw up a policy and publish a report that would have an influence far beyond the immediate purposes of the Foundation'. The pattern had a clear trajectory: 'to engage, network, enquire, deliberate and then act'.[43]

Later reports included *The Arts Britain Ignores*, an examination by Naseem Khan of the neglected status of the work of artists from minority ethnic communities, and *Support for the Arts in England and Wales*, which came to be known as the Redcliffe-Maud Report, both of which were published in 1976. The Gulbenkian Foundation also commissioned or, in the latter case, co-sponsored, two highly influential studies, which helped to encourage the emphasis on the instrumental value of the arts that has taken root in this country over the last two decades. Towards the end of the Thatcher period of government it initiated John Myerscough's seminal, largely quantitative, analysis *The Economic Importance of the Arts in Britain*, published in 1988, which highlighted in more detail and with more authority than ever before the fiscal benefits that result from subsidies for the arts. A decade later, it co-funded Comedia's major research project focused on the qualitative social impacts of participation in the arts, which culminated in François Matarasso's influential and controversial report of 1997, *Use or Ornament?*, a report which found an immediate resonance in the nascent 'social exclusion' agenda of the new Labour government.

The UK Branch of the Gulbenkian Foundation has exerted great influence in practice, as well as in theory. It is credited by Hewison and Holden with, amongst other things, 'virtually creating the contemporary dance scene in Britain' in the 1970s and, in the 1990s, of recognising before most others did the social deprivation that existed in the countryside, to ameliorate which it introduced 'an exemplary and innovative scheme to stimulate small-scale, largely non-professional rural arts activities'.[44]

Sian Ede, the Deputy Director of the UK Branch and the manager of its arts programme, believes that the Gulbenkian Foundation has succeeded, through its ability to connect with and to draw upon people with a high level of influence and expertise, in achieving an impact on the arts that seems out of proportion to its scale and resources. Ede describes the Gulbenkian's approach as 'informed philanthropy'. 'It is strategic and directed,' she says, 'but attempting to do what nobody else is doing. We always had independent advisors from outside: liberal progressive people who would tell us "nobody's doing this", or "nobody's doing that".'[45]

The areas in which nothing is being done tend, necessarily, to coincide with blind spots in the purview of the UK Arts Councils. For example, one area of lack which has recently been taken up by some independent grant-makers is the touring of artistic work across the borders of the countries which make up the United Kingdom. Since the abolition of the Arts Council of Great Britain in 1994, each of the Arts Councils that replaced it (plus the Arts Council of Northern Ireland, which already existed) has had an exclusive remit for its own territory. Consequently, it has become easier for independent foundations (most of which fund UK-wide) than it is for the respective Arts Councils to observe and to support work across UK boundaries. 'We have a bird's-eye view that the national funders no longer have,' was how one foundation manager described it to me.

If the way that boundaries and spheres of influence are defined can limit the strategic agency of public funding bodies relative to that of independent funders, so too can the mechanisms they design to organise the distribution of their grant funding. 'Arts Council England is turning everything bottom up through its Grants for the Arts programme,' observed one commentator, referring to the Council's decision, in 2003, to corral the majority of its funding for projects into a one-size-fits-all application-driven funding scheme. 'It is losing its flexibility to be strategic, which is where trusts and foundations can have an edge.'

At a policy level, too, gaps sometimes appear that independent funders are apt to recognise and may instigate measures to address. Within the visual arts, for example, the contemporary crafts have recently been the focus of developmental projects initiated by an informal network of grant-giving foundations. Responding to a perception that strategic work in this field of arts practice was being held back by a dearth of new policy development at a national level, following the transfer of the policy remit for the applied arts from the Crafts Council to Arts Council England in 2000, the Esmée Fairbairn, Foyle and Northern Rock Foundations have worked in partnership with each other and with a range of crafts organisations to kick-start a number of projects which aim to raise the profile and ambition of work in this area. One foundation manager commented that: 'Nobody could tell me what we wanted to achieve as a country for the crafts; crafts' policy kept slipping off the agenda. ACE can be a useful resource, but sometimes it can be frustrating where there is a policy vacuum or silence.' In the absence of a national plan, which would help to trigger and shape development, independent foundations have decided to use their combined resources to try to stimulate change, particularly in the English regions.

Whilst independent grant-making foundations appear increasingly inclined to use their expertise and their resources to act developmentally (and feel emboldened to do so), there remains also a need for independent funders who are prepared to be responsive to what arts practitioners themselves have identified as the priorities. Some foundations take the view that funders who develop temporary schemes and initiatives in order to achieve a particular strategic goal that they have identified may, in fact, create a detrimental impact: they might encourage an arts organisation to distort or to depart from its mission; or they might lead it to embark on a branch of activity which, when the funding dries up, proves to be unsustainable.

One foundation director, whose organisation's approach to funding was described as being 'driven by the sector', did not see the point of trying to invent strategic programmes that risked deflecting organisations that already had a clear sense of what they wanted to achieve from pursuing their core interests. 'The whole process of reinventing projects in order to get funding is par for the course for many organisations,' s/he said. 'They describe themselves back to the funders in the terms that the funders want to hear and then the funders feel reassured that they are actually doing what they ought to be doing. It is a sort of smoke and mirrors routine.'

Another trust director, who had recently developed a deliberately inclusive arts funding programme, told me that: 'We decided not to set up specific schemes because when we talked to the sector, they said that was their worst nightmare. Many of them believe now that they cannot target or approach the majority of trusts and foundations who support the arts because most of them have developed highly specific schemes, and unless you are part of a very exclusive group that meet their criteria you feel that you are excluded. We decided to spread our largesse as widely as possible, which is a bit different perhaps from most other trusts.' The same director cautioned against setting up special time-limited schemes designed to 'plug a gap for three or four years': 'The danger,' s/he said, 'is that you create an unsustainable momentum and then your source of funding disappears. We want to fund sustainably, not encourage stable organisations to over-reach themselves.'

Whilst some foundations retain a commitment to the more traditional hands-off, responsive approach of the independent grant-maker, other foundations are starting to emerge whose practice and philosophy shows the influence of the highly engaged, developmental approach characteristic of US-style venture philanthropy. In the domain of arts and culture, the most conspicuous example is probably the Louise T Blouin Foundation. Launched in May 2005, with a prestigious awards ceremony in New York that honoured, among others, former US President Bill Clinton for his contribution to creativity, the Foundation describes itself as 'an international not-for-profit organisation, working as an investor, originator and partner to pursue our goals', which are 'promoting culture and enhancing creativity across the world'. 'We will encourage efforts to better understand how creativity enhances culture, and generate a dialogue about how culture can inspire solutions to the world's challenges,' said the Foundation's President and donor, the international publishing magnate Louise T. Blouin MacBain.[46]

Early initiatives of the Louise T Blouin Foundation, which has its headquarters at the Louise T Blouin Institute in London but which aspires to have an impact globally, have included: a research project with the OECD (Organisation for Economic Cooperation and Development) to determine whether there is a correlation between the GDP spent on culture and the economic prosperity and quality of life in different countries; and a Global Creative Leadership Summit at which creative leaders from diverse fields, including business, technology, government, science and the arts, came together in November 2006 in New York to propose solutions to some of the major challenges currently facing the world.

The Director of the Louise T Blouin Foundation, Jeremy Newton, was formerly the inaugural Director of NESTA (the National Endowment for Science, Technology and the Arts), a non-departmental public body set up by the government in 1998 to stimulate a more receptive climate for innovation and creativity in the United Kingdom. There appear to be significant similarities between the two organisations. Both are endowment-based foundations which promote an expanded notion of culture and creativity – having a locus in the arts, but eager to embrace connections with science and other fields of human endeavour. Both organisations represent a new attitude to subsidy, which they term 'investment', in which the boundaries between commercial and not-for-profit activities are blurred or flattened. Both aspire to be 'thought leaders'.

Newton is clear that the modus operandi of the Louise T Blouin Foundation should be proactive and hands-on. It will: broker and initiate projects through partnership working; maintain links and have an input throughout the development process; try to lever additional resources and, wherever possible, to benefit from the commercial and intellectual exploitation of project outcomes. The Foundation's projects may, for example, provide editorial content for MacBain's publishing company, LTB Holding Limited. 'We will work in a devolved, but engaged way,' says Newton. 'Our model is to work with trusted partners to turn ideas into projects, building on existing expertise and high level contacts in the arts and in government in many countries. We want to help to promote change and policy development through research, discussion and example.'[47]

The Louise T Blouin Foundation is in its infancy, and it remains to be seen to what extent it can be successful in meeting its lofty ambitions. The fact that it exists, however, confirms that there is still a place, in the 21st century, for the kind of foundation which believes that organised philanthropy can help to effect significant positive change. In its emphasis on new thinking and creative research, and its belief that global problems and international conflicts might be addressed and resolved proactively through discussion and exchange, the approach favoured by the Louise T Blouin Foundation seems highly contemporary and determinedly future-oriented. In some ways, however, it could be regarded as the latest manifestation of an august tradition. According to Anheier and Leat: 'In an important sense, creative foundations act as the 21st-century equivalent of the 18th- and 19th-century European salons and coffee shops, generating new ideas and conversation about social and policy issues. In another sense, creative foundations are akin to the patrons of Renaissance thinkers, inventors and artists. Creative foundations act as both entrepreneurs and underwriters of new conversation, debate and exchange.'[48]

*How do trusts evolve?*

Some interesting questions arose during the course of my research concerning both the life cycles of individual trusts and foundations, and the stage to which the higher value foundations – those with sufficient income to warrant the employment of paid staff – have evolved. Is it a good thing that most trusts and foundations are created to exist in perpetuity, or is there an argument for setting a limit to the period of their existence? If trusts and foundations are of sufficient longevity to evolve over several generations of trustees and staff, is there a discernible pattern to the way that they tend to develop? Would it be true to say that the major trusts and foundations that fund the arts are more professional in their approach today than used to be the case? If so, how does this professionalism manifest itself? These are the questions that I will consider in this section of my analysis.

*Forever or for now: is there a fashion for avoiding perpetuity?*
It was explained in Volume I of this publication how the Rootstein Hopkins Foundation, which was originally expected to continue in perpetuity, took a strategic decision at a certain point in its evolution that it should wind up its affairs before it became necessary to hand over the reins to a new generation of trustees, who would not be familiar with the founders. Although the Rootstein Hopkins Foundation is still in a minority in this regard, there is some evidence to suggest that an increasing number of foundations are beginning to be set up with the deliberate intention of 'spending out' their assets over a time-limited period.

One commentator was of the opinion that there had been a growing trend in recent decades towards the creation of expendable endowments, where the trustees are not required to protect the value of the capital, but are permitted to spend it. 'More people are now wanting to see their wealth achieve something in their life-time,' s/he said, citing the example of Bill and Melinda Gates. 'They are prepared to use more of their money today, not keep it for tomorrow.' Recognising that there is a value in this trend, which makes resources available more immediately for charitable purposes, the Charity Commission now appears more willing than was formerly the case to convert a permanent endowment into an expendable one, should the trustees of a foundation request it.

In the United States, there is a 'five per cent rule' whereby all charitable founda-tions are required to expend the equivalent of at least 5 per cent of their total assets each year. The rule exists to ensure that foundations maintain a habit of active spend-ing and it has created a climate in which foundations have become used to the idea of budgeting to spend more than they may be guaranteed to earn in income. This attitude to endowment use, which involves an element of risk, is not necessarily one that all British trusts and foundations would find it easy to embrace. The director of one foundation which specialises in funding the arts told me that: 'We will not take more out of our endowment in any year than we think will be necessary for it to retain its value, plus inflation. We believe we can take 4.5 per cent per year and sustain the level of the endowment, but the trustees took the decision to reduce that to 4 per cent in 2004 because of the shaky financial markets, and that half a per cent meant the end of one of our programmes.'

There are, however, examples of grant-giving trusts that support the arts where the trustees are content for their endowments to depreciate over time. The Foyle Foundation, for example, which began operating in 2001 and which currently allo-cates around 40 per cent of its grants budget to the arts (around £2 million in 2005), is forecasting to spend more year on year than it anticipates that it will generate in income. The legacy through which the Foyle Foundation was created was in the form of unrestricted funds, which allows the trustees the discretion to spend capital as well as income. 'As a new foundation,' says its Chief Executive, David Hall, 'we are trying to break new boundaries and we don't want to be boxed in by traditional ways of doing things. In 2004 we gave away 7 per cent of our asset base. We would probably anticipate an annual income of between £3 million and £3.5 million, but we are projecting to spend £5 million.'[49] The Foyle Foundation expects to be a time-limited foundation, but there is for the time being no specific wind-down plan. 'Our policy,' says Hall, 'is to be as effective as we can be while we're here and to maximise what we try to achieve.'

Some commentators on philanthropy believe that the expectation of perpetual existence can encourage complacency in some foundations, because they may feel little pressure to perform to competitive standards. A 'sunset' model, such as that which appears to have been adopted by the Foyle Foundation, is perhaps one method by which a foundation can keep its thinking nimble and its spending flexible. The fact that the end is always in sight could make it easier for a foundation to retain a clear and strategic focus on the pursuit and achievement of its founding ideals.

*The influence of the donor*

The influence of the donor on the culture of a foundation will vary from trust to trust. In the case of the Foyle Foundation, the decision to use the vehicle of a charitable trust to organise the distribution of a wealthy individual's legacy was taken after the death of the donor, by the executors of the estate of Christina Foyle. In this instance, the donor has not had a direct influence on the direction that the Foundation which bears her family name has chosen to take. I have been advised of other instances where the donor of a foundation 'completely dictates the decisions', and of yet others where the living donor has been content to take a back seat and has delegated the decision making entirely to his or her appointed trustees.

Many trusts and foundations seem to go through a common trajectory as, with the passage of time, the influence of the initial donor wanes. One commentator told me that: 'Private foundations begin by fulfilling the interests of the founders, then they are passed on to their relatives, and later become more independent. Over time they become institutionalised. The trustees take more control and, as they move away from the influence of the original creator, there might be changes to priorities to meet new needs.'

The evolutionary process tends to be one of increasing professionalisation. This might involve the recruitment of trustees who have no personal connection to the founder and who have a greater level of expertise in the chosen areas of giving, as was the case with the Rootstein Hopkins Foundation (the details of which are described in Volume I). In trusts which have sufficient income to necessitate a full-time professional staff, there appears to be an increasing tendency towards specialisation. For example, senior paid employees of trusts and foundations that are major supporters of the arts now often have had significant prior experience of working for public sector arts funding bodies and policy-making agencies.

The director of a second generation foundation, where the donor had died but a connection remains with younger members of the donor's family, told me, drawing on direct experience of a number of different trusts, that: 'The first generation tends to be based more around the interests and enthusiasms of the founder, and his or her personal networks, and it is less likely to have detailed research, strategic plans and a sense of working in partnership with others. The sort of people who have money to give away don't tend to behave like that when they are setting up foundations.' This particular foundation continues to be motivated by the values of its founder but, when it has come to redefine its areas of priority, target potential grant recipients, and design its grant programmes, a more professional and reflexive approach has latterly been adopted. 'We now have permanent internal expertise to draw on – our staff are a mix of focused specialists and cross-programme generalists – and we also get external input in designing our programmes,' said my interviewee. 'We are more proactive in defining the type of organisation that we want to apply and in going out and talking to possible applicants.'

*A decade of professionalisation and specialisation*
There is a sense now that the expertise and sector-specific knowledge of the employees of the leading trusts is at a higher level today than might previously have been the case. One commentator, who has maintained close links with a variety of arts supporting trusts and foundations over a number of years, told me that: 'Current directors of trusts are very different than was the case ten years ago. They are much more aware than they used to be about the context in which they are funding. They really know their fields and can judge the particular contribution that a grant-making trust can make. They're not designing programmes in a vacuum.'

The director of an arts supporting foundation which was set up in the 1970s felt that both the way that it approached its work, and the culture of the independent funding sector as a whole, had changed significantly in the last decade. 'There is more mutual awareness and communication happening between trusts and foundations now,' s/he said. 'We are beginning to work more in partnerships; networking has become much easier. The sector has become more professionalised. People now see it as a career option.'

Another arts programme manager in a leading foundation felt that although ad hoc partnerships had sometimes previously been forged with others, the dominant mentality used to be: 'We're independent and we do what we do, and you do what you do.' There is now felt to be more dialogue and a greater willingness to cooperate. Use of e-mail and the growth of the internet means that, even with limited personnel, trust managers are able to stay better informed about the activities of their peers.

An example of an independent funder which has adopted a more reflective and specialist approach in the last decade is the Esmée Fairbairn Foundation. At the turn of the millennium, the resources available for the Foundation to spend each year more or less doubled, from around £13 million to around £25 million. To increase its professional capacity and to ensure that the efficiency of its grant-making would be commensurate with its enhanced resources, the Esmée Fairbairn Foundation took on specialist staff and, for the first time, created dedicated teams for each of its four programme areas. The new manager of its Arts & Heritage Programme, Shreela Ghosh (who has since moved on to become the Director of Programmes at the Louise T Blouin Foundation), felt that the Foundation's strategy for the future allocation of its resources would benefit from a greater awareness of how its funding for the arts had been deployed in the past. An audit of the Foundation's spending on the arts during the period from 1998 to 2000 revealed a major bias towards the performing arts (and in particular towards classical music), the extent of which the trustees had previously been unaware. A further audit, of the grant-making of other foundations which support the arts, revealed a comparative lack of project funding available across the independent sector to support the visual arts. Having been through this reflective process, the trustees decided in 2004 to reorient the priorities of the Esmée Fairbairn Foundation's arts programme. From April 2005 until April 2008 they agreed that its key focus should be the contemporary visual arts.

*Cultures of change*

One programme manager suggested to me that the bias that has historically existed in the independent sector towards funding the performing rather than the visual arts may be linked to the social background and education of the people who tend to run trusts and foundations. 'The visual arts have some very powerful and starry support- ers,' s/he said, 'but by and large the classical and privileged education of people who go into positions of power is still skewed towards music and the performing arts.' My interviewee felt, however, that as trusts and foundations begin to adopt a more professional outlook, there are signs that things might be changing. 'Trustees used to be recruited through an old boys' network,' s/he observed. 'Now, increasingly, there is the notion of skills auditing and the recognition of a need to diversify and refresh board membership with people from different generations and representing differ- ent areas of society.'

Changes in the culture of trusts and foundations are a response not only to inter- nal stimuli – the death of the donor, for example, or an increase in the size of the endowment – but also to the external landscape within which they must conduct their business. The Annual Report for 2005 of the Gatsby Charitable Foundation (a notable supporter of the arts and one of a number of foundations associated with the Sainsbury family) reflects on how that landscape has changed since the Gatsby Foundation was established in the mid-1960s. The report identifies substantial changes to the public context in which a grant-making trust must operate. 'Forty years ago,' it says, 'the major philanthropies operating in the UK were still largely Victorian creations. Grant-making was a discreet activity, with little taste for publicity … Grant-makers face changing expectations from commentators and regulators; the result is a situation today where philanthropists who use the trust route are required to be entirely public about the focus of the activity undertaken in their names – a complete turnaround from the social conventions which applied forty years ago.'[50]

The report also recognises the benefits of operating with a professional staff, which can provide an informed link between the trustees and the agencies that they seek to support. 'Trusts,' it says, 'can employ staff to research the trustees' fields of interest and to maintain working links with beneficiaries and others, as proxy for settlors and trustees whose primary time commitments lie elsewhere.' This enables trusts successfully to carry forward the philosophy of their founders well beyond the founders' lifetime, should the trustees so wish.

Notwithstanding the progress made towards greater professionalisation within the independent grant-making sector in recent years, the Gatsby Foundation report concludes with a 'fear for the future', which derives from a concern that the combination of over-intrusive regulation and the availability of lighter-touch tax efficient mechanisms for giving, such as Gift Aid, may discourage the formation of new foundations. 'We wish,' it says, 'to see new efforts made to encourage the release of more assets into grant-making charities ... There is a powerful need for a more sympathetic regulatory regime to encourage potential supporters of UK charitable activity both to create new trusts and foundations and to add to the resources available to those which already exist.'[51]

*Artist-initiated trusts and foundations: purposes and distinctions*

I shall conclude my survey of the current state of independent trust and foundation support for the arts in the United Kingdom by considering the small but significant niche occupied within this sector by the artist-initiated trust. The artist-initiated trust is not a widespread phenomenon, but it is worthy of consideration because, through the work of the Henry Moore Foundation and the Elephant Trust, it has given rise to some of the most focused and sympathetically informed support for, in particular, the visual arts in this country. As both the Henry Moore Foundation and the Evelyn Williams Trust demonstrate, charitable trusts can also play a vital role in the estate planning of artists, whether they hold the lofty ambition of preserving their artistic legacy for posterity; or whether they have more prosaic concerns, such as to avoid the complications associated with their posthumous obligation to the tax authorities.

*The Henry Moore Foundation*

The Henry Moore Foundation was set up in 1977 by the sculptor himself. Henry Moore (1898-1986), who was then 79, had become an extremely successful artist, to the extent that he is thought to have been the highest paying individual taxpayer at that time in the United Kingdom. 'Being a Yorkshire man,' says Timothy Llewellyn, the Director of the Henry Moore Foundation from March 1994 until May 2007, 'Henry didn't much like this. He lived modestly and found the tax regime for artists repressive, which it was.'[52] Moore was advised that if he set up a foundation, although he would be at arm's length from its assets, he could manage the charity as its employee and could encourage the trustees of the foundation to pursue, in a more structured way, the philanthropic activities that he had spontaneously engaged in as an individual.

Moore lived on until he was 88 and, whilst simultaneously directing the Foundation, he continued to work as an artist until his mid-80s. In those few remaining years of Moore's life, the Foundation turned out to be extraordinarily successful. 'He had given his means of production to the Foundation,' says Llewellyn, 'his own collection, his land and buildings; he also gave it some cash. Then he generated a lot more income for it as a result of these late years of work.' Because it started to wield real financial clout, Moore realised that he could accomplish much more than initially had been envisaged and he started to define what he wanted the Foundation to achieve after he was gone. The preservation and continued display of Moore's own work was the principal aim. Then, when the potential wealth of the Foundation became apparent, other things became possible. 'Henry gave pretty clear, if broad, guidance on what those things might be,' says Llewellyn.

Guided by the priorities set out by its founder, there are currently three key elements to the work of the Henry Moore Foundation: conserving and exhibiting the work of Henry Moore, through activities focused on the Henry Moore collection and archive at Perry Green in Hertfordshire; support for the study and display of sculpture from antiquity to the present day, through the Henry Moore Institute, an international centre for the discipline of sculpture based in Leeds; and support for institutions and individuals working in the field of fine art through the provision of grants to support artistic production, display, publication and scholarship. Moore was still alive when the forerunner of the Henry Moore Institute, the Centre for the Study of Sculpture, was set up in the city where he began his education as an artist. 'It was filling a gap that was important for him,' says Llewellyn, 'a lack that he felt when he was a young sculptor starting out in Leeds.'

The Henry Moore Foundation currently generates more than £4 million in income, which (after running costs are deducted) it apportions in three roughly equal measures to its operating activities at Perry Green and at the Henry Moore Institute and to its Grants Programme. Grants are available to support a range of projects, including exhibitions, new commissions, publications, artists' residencies and post-doctoral research fellowships. Although historical exhibitions and publications are supported, the main emphasis is given to the encouragement of new experimental work. 'We've always strongly supported what used to be called avant-garde art,' says Llewellyn, 'because Moore himself was a significant avant-garde artist in the earlier part of his career and often encountered critical opposition. We're trying to help artists who are breaking new ground and moving things forward. I'm very confident that Henry would support that, because it is in the spirit of his own career, even though he might not necessarily have liked some of the work.'

As the product and legacy of an artist who was committed to creative experimentation, the Henry Moore Foundation feels a clear sense of obligation to what has been referred to elsewhere in this essay as 'art for art's sake'. 'We have no other remit than the work,' says Llewellyn. 'We're less interested in the number of people who attend the exhibitions; we're less interested in the education programme. There are many who do care about these things and that's fine, but we were started by an artist and our principal focus is on the work of the artist. We may make mistakes from time to time and choose the wrong thing, but you have to take risks and artists will occasionally fail to pull-off what they plan. We want to encourage the artists of today who we believe have something important to say to make and show things and, through scholarship and exhibitions, to help the public understand the sculpture both of the present and of the past.'

Reflecting the specialist focus of the Foundation, the board of trustees includes a strong representation of scholars and other professionals from the fine arts, including a range of art historians, curators and collectors. There has been a conscious decision, however, not to include artists. 'This issue has been periodically debated,' says Llewellyn, 'and the view taken is that Henry Moore was very supportive of other artists, but he also sometimes had a difficult relationship with his peers. He was his own man. Some artists resent the Henry Moore Foundation, they think it provides unbalanced support for one artist over others; and many younger artists aren't very interested in Henry Moore. So, so far, we have thought it better not to involve artists. No doubt that is a debate which will continue.'

Through the recognition and acclaim that he achieved in his lifetime, Henry Moore helped to create a more receptive climate for new art work in this country; a climate in which the artists who followed on from Moore could flourish. This is something that the Foundation which bears his name has been keen to perpetuate. 'Moore's own success changed opportunities for sculptors coming after him and all have benefited from that,' says Llewellyn. 'If the Foundation has done something to help other artists to take further the approach that he himself took, that's what Henry would have wanted.'

### The Elephant Trust

The Elephant Trust was set up in 1975 by the artist and visual arts impresario Roland Penrose (1900-1984) and his wife, the photographer Lee Miller (1907-1977). Its aim is 'to develop and improve the knowledge, understanding and appreciation of the fine arts in the United Kingdom'.[53]

Roland Penrose was an English Surrealist painter and poet, who is perhaps best remembered for organising exhibitions and authoring books which profiled the work of his friends and contemporaries in the European avant-garde, including Pablo Picasso, Max Ernst, Joan Miró and Man Ray. Penrose organised the first International Surrealist Exhibition at the New Burlington Galleries in London in 1936. Later, in 1947, he was one of the co-founders of the Institute of Contemporary Arts (ICA), which was conceived as, and continues to be, a space for new and experimental art of all kinds. Penrose remained a guiding force at the ICA for 30 years until he resigned in 1976. Shortly before that, he founded the Elephant Trust with the proceeds from the sale of Max Ernst's first large-scale painting, *The Elephant Celebes*. Disillusioned by the increasing bureaucratisation that hampered his final years at the ICA, a charitable trust was suggested to Penrose as an alternative way to channel his support for the arts and, in particular, for artists.

The guiding ethos of the Elephant Trust was laid down by the original trustees – eminent friends and associates of Penrose who were, primarily, people of influence in the art world – and it remains the benchmark for its grant-making today. Reflecting the spirit of its founders Penrose and Miller, that ethos is: 'To bear in mind at all times an original, inquisitive, open-minded, generous and unshockable approach to art in all its forms, with a bias towards the visual arts.'[54]

Compared to the Henry Moore Foundation, the resources available to the Elephant Trust are modest. In the year to April 2004, for example, it had income of £102,707 and expenditure of £86,411. As its grant-giving capacity is limited, its approach has been to try to help artists to realise projects that otherwise might be 'frustrated by lack of funds'. It has sought to provide the critical amount of money that would make the difference to whether a project could happen or not, which might sometimes be as little as £2,000.

The late Joanna Drew (1929-2003) – a former Director of Art at the Arts Council of Great Britain, who was a founder trustee of the Elephant Trust and also a long-time trustee of the Henry Moore Foundation – commented, in 2002, in her oral history interview for the *Artists' Lives* project, on the Trust's empathy for the individual artist. 'The Elephant Trust,' she said, 'is small in financial terms but it is respected, particularly by artists. It likes to give to individuals, rather than institutions. Unfortunately, individuals don't often enough find their way to the trusts – they don't like asking for money for themselves.'[55] The Elephant Trust, along with the Rootstein Hopkins Foundation, is rare in the fact that it will support individual artists, as well as formally constituted organisations.

Joanna Drew was one of the founding generation of trustees chosen by Roland Penrose, which served from the Trust's inception in the mid-1970s until the millennium. Realising that as a cohort they were aging together, the trustees faced the dilemma of whether to secede to a new generation, or whether to wind the Trust up. Initially minded to do the latter, Drew recalled that, in the end, it was decided 'to hand over to people with a more pressing interest in what is happening now'; to people in the prime, rather than the twilight, of their careers who were 'at the sharp end of things'. The new generation of trustees, which came together in the first years of the 21st century, include the art historians Sarah Whitfield and Dawn Ades, both of whom are authorities on Surrealism, the artist Richard Wentworth, and Matthew Slotover, the Co-Director of the Frieze Art Fair and *Frieze Magazine*. 'When you are dealing with very young art, which we mostly are,' says Sarah Whitfield, the current Chair of the Trust, 'you've got to be somehow in touch with it, and I think that the previous trustees felt that they were no longer sufficiently in touch. The choice was either that they could wind up the Trust and give away the funds to various deserving causes, or that they could renew the trustees, and they decided that that was what they would do.'[56]

Along with the younger emerging artist, another significant category of artist that tends to attract Elephant Trust support is the mid-career artist, whose profile may temporarily have declined. 'They may be going through a period where they're not getting as much support as they deserve, or had been used to in their younger days,' says Whitfield. 'They are still making work that is very exciting but somehow, for the moment, fashion has passed them by.'

Whitfield reiterates the Trust's philosophy of seeking to gain the maximum benefit from its restricted funds. 'We want to provide the funding that will make a difference, that is the key thing,' she says. 'That's why individuals have a chance, because it will make a huge difference to them. If a project shows that it already has substantial backing from the Arts Council it's going to happen anyway.' Support for emerging talent is often routed through artist-led spaces, such as Matt's Gallery, Gasworks Gallery and Cubitt, rather than through more high-profile public venues. Many artists who are now well established were recipients of Elephant Trust funding in their early careers. They include several former winners of the Turner Prize: Rachel Whiteread, Gillian Wearing and Steve McQueen.

*The Evelyn Williams Trust*

It appears to have been a coincidence that the two pre-eminent artist-initiated trusts and foundations, the Henry Moore Foundation and the Elephant Trust, should have been established at around the same time, in the mid-1970s. The fact that their auspicious example has not been emulated led one of my interviewees to speculate that, perhaps, 'today's artists are not as civic minded as their predecessors'. The example of the Evelyn Williams Trust, however, suggests that that is not necessarily the case.

The origins of the Evelyn Williams Trust lay as much in its founder's concern to leave her artistic and financial affairs in order as in a wish to create a legacy of support for the arts. 'I became worried about what was going to happen to my work when I died,' says Williams, 'particularly from the point of view of inheritance tax. I wanted to get my work into responsible, independent hands; I didn't want my children to be encumbered with it. Now, when I die, all the work will go into the Trust and the trustees will do the best with it that they can.'[57]

Williams's partner Anthony Perry, who has extensive professional knowledge of the charitable sector, recommended setting up a trust; it would resolve the taxation dilemma and at the same time would create a positive legacy of support for the visual arts. 'A significant question when an artist dies is how their work is to be valued for inheritance tax purposes,' says Perry. 'A dealer can give the paintings on show in a commercial exhibition a certain price and then not sell them all. How do you determine the value of the work that remains unsold? This example demonstrates the problem that the executors of an artist might face if the artist's work is judged to be of value. If you have a charitable foundation, however, and believe that someone else should benefit when you die, you can put the work into a trust and there will be no problem about valuation. It side-steps the question.'[58] All of the work of Evelyn Williams which remains unsold in her lifetime will go into the Trust when she dies. A modest initial endowment was gifted by Williams to the Trust to enable it to begin to address its mission during her lifetime.

The Trust was set up in 1993, when Evelyn Williams was in her mid-sixties. Its charitable purpose was to support the fine arts. Initially, the focus was on the discipline of drawing, particularly through the encouragement of young and emerging artists. 'At that time, as far as I could see, there was no drawing going on in art schools,' says Williams. 'By drawing, I don't mean just drawing from the model; I mean making plans for what you're going to do. It's a process of thinking; it starts in your head and it comes out in your hands, in whatever medium you happen to be using. It is fundamental to all good art.'

During the period from 1995 to 2004, seven one-year Evelyn Williams Drawing Fellowships were set up, each at a different provincial art college in England. The purpose was to support and encourage the discipline of drawing within higher education, where, in the mid-1990s, it was perceived to have become an embattled medium; a concern which the Evelyn Williams Trust shared with the Rootstein Hopkins Foundation. The Fellowships were awarded to emerging artists, usually in their late-twenties, who were in the process of establishing themselves professionally and who would benefit from a period of time working on their practice within the supportive and stimulating environment of an art college. By 2004, the perceived gap which had led to the development of the Drawing Fellowships was no longer felt to exist and the Fellowships were discontinued. At the time of my research, the activities of the Trust were at a point of hiatus while alternative possibilities were being considered.

Evelyn Williams is not aware of any other living contemporary artists who have chosen to follow her example. 'A number have made enquiries,' she says, 'but they possibly lack the know-how to proceed. Setting up a trust is a very practical thing, but I think it is also a decent thing. I like the idea that any money that comes out of my estate will help some other artist when I am no longer around.' With a rising market for contemporary art creating a small but significant crop of affluent artists, and with a growing focus on the creative possibilities of organised philanthropy, perhaps the time is approaching when more artists will choose to follow the example of Williams and her eminent predecessors Moore and Penrose.

Within the present context of diminishing public subsidy, private sector investment in the arts, which includes funding from trusts and foundations, becomes increasingly significant. In an ever more competitive fundraising environment, the challenge for the arts will be to increase its market share of the £2 billion that trusts and foundations are estimated to give away each year. To achieve this, the arts sector must make a collective effort to get to know more about how trusts and foundations think and operate. Above all, it must learn to recognise that every trust and foundation is different, and that each individual case for support must be tailored to address the specific aims and priorities of the organisation from which funding is sought.

Notes

[1]   From 'The only trustworthy book...' Art and public value, the transcript of a speech to the Royal Society of the Arts, 16 February 2005, p.11.
[2]   The ACE website (www.artscouncil.org.uk, page title: 'Six decades of the arts') confirms that in 2000 'the Arts Council receives an extra £100 million from the Treasury in the Spending Review.'
[3]   ACE, Turning Point, p.9.
[4]   Ibid., p.10.
[5]   Hewitt, P., 'Council of Despair', the Guardian, 7 April 2007.
[6]   A&B, Private Investment Benchmarking Survey 2005/06, p.4.
[7]   A&B, Private Investment Benchmarking Survey 2004/05, p.1.
[8]   The A&B Benchmarking Survey for 2005/06 found that the figure for Trusts and Foundations investment had risen sharply again, to an estimated £113.7 million
[9]   This quotation, which is widely used by organisations wishing to promote philanthropy, such as the Institute for Philanthropy, is thought to be apocryphal; I was unable to trace a definitive source.
[10]  Breeze, 'The Return of Philanthropy', p.1.
[11]  Op. cit., p.8.
[12]  Op. cit., p.1.
[13]  Ibid., p.2.
[14]  Lloyd, Why Rich People Give, p.23.
[15]  Lloyd, Why Rich People Give, p.11. The survey sample was made up of '76 people of high net worth (largely between £5 million and £100 million) currently living in England and Wales. Additional interviews were carried out: 10 volunteer fundraising leaders ('askers' – many also with significant assets) and 14 leading professional advisers to the wealthy, also high earners.'
[16]  Ibid., p.16.
[17]  Bishop, The business of giving, p.1.
[18]  Ibid., p.4.
[19]  Quoted in the Philanthropy UK Newsletter, December 2006, p.11.

[20] From an interview with the author, 13 May 2005.

[21] Carrington, *Corporate Foundations and the Not For Profit Arts Sector*, p.4.

[22] Ibid., p.22.

[23] Ibid., p.16.

[24] Ibid., p.16.

[25] Ibid., p.34.

[26] Ibid., p.25.

[27] Quoted by Hewison and Holden in *Experience and Experiment: The UK Branch of the Calouste Gulbenkian Foundation 1956–2006*, p.25.

[28] Frayling, 'The only trustworthy book...' Art and public value, p.16.

[29] Ibid., p.19.

[30] From an interview with the author, 27 June 2005.

[31] All the quotations attributed to Paul Hobson in this essay are from an interview with the author, 4 July 2005.

[32] Information about the award schemes offered by the Paul Hamlyn Foundation has been taken from the Foundation's website: www.phf.org.uk

[33] From an interview with the author, 29 June 2005.

[34] All the quotations attributed to Robert Dufton in this essay are from an interview with the author, 29 June 2005.

[35] The paper referred to here was produced by the Northern Rock Foundation for internal use only and is not in the public domain.

[36] From the Northern Rock Foundation website: www.nr-foundation.org.uk

[37] Anheier and Leat, *Creative Philanthropy*, p.9.

[38] Ibid., p.11.

[39] Ibid., p.12.

[40] Ibid., p.10.

[41] Hewison and Holden, *Experience and Experiment*, p.9.

[42] Ibid., p.11.

[43] Ibid., p.15.

[44] Ibid., p.21.

[45] From an interview with the author, 6 June 2005.

[46] Quoted on the website of the Louise T Blouin Foundation: www.ltbfoundation.org

[47] From an interview with the author, 29 September 2005.

[48] Op. cit., p.251.

[49] All the quotations attributed to David Hall in this essay are from an interview with the author, 21 July 2005.

[50] The Gatsby Charitable Foundation, *Annual Report 2005*, p.2.

[51] Ibid., p.3.

[52] All the quotations attributed to Timothy Llewellyn in this essay are from interviews with the author conducted on 13 July and 8 September 2005.

[53] Stated on the Elephant Trust's website: www.elephanttrust.org.uk

[54] Ibid.

[55] The Joanna Drew oral history interview for the *Artists' Lives* collection can be accessed at the British Library.

[56] All the quotations attributed to Sarah Whitfield in this essay are from an interview with the author, 12 September 2005.

[57] All the quotations attributed to Evelyn Williams in this essay are from an interview with the author, 14 June 2006.

[58] From an interview with the author, 14 June 2006.

# TRUSTS AND FOUNDATIONS:
# TOWARDS NEW STRATEGIES FOR VISUAL ARTS
# FUNDING IN THE UNITED KINGDOM

by *Marjorie Allthorpe-Guyton*

## Public value: the challenge

The post-war changes in the visual arts, from those that fall into the category of 'heritage' to the directly contemporary, are dramatic and on-going. They range from the growth and pluralism of art practices and arts organisations, to the institution of new and refurbished public venues, and to the unprecedented expansion and globalisation of the art market. The public sector has made great strides in developing participation in the arts, and in demonstrating the wider social benefits of an active engagement with art and with artists. These changes in the landscape of the visual arts in the United Kingdom are widely acknowledged but not well understood. The 'public value' of visual art may be described in a number of ways, from its importance to economic and social regeneration in areas where new or revived venues attract new forms of investment in tourism and leisure and generate an enhanced public attendance, to the crucial but less easily measured social and cultural benefits in terms of environment, education, recreation, general culture and personal 'quality of life'.

The need to present hard evidence of the economic, social and cultural value of public investment in the contemporary visual arts in England lay behind the Arts Council's important review and strategy document, *Turning Point*, which was published with supporting research reports in 2006.[1] In the United States, the Rand Corporation report, *A Portrait of the Visual Arts, Meeting the Challenges of a New Era*, published in 2005 with the support of the Pew Charitable Trusts, was altogether more wide-ranging in its address to complex national and international socio-economic, political and cultural factors in the visual arts sector.[2] This groundbreaking survey revealed significant differences between the operating contexts of the visual arts and those of the performing arts, and between the determining conditions of the visual arts economy in the United States as contrasted to those in the United Kingdom, especially in relation to tax regimes and to corporate and private giving. In general terms, however, the Rand report's findings on the dynamics of the visual arts economy are relevant to the United Kingdom because of the increasingly international nature of this sector and the growing tension generated by the overlap of public and private elements in the global economy. With pressure to meet government agendas, public funding is increasingly conditional. It is also more difficult for the publicly funded visual arts organisation to uphold its distinctiveness from the commercial sector, where the core business is profit not public benefit.

The greatest challenge facing those concerned with the support and dissemination of the visual arts at this time is to respond appropriately to these volatile conditions of continual change and development. Central to the effectiveness of that response and to sustaining true public value is the role and impact of trusts and foundations.

### Charitable funding for the arts: a more strategic approach

The visual arts, especially contemporary art, have enjoyed an unprecedented decade of growth and success, making the most of public subsidies and attracting private support and investment. But the challenges of responding to a fast and competitive funding environment are daunting, particularly for those involved in the kinds of risk-taking art practice embraced by many contemporary artists and organisations. Individual giving, especially from a newer breed of venture philanthropist, is becoming much more significant as a source of private support for the visual arts, as it is for the cultural sector as a whole. As legislative reforms in taxation relief are implemented, more individuals may choose not only to gift charities but to establish new trusts with arts-related missions. This could well lead to a broadening of the impact of established trusts and foundations, which traditionally have been relatively conservative and most usually focused on issues of disadvantage, education and quality of life, rather than on direct investment in the arts themselves or on support for the individual artist.

Any analysis of the current workings of charitable trusts in the context of the visual arts in the United Kingdom needs to broadly survey visual arts developments in order to assess whether public and private support is being truly maximised. The support of trusts and foundations for visual arts has become increasingly important as need and activities expand, but much could be gained from the definition of a clearer rationale for their investment and a more strategic approach to funding. This would enable a more effective fulfilment of their own missions as well as better serving the central purposes of their beneficiaries and enhancing public value.

This paper argues that the focus on repeated project funding, often through small grants, with less attention to broader ongoing artistic and business development and capacity-enhancement, fails to maximise the value of the distinct, and essentially complementary, role of trusts and foundations in the arts funding economy as a whole. As the ratio of public subsidy decreases to the point where it barely covers core operating costs, visual arts organisations have to raise additional funding not only for their artistic programmes and the production of new work, but for dedicated staffing in education and resource development. Evaluation of economic impact, audience profiling and strategic research are other important aspects of effective operation that are not easily covered by funding from inadequate public subsidy. But these are the very areas of activity that might most appropriately fulfil the social aims of private trusts and foundations. Some trusts are now recognising this as a proper use of their funds: the Rootstein Hopkins Foundation, for instance, has recently awarded £500,000 to the BALTIC Centre for Contemporary Art to support capital costs, training and the programme for its new education space.

The charitable contribution is, then, critical to developing and sustaining those aspects, so important to public value, which are threatened by the hybridisation – even privatisation – of public institutions.[3] This erosion of public support is particularly acute in the visual arts where the power of the art market and the imperative need for institutions to generate income in order to supplement subsidy is compromising their integrity and adversely affecting their ability to fulfil their core mission, which is the support and presentation of good work and balanced programmes. In the current circumstances it is very difficult to present those seminal exhibitions which may attract small audiences but which can exert a profound influence on the course of art. It is also hard to raise programme funding to exhibit the work of those mid-career or senior British artists whose moment of fame has perhaps come and gone, but whose current work is of high quality and continues to deserve public exposure. Support is more readily available, paradoxically, for presentations of the work of successful younger artists who presently enjoy celebrity in the commercial and media spotlight, or for that of fashionable international names from abroad.

Fortunately, trusts in the United Kingdom are beginning to follow the American lead in looking more closely at the feasibility of investment that allows for long-term mission-related expenditure as well as continuing with the more traditional, project-related, grant-giving. This welcome development could encourage a more pro-active partnership between the funding body and the receiving institution in the promotion of public value through staffing, education and research as well as in supporting the art programmes as such. Trusts have not traditionally involved themselves this closely with the governance and business of the bodies they choose to support, and to engage in this way will require a deeper knowledge of the issues that concern the visual arts sector than has hitherto been the case. A recent seminar paper, published by the Esmée Fairbairn Foundation, considers this challenge to the orthodox model of grant-giving and argues persuasively for the positive potential of such new approaches, including the use of specialist intermediaries, such as Charity Bank, to reduce risk and exposure.[4]

## Trusts and the visual arts now

There is some evidence that charitable trust giving to the visual arts in Britain, with some notable exceptions, may be in decline. The Arts & Business report on Individual and Trust Giving to the Arts 2002/3, for example, showed a fall in overall giving to the arts from trusts and foundations.[5] Visual arts received just £1.7 million, compared to £10.9 million for Theatre, although Museums and Galleries received £14 million. Of this funding, a disproportionate share went to London-based organisations, whereas the visual arts in the East Midlands region, for example, received nothing. This inequitable pattern of national versus regional provision is confirmed by the research undertaken for the Art Council's visual arts review.[6] In fact, no large awards (i.e. over £1 million) were reported from trusts and foundations to the visual arts in 2005/6.

While trust and foundation funding represents a relatively small proportion of the income received by arts organisations, its power of leverage in this sector is nevertheless considerable, and continues to grow.[7] The impact in the United Kingdom of ten years of the National Lottery has been profound, creating new opportunities for the wider participation of both artists and audiences. And the imperative to find 'matching funding' for Lottery-funded projects has led to a significant rise in financial support from both public and private sources.[8 & 9] Many of the visual arts organisations in London and the regions, which collectively received over £230 million for large capital projects, also received funding from charitable trusts.

Now that the boom years of National Lottery funding for the arts are over, charitable trust support for new capital projects is increasingly critical, especially for London-based organisations, which do not generally benefit from substantial local authority and EU funds. A good example is provided by the current £10 million Whitechapel Project for the redevelopment of the Whitechapel Art Gallery and adjoining Library, which in addition to Lottery funding has raised almost £2 million from charitable trusts to supplement the exceptional local authority capital award from Tower Hamlets of £1.3 million.[10] Trusts and foundations have also provided funding towards the redevelopment of Camden Arts Centre. In both cases this funding has been largely targeted for education facilities and disabled access.

The success of an application to a trust may depend on established connections with trustees of charitable bodies and an awareness of the levels of awards that might be expected for a given purpose. This accords with the perception amongst visual arts organisations that trusts are usually risk-averse, generally wary of contemporary art initiatives, and tend to favour large established organisations and national institutions with the most generous awards. Other visual arts organisations, smaller or less prestigious, are most likely to benefit when they are able to demonstrate their abilities to address the problems of disadvantage in the area of their local audience, or to reach out to a public broader than that of the usual attendance, or to deliver programmes that link with government agendas such as social inclusion and support for the national curriculum. Middlesbrough Institute of Modern Art, for example, which opened at the beginning of 2007, has achieved significant capital support of £500,000 from the Northern Rock Foundation, which supports projects whose aim is to improve the quality of life of people in the North East and Cumbria. On this basis, the same foundation also allocated a major award of £1 million to Gateshead's BALTIC Centre for programme support.

While there are a small number of trusts and foundations that have given particular support to capital development in the visual arts field, and others which have been more inclined to fund one-off projects, strategic awards for revenue programmes have been few and far between. Those contributing particularly to the contemporary visual arts are the Henry Moore, Esmée Fairbairn, Paul Hamlyn and Jerwood Foundations. The Calouste Gulbenkian Foundation and the Wellcome Trust are also significant funders of projects and programmes connecting art and science. The Art Fund (established in 1899 as the National Art Collection Fund) is unique as a membership body focused on support for the acquisition of works of art of all periods for public collections, and is taking a leading role in campaigning for government funding and for tax reform to encourage private donation. The recently established Public Catalogue Foundation has a long term programme for the publishing of comprehensive catalogues of oil paintings in public ownership.

There can be few visual arts organisations in Britain that have not benefited from the support of the Henry Moore Foundation, which is exceptional among charities in its dedicated and uncompromising focus on the promotion and appreciation of the fine arts, particularly sculpture, and on artistic and critical quality as a determining criterion for project and publication funding. Alongside its management of the Henry Moore estate and Institute, the Foundation is a mainstay of museums, galleries and of individual artists, especially outside London. Its judicious grant-making has enhanced immeasurably the range and quality of the presentation in the United Kingdom of new and historical work, and of associated publications. Special capital awards to provide new spaces at Yorkshire Sculpture Park have enabled greater access to the Arts Council Collection and for the presentation of exhibitions at the recently opened underground gallery there. Capital investment of this kind from other charitable trusts could unlock the great potential of many regional museum collections, addressing inadequate storage and display facilities.

The Esmée Fairbairn Foundation has taken an admirable lead in this respect by allocating funds to the Art Fund for the improvement of regional museum collections. It has also, significantly, entered into an innovative and unprecedented strategic initiative with the Henry Moore Foundation to channel funds into the promotion of contemporary visual art, effectively taking advantage of the accumulated experience and expertise of the latter in the field. This partnership of two major players in the world of charity foundations perhaps signals a more co-ordinated approach to visual arts funding, and one which will more effectively complement public subsidy. While project funding from Arts Council England has substantially increased through Grants for the Arts, and the visual arts have received £9 million over the last two years, funding for large-scale and ambitious projects remains highly competitive. The dramatic cut to the Grants for the Arts programme announced in March 2007, however, threatens to undo recent investment and the gains of greater partnership between trusts and public funding.

By giving priority to the contemporary visual arts, allocating £4 million – no less than half of its arts programme budget – to core and revenue costs, including loans through the Charity Bank, Esmée Fairbairn has effected a step-change in private trust funding of the sector. And the Foundation has sought to gain an appropriate understanding of the key issues affecting the promotion and presentation of visual art. For example, one of its strategic initiatives is to support exhibition programmes and the necessarily complementary curatorial development in regional museums (for which purpose it has committed £800,000); another is its partnering of Arts Council England in the Inspire programme whose aim is to widen the cultural diversity of staff in museums and galleries. The challenge faced by the Foundation and its partner organisations is to evaluate the effective outcomes of these pioneering programmes, and to sustain support for them, even if this means the reduction of more immediately reactive and popular small project awards. It would be a great pity if the implications of the big picture focus of these significant strategic investments were not fully grasped. These initiatives represent the kind of private/public collaboration of which the Clore Duffield Leadership programme is the prime exemplar, and from which the visual arts are already showing evidence of benefit.

The rising level of trust funding for programme development of arts organisations is not matched by grants to individual artists. Since its inception in 1998, the Paul Hamlyn Foundation Awards for visual artists in the United Kingdom have been exemplary in this respect. Artists are selected through a wide-ranging and carefully professional process of nomination, and receive a generous £30,000 spread over three years, awarded without conditions. The criteria for the award are talent, achievement, promise and need, each of these variables being relatively pertinent to the consideration of individual cases, and there is no age limit. Unlike artists' prizes, which are often problematic – variability of juries, arbitrary conditions of eligibility, the difficulties that come with too much attention, too late, too soon – the Paul Hamlyn Awards make a serious intervention through considered support for artists at significant moments in their careers. Like those of the Pollock-Krasner and Gottlieb Foundations in the United States, the Hamlyn Awards recognise that some artists may not always benefit from the market or from frequent exhibition, or be enjoying current attention and success, but may nevertheless have an enduring practice and a deserved reputation. The greatly distinguished Gustav Metzger, for example, born in 1926, was an award winner in 2006.

The greatest range of visual arts prizes, including those for Drawing and for Painting, often supported by high profile exhibitions at the Jerwood Space and elsewhere in London, are awarded by the Jerwood Charitable Foundation, which makes a powerful contribution to the arts in general through a range of funding and strategic initiatives. The Jerwood Applied Arts Prize, organised in partnership with the Crafts Council, and Jerwood's investment in Innovative Craft, a new organisation whose purpose is to generate exhibitions for craft work, are crucial to the development of a much-needed infrastructure for the crafts sector. This more strategic approach also underpins Jerwood's purposive participation with Arts & Business, Arts Council England and other charitable trusts and foundations in the seminal Mission, Money, Models, a recent initiative to create conditions conducive to a healthy arts environment in this country.

As I have already suggested, it is arguable as to whether the proliferation of fine art prizes best serves the purpose of giving both emergent and senior artists appropriate recognition and serious assistance for professional development and a sustainable career. These might better be secured, as I have indicated, through long-term programme support for those under-resourced but well-established and respectable venues and organisations that might then provide studio facilities, exhibition and publishing opportunities for a wider range of artists than is possible in the current conditions that favour short-term funding.

There is a particular and underdeveloped potential for trusts to consider opportunities for programme-related investment in artist-run spaces and artists' studios, which are among the areas of most acute need in the field of the visual arts, but which have often proved to be crucial elements in urban and rural regeneration. Such investment could be facilitated by specialist intermediaries with experience in this sector, such as the ACME or Space studios organisations in London. A useful model might be the Creative Foundation, established by Roger De Haan to contribute to the rejuvenation of Folkestone by way of a mix of commercial enterprise and low-cost housing and creative workspaces. Trusts with a national remit might be deterred from an investment with such limited geographical focus, but might well feel confident if they were working in partnership with other funding bodies as part of a national strategy to invest in a number of carefully selected places and with collectives constrained by agreed criteria and carefully determined aims and objectives.

Since 2004, the Jerwood Charitable Foundation has partnered the Cell Project Space for the Jerwood Artists Platform. And another very welcome initiative is the exceptionally generous £1 million award for the Jerwood Artangel Open, which, in creative partnership with Channel 4, is a positive response to Artangel's long-established reputation as the imaginative initiator of seminal art events and unusual collaborations. This will fund three new commissions by artists for site-specific projects across Britain.

It seems clear from the foregoing that, in the long run, it is sustained long-term funding, and investment in proven venues and facilitating organisations, that will create the conditions most helpful to individual artists in their creative endeavours and most conducive to a healthy environment for the visual arts.

## Postscript: a quiet philanthropist

The Jerwood name, like that of Bloomberg (for the Bloomberg New Contemporaries and Bloomberg Space), has become something of a key brand word for contemporary art in the United Kingdom. Much less widely known, but perhaps no less significant, is the A Foundation, established by the philanthropist James Moores with support from the Nigel Moores Charitable Foundation. The A Foundation has established new artists' studios and an exhibition space at Rochelle School in East London, and set up the great new Greenland Street venue in Liverpool, which was inaugurated at the Liverpool Biennial 2006. James Moores was a major funder of the first Liverpool Biennial in 1999, and Greenland Street constitutes a significant development, unprecedented in its scope and opportunity, for the contemporary visual arts in the city. It is also an important strategic contribution to the city and region in advance of Liverpool's year as the European Capital of Culture in 2008.

The rehabilitation of 2500 sq. ft. of industrial space at Greenland Street, and its appropriation for the visual arts, and as an umbrella space for other arts organisations, is a demonstration of altruism and of visionary commitment to the idea that art and artists belong at the heart of local communities. The A Foundation provides a highly relevant contemporary example of the way in which charitable trusts and foundations might find ambitious long-term projects to invest in and to support on a continuing basis. Funding for such fit-for-purpose projects and organisations is in perfect accord with the primary aims of the wider charitable trust community to bring social, economic and cultural benefits to our cities and countryside, and to create public value in raising the quality of life of those who live here in our time. It is consistent also with the history of generous and responsible benevolence that has characterised the traditional kinds of support that trusts and foundations have provided for the visual arts in the United Kingdom.

## Notes

1. Arts Council England, *Turning Point: a strategy for the contemporary visual arts in England*, London, 2006.
2. McCarthy, Kevin et al, *A Portrait of the Visual Arts, Meeting the Challenges of a New Era*, Rand, 2005.
3. Shuster, Mark, 'Neither Public nor Private: The Hybridisation of Museums', *Journal of Cultural Economics*, Vol. 22, 1998.
4. Bolton, Margaret, *Foundations and Social Investment*, Esmée Fairbairn Foundation, 2005.
5. Arts & Business, *Individual and Trust Giving to the Arts 2002/3*, London, 2004.
6. *Turning Point*, p.26.
7. See Arts & Business, The Maecenas Initiative, a three-year research project set up in 2004
8. *Turning Point*, p.30-39.
9. Arts Council England, *Pride of Place, How the Lottery Contributed £1b to the Arts in England*, London, 2002, pp.40-43, 65.
10. The major trust awards towards the Whitechapel Project are from the Garfield Weston Foundation, the Clore Duffield Foundation, the Foyle Foundation, the Bridge House Trust, the Mercers Company, the Stavros Niarchos Foundation and the Fidelity UK Foundation. Garfield Weston, Clore Duffield, Bridge House, Foyle and Fidelity UK also provided funding towards the redevelopment of Camden Arts Centre. Fidelity UK specifically requested planning for capacity building and business growth.

# CHARITABLE TRUSTS AND THE
# VISUAL ARTS UNDER NEW LABOUR

*by* Tim Llewellyn

Why has there been such an extraordinary development of interest in contemporary visual art over the last ten or fifteen years? There are many answers: the ambition and vision of artists; the perceived quality, nature and interest of the art; its availability in public displays, the media and the market; and economic prosperity, which facilitates creation and participation in whatever form. There is another less tangible reason: the most prominent contemporary art of recent years has, by intention or chance, exemplified or reflected the New Labour zeitgeist. Its preoccupations and those of official agencies and government itself have come together in a potent mix. Has this been a deliberate partnership or a random conjunction? Analysis of the sources of funding perhaps provides a clue. Large amounts of money are needed to create public displays of visual art. In the non-profit arena, most financial support comes directly or indirectly from government, with lesser amounts coming from charitable trusts and commercial sponsorship. In this essay I shall look at the recent history of government funding of contemporary visual art and then consider how other funding agencies have responded.

New Labour has sought to influence aspects of our lives which had previously seemed beyond direct political intervention. In pursuit of a radical agenda, empowered by landslide election victories and overwhelming parliamentary majorities, the ambition of Tony Blair and his colleagues to be seen to introduce change frequently prevailed, not always with the desired results, over the experienced views of a wide range of professional experts in the formulation and delivery of public policy. The media has often carried stories, prompted by leaked emails and memoranda, about severe tension between elected ministers and, especially, their appointed political advisers on the one hand, and seasoned civil servants or members of other bodies delivering public services on the other. The attack on Gordon Brown by recently retired senior civil servants at the time of the 2007 Budget exemplified this.

In the cultural field, relationships have been uneasy between the Department of Culture, Media and Sport and both Arts Council England, whose very existence seems sometimes to have been under threat, and the trustees and directors of national and other galleries and museums. It is not within the scope of this essay to assess whether this tendency to conflict has been justified or indeed whether the Blair administration's 'modernising' agenda achieved success. We need to recognise however, that the Government has developed an unprecedented armoury of means to pursue its agenda, of which its relationship with the media has been the most potent, but which extends also to patronage in the arts and the closely allied so-called creative industries.

It is not difficult to see why significant aspects of contemporary visual art would appeal to New Labour's desire for radical change. Avant-garde art is frequently characterised as 'challenging': challenging to all manner of established views, particularly to perceptions of what art might be and for whom and by whom it is made; challenging to racial and social prejudice, and challenging to indifference about social injustice. In engaging directly with a wide range of social and personal issues previously little touched by art, contemporary artists have sought not only to amplify their own voices, but also to transform the significance of the medium itself in the nation's attention. David Lammy, Minister for Culture, in a speech at the opening of the 2006 Liverpool Biennial, recognised the tendency for artists to identify with the disadvantaged in society and welcomed this as a stimulus to change. This view reflected his Department's stance in *Culture at the Heart of Regeneration*, 2004, which echoed a statement published by the Social Inclusion Unit in 2001: 'Art ... can not only make a valuable contribution to delivering key outcomes of lower long-term unemployment, less crime, better health and better qualifications, but can also help to develop the individual pride, community spirit and capacity for responsibility that enable communities to run regeneration programmes themselves'.[1]

Mr Lammy's predecessors were titled Ministers for the Arts. The change to Minister for Culture suggests where the Government wishes to place emphasis and also hints that artistic quality alone has a lower priority in its agenda than broader cultural, educational or social benefit. This view is supported by the statement on the Department's website: 'We aim to improve the quality of life [n.b. not art] for all through cultural ... activities.' Improving the quality of life for its citizens is clearly a goal which any government should espouse, but it is only sometimes, and then indirectly, the purpose of art. Those who have been critical of New Labour's approach, seeing it as devoid of substance and obsessed with headlines and media manipulation may also have levelled the same criticism at some contemporary visual art, which often seems self-obsessed and in which all aspects of popular culture – fashion, pop music, sport, computer games and digital imagery, film and even pornography – may play active roles. Government and artists alike have understood that to address a wide audience, a popular language is required. While the Government has not created this tendency among artists, it has certainly nurtured it and harnessed it.

In the visual arts, as in many areas of activity where public spending plays a key role, Government has sought to broaden participation. It has enabled the widening and enlarging of audiences by ending museum entrance charges and this has stimulated an appetite for new kinds of exhibitions dealing with subjects outside the traditional canon of visual art, whether it be football, the clothes of Kylie Minogue, Kate Moss or Princess Diana or photographs of 'celebrities'. In thus encouraging the extension of the range of exhibition programmes, the Government has emphasized the desirability of accessibility, cultural diversity and popular appeal. It has also worked to improve management by requiring greater accountability and transparency. An issue to be explored is whether, in pursuit of larger audiences and therefore a better return on public investment, government policy has encouraged museum directors and curators, intentionally or unintentionally, to distort or ignore the criteria they would previously have adopted in creating their exhibition programmes and thereby influenced artists in the development of their work.

In the arena of accountability and transparency of management those bodies responsible for funding cultural organisations have been encouraged and empowered to play a more active role in reviewing governance issues. The same is true for charitable trusts. Most institutions of both kinds publish, no doubt at great cost, significantly more information about themselves in much more readable and better illustrated virtual and printed form than used to be the case. Thanks to the new Statement of Recommended Practice and the encouragement and empowerment of the Charity Commission, much more is known about the aims, policies and activities of both the funding bodies and the recipients of their generosity. While this is doubtless desirable from a number of points of view, the resulting cost of increased administration and public accountability is very heavy in human and financial terms and, for small organisations, often disproportionate. It is not clear that the concept of 'value for money', which has rightly become an important focus in all sectors of public spending, has yet been adequately applied to accountability.

Widening participation, communication and accountability are not the only priorities to have changed under New Labour: the role of education in any project in receipt of public funds has developed greater prominence and is often as carefully examined and resourced as any other aspect. This has been stimulated by an understandable desire to extend the public benefits flowing from the funding as well as to provide opportunities for school children and students in fields of cultural study that are not now widely available as part of the school curriculum.

Overall, this approach to visual art, as no doubt to other art forms, has been projected as the logical extension of democratic principles: the outcomes of public expenditure must be seen to be open to all. In the cultural field, the policy has been designed to lead to the elimination of 'elitism' and outmoded patterns of patronage and to reflect more faithfully the preoccupations, characteristics and interests of particularly the younger members of a multi-racial society, in which minorities groups are deeply sensitive to and proud of their diverse traditions, languages and standards.

New Labour's approach has had a profound impact on two key agencies, the Arts Council and the British Council. The Arts Council of Great Britain was a body created soon after the Second World War in response to the perceived need for informed public funding of art, which recognised from the outset the desirability of keeping politicians at arm's length from its detailed disbursement. In 1994, the Arts Council of Great Britain was split and funding and policy responsibilities were devolved to parallel agencies in Scotland, Wales and Northern Ireland. Under New Labour these arrangements were cemented into the newly devolved governments of these countries and, recently, important aspects of the remit of the remaining Arts Council England have been devolved to the English regions in parallel with the development of 'hubs' in the regional museum sector. While access to greater funding for the regions has been desperately needed, especially in municipal galleries, it is probably too early to know how this strategy has influenced the quality and nature of visual arts programmes up and down the country. It is difficult to be optimistic. The almost total disappearance of the Arts Council's central Visual Arts Department, which since its establishment had trained and nurtured many of the brightest talents in the field has, certainly not by chance, been mirrored by developments at the British Council, whose role in the promotion of understanding of British culture overseas has been subjugated to New Labour's political agenda and whose distinguished Visual Art Department has also been decimated.[2]

All the above policies have been promoted through legislation, directive, exhortation and, most importantly, where government controls the purse strings, carefully directed funding. How successful have they been? As in other aspects of government activity, much effort has been made to measure the success of the policies and the funding. Sara Selwood, editor of the academic journal *Cultural Trends* has observed: 'The gathering of evidence about the impact of the sector has assumed centre stage in the management of the subsidised cultural sector in England. It is closely associated with an extension of government control over the sector, and the tendency to value culture for its "impact" rather than its intrinsic value'. Selwood concludes: 'Until the collection and analysis of data is carried out more accurately and objectively, and until the evidence gathered is used more constructively, it could be argued that much data gathering in the cultural sector has been a spurious exercise.'[3] Estelle Morris, a former Minister for the Arts, admitted that in the cultural field the setting of targets is often difficult if not impossible: 'I know that arts and culture make a contribution to health, to education, to crime reduction, to strong communities, to the nation's well being, but I don't know how to evaluate it or describe it. We have to find a language and a way of describing its worth. It's the only way we'll secure the greater support we need.'[4] The Secretary of State for Culture, Media and Sport in the Blair Government, Tessa Jowell, also voiced her concern about this difficulty.[5]

Participation, that is, size and diversity of audience, has been the most important measure of success for the Government, not least no doubt because it is a quantitative concept readily comprehensible to the voter. For those who believe that visual art is principally neither entertainment nor education, although of course it can both entertain and educate, artistic excellence cannot be demonstrated by the numbers of adult or junior visitors to any particular exhibition, still less by the proportion or scale of the audience from ethnic minorities or socially deprived backgrounds.

It would be logical to expect that the characteristics of those participating in the making and showing of art would mirror those of the audience. This is also difficult to establish, but one rough and ready measure suggests that all may not be what it seems. The Bloomberg New Contemporaries exhibition is open to all final year undergraduates and current postgraduate students of Fine Art at colleges in the United Kingdom and to those artists who graduated in the previous year. Of the thirty-six artists shown in the 2006 exhibition, very nearly half have family names which suggest that their grandparents or parents were probably not born in Britain. This remarkable proportion, which is almost matched by an equivalent assessment of the artists chosen both for the 2006 British Art Show and the John Moores Painting Prize, might indicate that visual art has provided extraordinarily fertile ground for talented people from ethnic minorities to make their mark in the United Kingdom.

While there may be truth in this, closer inspection reveals that fully a third of all the New Contemporaries artists were born outside the United Kingdom. It would take further, rather sensitive research to discover whether these young artists have been living in this country since childhood. However, their age and the disproportionately large numbers suggest that for the most part they have been attracted here as students by the country's 'cool' reputation and the dynamic art scene which has enlivened the art colleges and provided many opportunities to show work.[6] This is clearly admirable, desirable and a great benefit to this country, but it is not proof of any long-term benefits of strategies of ethnic inclusion to artists working in the United Kingdom itself.

Whatever the identity of the participants, there can be no doubt that there has been an explosion of interest in contemporary visual art, particularly as represented by younger artists and a rapid increase in the opportunities for practising artists to exhibit their work; but which artists? The phenomena of Tate Modern and the Turner Prize have been matched not only in London at the Camden Arts Centre, the Serpentine Gallery, the South London Gallery and the Whitechapel Art Gallery, but all over the country with new or refurbished galleries in Bristol, Oxford, Walsall, Milton Keynes, Gateshead, Dundee, Colchester, Glasgow, Birmingham and most recently Middlesbrough. In addition, it has become a frequent strategy for museum directors and curators seeking to build visitor numbers, a key measure for Government support, to introduce contemporary work to historic displays of art, as for example at the National Gallery, or by showing contemporary art in the context of quite different collections, as at the British Museum, the Freud Museum, the Bowes Museum, the Science Museum and the Natural History Museum. While some of these projects have seemed opportunistic, where they have been well thought through and executed the results have often been stimulating and successful in attracting new audiences.

Charitable trusts, which generally have been created by or in the name of wealthy individuals to promote values they themselves considered important, place emphasis on their independence from government. Nevertheless, unless they take the unusual step of devising and running their own programmes, their philanthropy will be limited according to what applications for support they receive. Those like the Elephant Trust and the Henry Moore Foundation that focus exclusively on supporting visual art are chiefly motivated by the desire to help artists achieve their goals. It is vital that the institution presenting an exhibition has the space, technical resources and curatorial expertise to show work in a manner that best reflects the artist's intentions. These trusts give the highest priority to the purely artistic outcome of any grant or project. They do not principally measure their success in grant-making by the size, age or origins of the audience, but by the nature of the artist's intention and his or her ability to realize it.

On the other hand, the fertile conjunction of circumstances that has raised the stakes for contemporary art in the field of public funding for contemporary art, has also stimulated increased support for the visual arts from other trusts and foundations with a special interest in education, young people, increased access to the arts, social welfare and social change, especially the Paul Hamlyn Foundation, the Calouste Gulbenkian Foundation and the Esmée Fairbairn Foundation, which, perhaps significantly for a trust with a strong emphasis on education and social change, has only recently adopted contemporary visual art as a special objective of its grant programme. This development has been particularly valuable to institutions outside London where commercial sponsorship for avant-garde art is very difficult to find and where exhibition budgets even in the newly created galleries up and down the land specialising in contemporary art are very small indeed. Recognising this, the Esmée Fairbairn Foundation and the Henry Moore Foundation have shown themselves ready to work together to give priority to ground-breaking visual art projects outside London.

The artists or projects that trusts choose to support will depend on whether they regard art and artists in themselves as especially worthy of funding, or are more interested in the benefits that may accrue to society in general by making art available to the public. Those trusts concerned with creating and increasing opportunities for minority groups and the socially and economically disadvantaged will focus on grants for locations, venues and programmes that most effectively meet the greatest needs of those audiences. Other trusts, such as the Henry Moore Foundation, will look for circumstances offering artists the greatest possible stimulus to their invention and energy regardless of the size or type of audience their work may attract. However, trusts and foundations can for the most part only make awards to the projects that are proposed to them and it is at this point we encounter an ironic twist brought about by the developments in contemporary visual art described in the earlier part of this essay.

Whatever criteria trusts wish to adopt, for the most part the opportunities they will be offered will have been contrived to fit the Government's agenda. As we have seen, these will in most cases reflect the interests of the majority of artists whom most galleries want to show, because in turn these are the most likely to receive official funding. A circular phenomenon is thus created whereby a particular group of artists is shown with a relatively high frequency in a large number of venues and other artists of great quality are given little scope to do so. These latter are likely to be mature artists or those lacking a discernible political or social agenda, artists whose works do not yield their secrets easily, demanding critical attention over time, or which are informed by more traditional artistic values, being concerned perhaps with form, surface or colour rather than social or political meaning.

There are, of course, many exceptions to this pattern of officially supported preferences, but a trend is clear. This observation is not intended to suggest any criticism of the artists whose work has been widely shown. On the contrary, many are among the best we have and are rightly admired. What I believe the trend indicates is that New Labour, by a variety of means, has successfully harnessed the imagery, power and popularity of visual art to its own agenda. This may be of great service to charitable trusts that share the Government's aims in the social field; others, whose interests are largely concentrated on the promotion and nurturing of visual art for its own sake, may find that remaining truly independent in their grant-giving is more difficult than it seems.

# Notes

1  Social Exclusion Unit, Policy Action Team 10, DCMS, 2001, quoted in John Holden, *Capturing Cultural Value*, Demos, 2004.

2  Editorial, 'The betrayal of the British Council', in *The Burlington Magazine*, CXLIX, March 2007, p.147.

3  Sara Selwood, 'The Politics of Data Collection' in *Cultural Trends 47*, Policy Studies Institute, London, 2002, quoted in John Holden, ibid.

4  Estelle Morris, Minister for the Arts, in a speech to the Cheltenham Festival of Literature, October 2003, quoted in John Holden, ibid.

5  Tessa Jowell, 'How, in going beyond targets, can we best capture the value of culture?' in *Government and the Value of Culture*, DCMS, 2004, quoted in John Holden, ibid.

6  This impression was supported at a seminar organised by the Esmée Fairbairn Foundation in London to provide information to artists about sources of funding in the United Kingdom, where English was the first language of very few of the participants.

# BIBLIOGRAPHY

AEA Consulting, *A Review of Charitable Giving Vehicles and Their Use in the US and Canada*, Arts & Business, London, 2004.

Anheier, H.K. & Leat, D., *Creative Philanthropy*, Routledge, London & New York, 2006.

Anheier, H.K. & Leat, D., *From Charity to Creativity: Philanthropic Foundations in the 21st Century*, Comedia in association with the Joseph Rowntree Reform Trust, 2002.

Arts & Business, *Individual and Trust Giving to the Arts 2002/03*, Arts & Business, London, 2004.

Arts & Business, *Results of Arts Sector Qualitative Research*, Arts & Business, London, 2004.

Arts & Business, *Private Investment Benchmarking Survey 2003/04*, Arts & Business Research and Information, London, 2004.

Arts & Business, *Private Investment Benchmarking Survey 2004/05*, Arts & Business Research and Information, London, 2005.

Arts & Business, *Private Investment Benchmarking Survey 2005/06*, Arts & Business Research and Information, London, 2006.

Arts Council England, *Pride of Place, How the Lottery Contributed £1b to the Arts in England*, London, 2002.

Arts Council England, *Turning Point: a strategy for the contemporary visual arts in England*, London, 2006.

*Arts Professional*, 'Council cuts hit arts services', Issue 130, 25 September 2006.

'Arts and Culture in the New Economy', *The Journal of Arts Management, Law and Society*, Vol. 32, No. 2, Summer 2002 (special edition).

Belfiore, E., 'Auditing Culture: the subsidized cultural sector in the New Public Management', *International Journal of Cultural Policy*, 10.2, 2004.

Benjamin, A., 'Trust Deeds', the *Guardian*, 27 November 2002.

Bishop, M., 'The business of giving: a survey of wealth and philanthropy', *The Economist*, 23 February 2006.

Bolton, M., *Foundations and Social Investment*, Esmée Fairbairn Foundation, 2005.

Breeze, B., 'The Return of Philanthropy', *Prospect* magazine, January, 2005.

Browne-Wilkinson, H., *Philanthropy in the 21st Century*, transcript of speech at Coutts Conference, 17 June 2004.

Calouste Gulbenkian Foundation, *Twenty-One Years: An Anniversary Account of Policy and Activities 1956-1977*, United Kingdom and Commonwealth Branch, London, 1977.

Carrington, D., *Corporate Philanthropy and the Not For Profit Arts Sector*, a report commissioned by Arts & Business Research and Information, London, 2005.

Carrington, D., *How Trusts and Foundations Can Be More Than Grantmakers*, transcript of speech, November 2003 (see www.davidcarrington.net).

Carrington, D., *Measuring Impact*, transcript of speech, NCVO conference, 18 November 2002.

Conrad, J., Preface to *The Nigger of 'The Narcissus'*, first published 1897 and republished.

Cooke, R., 'Welcome to the new cultural revolution', the *Observer*, 15 October 2006.

Cowling, J. (ed.), *For Art's Sake*, Institute for Public Policy Research, London, 2004.

Editorial, 'The betrayal of the British Council', in The *Burlington Magazine*, CXLIX, March 2007.

Frayling, C., 'The only trustworthy book...' *Art and public value*, transcript of speech, 16 February 2005, Arts Council England, London.

Glinkowski, P., 'Giving as Investment', *Arts Professional*, Issue 104, 29 August 2005.

Hewison, R. & Holden, J., *Experience and Experiment: the UK Branch of the Calouste Gulbenkian Foundation 1956–2006*,

Calouste Gulbenkian Foundation, London, 2006.

Holden, J., *Capturing Cultural Value*, Demos, 2004.

International Federation of Arts Councils and Cultural Agencies [IFICCA], *Encouraging Arts Philanthropy: Selected Resources*, D'Art report number 7, February 2003.

Jay, E., Lee, S. & Sargeant, A., *Major Gift Philanthropy – Individual Giving to the Arts*, a report commissioned by Arts & Business from the Centre for Voluntary Sector Management, Henley Management College, London, 2002.

Kressner Cobb, N., 'The New Philanthropy: Its Impact on Funding Arts and Culture', *The Journal of Arts Management*, 125, Summer 2002.

Lee, F. R., 'A New Arts Foundation With a Focus on Creativity', *New York Times*, 2 May 2005.

Lind, M. & Minichbauer, R. (eds), *European Cultural Policies 2015: A Report with Scenarios on the Future of Public Funding for Contemporary Art in Europe*, International Artist Studio Programme in Sweden [IASPIS], Stockholm, 2005.

Lloyd, T., *Why Rich People Give*, Association of Charitable Foundations, London, 2004.

Lloyds TSB Foundation for England and Wales, *A Measured Approach: Impact Assessment Report*, Executive Summary, May 2003.

Mauss, M. *The Gift: forms and functions of exchange in archaic societies*. First published in *L'Année sociologique*, 1924, and republished.

McCarthy, K., et al, *A Portrait of the Visual Arts, Meeting the Challenges of a New Era*, Rand, 2005.

Mirza, M. (ed.), *Culture Vultures: Is UK arts policy damaging the arts?*, Policy Exchange Limited, London, 2006.

Pauly, E., *The Role of Evaluation in the 21st Century Foundation*, International Network for Strategic Philanthropy [INSP], January 2005.

*Philanthropy UK Newsletter*, Issue 27, December 2006.

Reeves, M., *Measuring the economic and social impact of the arts*, Arts Council England, London, 2002.

Rochester, C. & Woods, Z., *Making a Difference Together: Impact Assessment, Lloyds TSB Foundation for England and Wales' Collaborative Grant-Making Programme*, Lloyds TSB Foundation, London, January 2005.

Selwood, S., *Public Funding, Private Contributions and A&B*, Arts & Business, London, 2007.

Selwood, S., 'The Politics of Data Collection', *Cultural Trends* 47, Policy Studies Institute, London, 2002.

Selwood, S. (ed.), *The UK cultural sector: profile and policy issues*, Policy Studies Institute, London, 2001.

Shuster, M., 'Neither Public nor Private: The Hybridisation of Museums', *Journal of Cultural Economics*, Vol. 22, 1998.

Unwin, J., *The Grantmaking Tango: Issues for Funders*, The Baring Foundation, London, 2004.

Unwin, J., *Fruitful Funding: a guide to levels of engagement*, Association of Charitable Foundations [ACF] and the Improvement and Development Agency for Local Government [IdeA], London, 2005.

Varcoe, L. & Sloane, N., *Corporate Foundations; building a sustainable foundation for corporate giving*, Business in the Community, London, 2003.

ANNUAL REPORTS/ANNUAL REVIEWS

Calouste Gulbenkian Foundation [UK Branch], Annual Report, 2004 & 2005.

Esmée Fairbairn Foundation, Annual Report & Accounts, 2004 & 2005.

The Gatsby Charitable Foundation, Annual Report 2005.

The Henry Moore Foundation Review, 2004 & 2005.

The Jerwood Foundation Annual Report, 2004 & 2005.

NESTA [National Endowment for Science, Technology and the Arts], Annual Report, 2003/2004 & 2004/2005.

Northern Rock Foundation, Annual Review, 2004 & 2005.

The Paul Hamlyn Foundation, Annual Reports, 2004/2005 & 2005/2006.

# SIGNPOSTING

WEB LINKS TO USEFUL SOURCES OF INFORMATION REGARDING ARTS FUNDING AND PHILANTHROPIC GIVING IN THE UK.

### Arts & Business (A&B)
www.aandb.org.uk
*Through 12 regional offices around the UK, A&B acts as a crucible where businesses and arts organisations come together to create partnerships to benefit themselves and the community at large.*

### Arts Council England (ACE)
www.artscouncil.org.uk
*Arts Council England is the national development agency for the arts in England. It distributes public money from Government and the National Lottery.*

### The Association of Charitable Foundations (ACF)
www.acf.org.uk
*The leading membership association for grant-making charities in the UK.*

### Charities Aid Foundation (CAF)
www.cafonline.org
*CAF seeks to 'put donors in control of their giving, and help charities make the most of what they get'.*

### Directory of Social Change (DSC)
www.dsc.org.uk
*The Directory of Social Change aims to be an internationally recognised independent source of information and support to voluntary and community sectors worldwide.*

### Guidestar UK
www.guidestar.org.uk
*Guidestar UK is an on-line database set up to provide, for the first time, a single, easily accessible source of detailed information about every charity and voluntary organisation in the UK.*

### The Institute for Philanthropy
www.instituteforphilanthropy.org.uk
*The Institute for Philanthropy works to develop a greater understanding of philanthropy and its place in modern society.*

### Philanthropy UK
www.philanthropyuk.org
*Philanthropy UK, an initiative of the Association of Charitable Foundations, aims to help develop new philanthropy by promoting and disseminating knowledge and best practice to all those involved in giving.*

WEB LINKS FOR SOME OF THE PRINCIPAL TRUSTS AND FOUNDATIONS THAT SUPPORT THE ARTS IN THE UK.

### Calouste Gulbenkian Foundation
www.gulbenkian.org.uk
*The UK Branch of the Gulbenkian Foundation offers funding programmes in Arts, Social Change and Education, and Anglo-Portuguese Cultural Relations.*

### Clore Duffield Foundation
www.cloreduffield.org.uk
*The Clore Duffield Foundation concentrates its support on education, the arts, museum and gallery education, cultural leadership training, health and social welfare, placing a particular emphasis on supporting children, young people and society's more vulnerable individuals.*

### Elephant Trust
www.elephanttrust.org.uk
*The Elephant Trust exists to develop and improve the knowledge, understanding and appreciation of the fine arts in the UK.*

### Esmée Fairbairn Foundation
www.esmeefairbairn.org.uk
*Esmée Fairbairn Foundation is one of the largest independent grant-making foundations in the UK. It offers grants in four areas: Arts & Heritage, Education, Environment and Social Change.*

### Foyle Foundation
www.foylefoundation.org.uk
*The Foyle Foundation distributes grants to UK charities whose core work is in the areas of Learning, the Arts and Health.*

### The Garfield Weston Foundation
www.garfieldweston.org
*The Garfield Weston Foundation is a general grant-giving charity. Categories of activity funded include: Arts, Community, Education, Welfare, Medical, Social, Religion, Youth and Environment.*

### The Henry Moore Foundation
www.henry-moore-fdn.co.uk
*The Henry Moore Foundation was set up 'to advance the education of the public by the promotion of their appreciation of the fine arts and in particular the works of Henry Moore'.*

### Jerwood Charitable Foundation (JCF)
www.jerwood.org
*The Jerwood Charitable Foundation initiates a range of grants and activities in the Jerwood name. The majority of the JCF's work is in the arts. The Foundation is dedicated to imaginative funding, particularly in the arts.*

### Louise T Blouin Foundation
www.ltbfoundation.org
*The Louise T Blouin Foundation believes in the unique power of culture and creativity to be catalysts for positive change. It has two main aims: to encourage a better understanding of foreign affairs and culture beyond borders through international cooperation, exchange and dialogue; to explore the broader practical significance of creativity and the creative potential of the human brain.*

### Northern Rock Foundation
www.nr-foundation.org.uk
*The Northern Rock Foundation aims to tackle disadvantage and to improve quality of life in North East England and Cumbria. To achieve these objectives it invests in charitable activities that help the disadvantaged, or that make the North East a place for everyone to enjoy and celebrate.*

### The Paul Hamlyn Foundation
www.phf.org.uk
*The Paul Hamlyn Foundation is one of the larger independent grant-making foundations in the UK. Its principal areas of funding are: Arts, Education and Learning, and Social Justice.*

### The Wellcome Trust
www.wellcome.ac.uk
*The Wellcome Trust is the world's largest medical research charity, funding research into human and animal health. Under its Public Engagement programme it offers Arts Awards to 'support and encourage imaginative and experimental arts projects that investigate biomedical science'.*

### The Wolfson Foundation
www.wolfson.org.uk
*The Wolfson Foundation awards grants to back excellence in the fields of Science and Medicine, Health, Education, the Arts and Humanities.*

More comprehensive information on trusts which support the arts can be found in the directories and web-based resources produced by the Directory of Social Change.

# INDEX TO VOLUME II